Force or Freedom?

Force or Freedom?
The Paradox in Modern Political Thought

William T. Bluhm

Yale University Press
New Haven and London

Designed by Nancy Ovedovitz and set in VIP Baskerville type by The Saybrook Press, Inc., Old Saybrook, Connecticut. Printed in the United States of America by Vail-Ballou Press, Binghamton, New York.

Library of Congress Cataloging in Publication Data

Bluhm, William Theodore, 1923–
   Force or freedom?
   Includes index.
   1. Legitimacy of governments. 2. Authority.
3. Liberty. I. Title.
JC328.2.B48 1984 320.2 83-51293
ISBN 0-300-03087-8

10 9 8 7 6 5 4 3 2 1

For Guy Howard Dodge,
my teacher and my friend

Nature has set no limit to the perfecting of the human faculties, . . . the perfectibility of man is truly infinite; . . . the progress of this perfectibility, henceforth independent of any power that might wish to arrest it, has no limit other than the duration of the globe on which Nature has placed us. . . . The time will come therefore when the sun will shine only on free men who know no other master but their reason.

M. J. A. N. Caritat
Marquis de Condorcet, 1795

NEW YORK—*A bomb blast rocked the Statue of Liberty last night, burying in rubble a plaque bearing the famous "Give me your tired, your poor" poem that symbolized a new life for millions.*

Police said callers claiming to represent three different terrorist groups said they had set off the bomb, which caused heavy damage in a room in the statue's base. No injuries were reported.

United Press International
June 4, 1980

Contents

Preface

The theses of modern political thought move uncertainly between the poles of force and freedom, for we lack today a persuasive and shared concept of fundamental right, a concept of legitimacy that might bind them together. To develop such a concept is imperative if we are to weave force and freedom into a persuasive system of free authority. This book is about our modern quest for a philosophy of freedom under law and about our failure to achieve it—a failure that has entailed as well the loss of a viable ideal of community. I write also about the ultimate irreconcilability of force and freedom within our present way of thinking about the world. And I try to show how these salient terms of our political vocabulary might be rendered compatible and a way opened toward free community. This book is lastly a call for a thoroughgoing revolution of our world view, a revolution that is necessary if the work of reconciliation is to succeed.

That every system of government requires the exercise of coercive force is not in question. But the distinction between coercive *authority*—legitimate force limited and controlled by law—and *mere* force is vital for our enterprise. Yet authority everywhere today rests on implausible myth. Three ironies are central to this book: (1) that force (both psychological and physical) should be conceived in some of our myth systems as the midwife of human freedom; (2) that the necessary processes of force should, in some of these myths, be identified with freedom; and (3) that in some of them the freedom of the many should be deemed incompatible with other salient values and therefore coercively eliminated. It is my thesis that these problematical conceptions result from our effort to understand reality from a world view bequeathed to us by René Descartes.

The first major classics of modern political thought—the writings of Hobbes, Locke, and Rousseau—were intended to signal the beginnings of a new freedom for the individual. The mission of each writer was to overturn past tyrannies of thought and action. Yet somehow, in the eyes of some of their interpreters, these men became instead theorists of lawless force and of mythical law. Challengers, both philosophical and political, appeared brandishing new theories. Hobbes, in working out the freedom of the individual from the terrors of the state of nature, produced the thralldom of absolute force. And Locke, having brought Hobbes's Leviathan within the constitutional limitations of parliamentary government under the "Law of Nature," was found only to have substituted for an absolute crown an absolute social majority. Rousseau, seeking to overcome the oppressions of ages of inequality, produced a polity of egalitarian virtue in which freedom is defined as national discipline by a charismatic "Legislator." Kant, in his turn, found a way back to individual freedom, but only as a freedom of the pure idea, a noumenal freedom that might approach realization in the phenomenal world only through conflict and force (the mechanism of nature). Hegel and Marx, in seeking to eliminate the bedevilling ambiguities of Cartesian dualism, ended up with the freedom of dialectical necessity in which the individual becomes variously a function of the "Absolute Idea" and a species-being whose freedom is realized in the mystical unity of classless togetherness. All was to be engendered by the imperial compulsions of history. Nietzsche inverted egalitarian freedom with the myth of an "overman" whose liberty is achieved by molding the many to his will. It was Cartesianism that provided the intellectual matrix from which each of these problematical ideas emerged.

The substantive freedoms achieved in our time for Everyman are paradoxically interwoven with new compulsions in the societies that have been intellectually formed (or at least expressed) by the writers we have named. In liberal America every repressed group has sought to find its way to new autonomy and dignity in the last fifty years—first working men, then blacks and Hispanics, now women and gays. But idealistic youth from many walks of life have found the new freedom spiritually empty—in fact, not freedom at all, but a new kind of force. It stifles them, and in the desperation of their anomie they are prepared to sacrifice it to technologists of the spirit, who are growing in number and attractiveness, for what they consider to be true freedom. To their parents, of course, this true freedom is the result of spiritual programming, that is, of mechanical force. And the parents are prepared to meet force with force, in order to reestablish their conception of freedom. They call in deprogrammers.

The mechanistic techniques of behavior modification, preached as a gospel of social salvation by Skinnerian psychologists, when applied by teachers and administrators in classrooms, prisons, and mental institutions, point in opposite directions of the force—freedom compass at the same time. They contribute in manifest ways both to the freedom and to the enslavement of the human spirit. Subliminal advertising, grounded in the same principles of behaviorism, is less ambivalent. It brings freedom to the manipulative few only at the expense of an unseen thralldom for the many.

Political paradox has many other forms. Most threatening at the moment is the form implicit in the problem of liberal democratic community, or coherence, in societies like the United States. The paradox derives from the fact that freedom has been won by many groups under a banner inscribed: "Do your own thing!" (interest group liberalism or the "politics of group process"). This has been achieved through peaceful warfare conducted within a field of separated, checked, and balanced legal forces, a freedom-producing mechanism that we have venerated since the writing of the Constitution. But free, individualist Americans find themselves increasingly incapable of aggregating a public interest on the basis of widely shared moral norms within this mechanism of distributed force. They cannot ensure the rational management of scarce energy resources, the conservation of a livable environment, security from violence at home or on the street, or respect abroad—shared values that can readily be described as aspects of meaningful freedom.

European mimics of American dreamers have succeeded beyond belief in creating middle-class freedom, defined as broad affluence and liberal democratic process. But they have not been able to give it legitimacy. As a consequence, they face a much greater problem of security for persons and property than do their American counterparts and also a deeper and more widespread spiritual despair. Despite the encouraging vitality of liberal Europeanism displayed in such institutions as the Common Market, the European future is darkly clouded by mindless terrorism at the hands of frustrated losers and anomic idealists and by the threat of Eurocommunist discipline. Herbert Muller, in his magisterial history of freedom, has made similar observations. He finds in the quest of liberalism a "basic theme of ambiguity or paradox: the multitude of individuals who have been emancipated in modern society, given extraordinary opportunities to discover and fulfill themselves, . . . at the same time . . . have been subjected to massive pressures, and . . . may look and act less like individuals than the much less favoured men of the past."[1]

Things are no better—indeed are considerably worse—east of the Oder-Neisse Line. In the Soviet Union and its satellites the average man and woman are told that they must submit to a regime of total force to prepare them for a reign of freedom. And even the "scientific" elite that presides over the regime of total mobilization finds its own freedom and power dwindling through policies that demobilize human resources by driving creative intellect into exile abroad. The Chinese oscillate between the destructive freedom of visionary anarchism (the "Cultural Revolution") and the disspiriting rigors of state capitalism. Elsewhere, the black and brown people of the globe, escaping from the illegitimate force of colonialism in pursuit of their own visions of freedom, have made themselves a prey to the extermination policies of sadists and power-crazy juntas. The paradox is found the world around. And as it moves toward resolution, force is becoming the dominant political reality.

In the academy we have for a long while experienced the tensions of force and freedom in the problem of relating behavioral political science to normative political theory as a single cognitive enterprise (in shorthand, the 'fact–value' problem).

---

1. Herbert J. Muller, *Freedom in the Modern World* (New York: Harper and Row, 1966), 539.

Much of my own professional life has been devoted to overcoming those tensions and to establishing a cooperative enterprise. But despite some progress, the solution has remained fundamentally elusive. A central difficulty has been to find a way to dovetail a conception of freedom in moral choice with the deterministic (nomological) categories of behavioral political science. Rational choice theory does not hold the key, for its principles are causal in character.[2] Nor do the very different humanizing and holistic efforts put forth by existential phenomenologists, by followers of the Wittgenstein of the *Investigations,* and by revisionists within the philosophy of social science suffice to resolve the problem, though they have certainly contributed to its clarification. For while all these latter efforts constitute a critique of the Cartesian world view, they are made within a paradigm of knowledge that remains fundamentally Cartesian in character. And if we try to resolve the problem of the normative–scientific dichotomy on Descartes's terms, with categories such as "mind" and "body" as the two fundamental and separate sources of knowledge, we shall never find a satisfactory way to do it.

I wish to be very clear about one matter at the outset of my enterprise. A critique of Descartes and of Cartesianism is not a criticism of natural science and its works. Who has any doubt that science and the liberating technology that is its instrument in the world have contributed vastly to the freedom and well-being of humanity? It is common knowledge that scientific technology has saved and eased a myriad of lives through the miracles of medicine, through a multiplication of loaves for the starving made possible by scientific agronomy, through the power of modern communications systems to distribute these good things as well as the goods of high culture with incredible speed to the ends of the earth. This book is not a critique of science but of an early philosophy of science that has developed into an entire world view and way of life that is with us still, a world view that has been more ambiguous in its benefits than the early science from which it grew. The practices of natural science had developed and

2. See William T. Bluhm, ed., *The Paradigm Problem in Political Science* (Durham, N.C.: Carolina Academic Press, 1982), especially 14–21, 136–37.

were successful before René Descartes penned his philosophy. Moreover, the working hypotheses and early statements of "law" that were the vehicles of its discoveries at the beginning—things erected by Descartes into a philosophy of life—have given way to quite different hypotheses and principles for understanding, predicting, and controlling the empirical world of nature that is science's field of endeavor. Even the concept of necessary laws that political thinkers, working even today with the categories legislated by Descartes, have made a pillar of their theories has been yielded up by the practitioners of natural science in favor of a quite different view of reality. From Cartesian observers, standing outside nature in order to understand and conquer it, scientists have recently begun to see themselves and their relationship to nature in a holistic and less imperial way. They surely no longer view the world as a great machine whose motions are governed by necessary laws. As Tom Ferris has written:

> The new insights coming out of particle physics tend to disprove the myth that the cosmos is an inexorable machine. To see the universe as evolving like life, like thought, as subject to chance just as our lives are subject to chance, is to deepen our sense that we have a rightful place in nature.[3]

Devotees of political, economic, and moral science and philosophy of a positivistic character, grounded in a dualistic, mechanistic world view, ought to reexamine that view as the practitioners of physical science already have done. This book is intended as a stimulus to reflection on what they are doing by scientists of society, by ethicists, and by political philosophers who still inhabit the world that Descartes created so many years ago. As I have indicated, some schools of thought, like that of existential phenomenology, have begun to search for a new world. But they have not sufficiently cleared the rubble from the field that is obstructing the view of all of us of a more viable theoretical future. This book is therefore designed to accomplish a little more of that "underlaborer" work. It is an invitation to begin to resolve the force—freedom problem by rethinking the categories within which that problem emerged in modern thought.

3. Tom Ferris, *New York Times Magazine*, September 26, 1982.

Another disclaimer is needed here. This book is not a single-cause analysis of all the political problems of modernity. The tensions of force and freedom I have sketched, tensions discoverable at every level of modern life, are a complex reality produced by an intricate complex of causes. To explain them fully would require inspired feats of psychological, economic, social, cultural, and political research. In the present book I shall essay only a beginning of this many-sided endeavor by spelling out the philosophical confusions that derive from the Cartesian foundations of modern intellectual life. This effort rests upon the assumption that what people think about reality has a profound effect on how they behave and therefore on the political and social reality in which they live. If the assumption is warranted, a faulty understanding of the nature of force, of freedom, and of fundamental right, and of the appropriate relationships of these concepts one to another, has importantly contributed to the dilemma we are in. To clarify our understanding of these terms may help us to escape the dilemma. It should prepare us for the necessary task of rethinking the idea of a free society.[4]

---

4. I have provided an extensive bibliography in the notes.

Acknowledgments

The initial research for this study was supported by a stipend from the National Endowment for the Humanities for the summer of 1976. I was granted a sabbatical leave by the University of Rochester for the spring semester of 1978 to continue work on the project. I am grateful both to the endowment and to the university for their aid and encouragement. My thanks to Isaac Kramnick, who reviewed the manuscript for Yale University Press, to Thomas A. Spragens, Jr., and to Hank Jenkins-Smith for their help. All of them read the entire manuscript in one or another of its several incarnations and made many useful suggestions for its improvement. I thank Walter Soffer for his helpful comments on chapter 2. The faults that remain in the book are, of course, my own responsibility. My gratitude also to Claire Sundeen, who patiently typed the penultimate and final versions of the manuscript, and to Mary Heinmiller, who helped with the typing. Thanks are due as well to Anwar Syed for permission to reprint in chapter 3, in somewhat modified form, my article entitled "Freedom in the *Social Contract*: Rousseau's 'Legitimate Chains,'" which appeared in the Spring 1984 issue of *Polity*. Loving thanks also to my wife, Elly, who encouraged and cheered me during the long gestation of this book. A great thanks to Marian Neal Ash, who is the finest editor with whom I have worked.

I should also like to acknowledge with thanks the permission of the M. C. Escher Foundations, Haags Gemeentemuseum, to reproduce the lithograph entitled "Cycle."

Force and Freedom in Political Philosophy: Controversy about the Classics

Philosophy and Popular Culture

Analogously to art and dress, philosophy has been democratized over the centuries of the modern age. Perhaps only professors and a bookish intelligentsia are familiar with the writings of Rousseau, Mill, Marx, and Nietzsche. But in our popular ideologies average men and women carry around simplified versions of their ideas, though sometimes in illogical mixtures and though unselfconsciously assimilated to their way of thought rather than as conscious doctrine. The prophecies of Nietzsche can be clearly discerned in the "punk-rock" songs of the *Sex Pistols*.[1] And social scientists have successfully tested for the popular currency of ideas drawn from the systematic philosophies of Rousseau, Locke, and other writers.[2] All our "isms" have their most elegant and subtle statement in the little-read pages of systematic philosophy.

1. See the lyrics of "Anarchy in the U.K.," reprinted in *Time*, January 16, 1978, 62:

I am an antichrist
I am an anarchist
Don't know what I want
But I know how to get it,
I want to destroy.

2. See, e.g., Robert E. Lane, *Political Ideology: Why the American Common Man Believes What He Does* (New York: Free Press of Glencoe, 1962); Donald J. Devine, *The Political Culture of the United States* (Boston: Little, Brown & Co., 1972).

It does not seem inappropriate, therefore, if we wish to get an understanding of the contradictions and paradoxes of force and freedom in our popular culture today, to examine the writings of the leading philosophers of modern times, in which the puzzling relationships of force and freedom have been framed in their sharpest terms. To understand the problem of our culture as it manifests itself in the clear air of the fifth level of abstraction may help us to comprehend what is going on in the heads of the people on smoggy Main Street.

Political Paradox: Hobbes to Nietzsche

One of the most arresting relationships of force to freedom in modern thought is the paradoxical identity that Jean-Jacques Rousseau establishes between the concepts in his political writings. Resolution of the paradox by reducing it to one or other of its terms has certainly been a favorite occupation of commentators for two hundred years—assigning Rousseau the status of either a patron saint of freedom or an apostle of despotism.

The most striking statement of the paradox appears in book 1, chapter 7 of the *Social Contract*, in which Rousseau has begun to delineate the concept of the "general will" and to explain its relationship to particular wills. He has just pointed out that every individual may be prompted by private interest to act against the common interest of the society to which he belongs or to enjoy his citizen rights without fulfilling his citizen duties. If such behavior becomes widespread, the body politic soon faces ruin, and all the citizens forfeit the precious value for whose sake they signed the social contract—their freedom from domination by other individuals. To prevent the frustration of the social pact's intent, therefore, the pact must be understood tacitly to include the following engagement:

> that whosoever refuses to obey the general will shall be constrained to do so by the whole body; which means nothing else than that he shall be forced to be free; for such is the condition which, uniting every citizen to his native land, guarantees him from all personal dependence, a condition that ensures the control and working of

the political machine, and alone renders legitimate civil engagements, which, without it, would be absurd and tyrannical, and subject to the most enormous abuses.[3]

But how is submission to force compatible with freedom? Does Rousseau define freedom differently in different contexts? Since in the passage cited, he seems to have something like "inner freedom" or "moral freedom" in mind, how can his statement be reconciled with other passages of his work in which he says clearly that "force is a physical power" only and has no "moral effect"?[4]

For more than two hundred years, commentators have attempted to resolve this paradox by showing that the burden of Rousseau's thought is the defense of human freedom or by arguing that Rousseau's freedom is false and illusory and that his philosophical and historical significance lies in an advocacy or

3. Jean-Jacques Rousseau, *The Social Contract*, Henry J. Tozer, trans., in Jean-Jacques Rousseau, *The Social Contract and Discourse on the Origin of Inequality*, Lester G. Crocker, ed. (New York: Simon and Schuster, Washington Square Press Pocket Books, 1967), 22. *The American College Dictionary* defines paradox as "1) a statement or proposition seemingly self-contradictory or absurd, and yet explicable as expressing a truth; 2) a self-contradictory and false proposition." Clarence L. Barnhart, ed., *The American College Dictionary* (New York: Random House, 1951), 879. For Rousseau the statement would be a paradox according to meaning #1; for anyone unable to understand its hidden "truth" it would be a paradox according to meaning #2. For a recapitulation of the passages in Rousseau's works that involve the paradox, see Guy H. Dodge, ed., *Jean-Jacques Rousseau: Authoritarian Libertarian?* (Lexington, Mass.: D. C. Heath & Co., 1971), vii–xi. This volume also contains extracts from the Rousseau canon in which these passages appear. Dodge describes the paradox as follows: "The key problem of this volume is centered around the famous 'libertarian–authoritarian' or 'force–freedom' paradox in the political theory of Jean-Jacques Rousseau, which has been the subject of intense controversy for more than two hundred years, thereby giving some indication of the influence and timeliness of his thought. On the one hand, passages of his work are cited where he opposes despotism, oppression, force, and injustice in favor of liberty, equality, and law, while, on the other hand, very different selections are referred to which have authoritarian, if not even totalitarian implications" (vii). See also John W. Chapman, *Rousseau—Totalitarian or Liberal?* (New York: AMS Press, 1968). Henry D. Rempel treats the force–freedom paradox in Rousseau and in J. S. Mill from a standpoint very different from my own in "On Forcing People to be Free," *Ethics* 87, no. 1 (October 1976): 18–34.

4. Dodge, *Rousseau*, viii.

prophecy of authoritarian (even totalitarian) control.[5] In the eighteenth century, Voltaire was one of the first to read him as a liberal, while Edmund Burke was an early adherent of the school that has held him to be a father of authoritarian politics. All through the nineteenth and twentieth centuries he has been attacked as an enemy of freedom by liberals, conservatives, and social anarchists (for example, Benjamin Constant, Sir Henry Maine, and Pierre Joseph Proudhon), while other liberals (for example, T. H. Green and John Chapman) have seen him as one of their own. The debate continues to this day.[6]

Though he was the first to deal with the problem of relating force to freedom by announcing a paradox, Rousseau was not the first to address the problem. A problematic relationship between force and freedom is also implicit in the political theories of Thomas Hobbes and John Locke, whose work predated Rousseau's by about a century. That it figures importantly in the thought of these philosophers is proved by the antithetical interpretations that have been given to their writings down through the years. The volume of the polemic about them has been smaller, however, and the enthusiasm of celebration and the acrimony of criticism not as marked as among the Rousseau controversialists.

C. E. Vaughan, a noted English student of political theory at the turn of the century, discerned a puzzling ambivalence in Hobbes's *Leviathan* and described it in these terms:

> The whole work of Hobbes breathes the bitterest hatred not only of individualism as a theory, but even of those elementary rights which none but the most backward nations now deny to the individual in practice. Yet this preposterous system is itself based . . . on assumptions representing an extreme form of individualism: an individualism more uncompromising than that of Locke himself.[7]

5. Dodge's volume contains an extensive digest of the entire literature of controversy. See ibid., 38–91.

6. Ibid., xi–xvii.

7. C. E. Vaughan, *Studies in the History of Political Philosophy* (London: Longmans, Green and Co., 1925), 22–23. Ramon M. Lemos in a much later study shows that while Hobbes's political theory displays as "thoroughly egoistic [an] approach as any that has ever been devised" in which every man has "but one unconditional natural obligation, . . . to act compatibly with his preservation, he

Vaughan was obviously no partisan of Hobbes, and he placed him at the authoritarian pole. A French scholar, Joseph Vialatoux, writing in the 1950s, has gone so far in this line of interpretation as to call Hobbes "the abstract theoretician of state totalitarianism." "Hobbes has deduced the abstract archetype of the totalitarian state," he writes, "—of the gigantic 'artificial animal' which absorbs man without reserve, totally, body and soul, subjecting to its control the spiritual personality no less than the organic individuality of man."[8] In striking contrast, George Catlin, a Canadian political theorist, contradicts both Vaughan's and Vialatoux's interpretations with the statement that "Hobbes remains, not a worshipper of despots, but an individualist to the core." And he calls Hobbes and John Selden "the first Utilitarians."[9] Many others as well have seen Hobbes essentially as a liberal of the utilitarian stripe.[10]

---

presents the most profound argument for political absolutism in the entire history of political philosophy." Lemos shows that this paradox is the logical result of Hobbes's fundamental egoism. See *Hobbes and Locke: Power and Consent* (Athens: Univ. of Georgia Press, 1978), 12, 69.

8. Joseph Vialatoux, *La Cité Totalitaire d'Hobbes* (Lyon: Chronique Social de France, 1952), vi.

9. George Catlin, *The Story of the Political Philosophers* (New York: McGraw-Hill, 1939), 241–42; cf. the much more recent work of Eldon J. Eisenach, *Two Worlds of Liberalism: Religion and Politics in Hobbes, Locke, Mill* (Chicago & London: Univ. of Chicago Press, 1981): "Hobbes bequeathed to liberalism a systematic structure, but one replete with paradox. Men are born to liberty and from 'Principles of Reason' can be shown the necessity of sovereign power. . . . Hobbes's hope is that most men would exchange their past servitudes and sacrifices for a safer but more constricted world of contractual liberty" (71).

10. See Dante Germino, *Modern Western Political Thought* (Chicago: Rand McNally, 1972), 90; Sterling Lamprecht, "Hobbes and Hobbism," *American Political Science Review* 34 (February 1940):34. Rejecting Hobbes's absolutistic conclusions and the psychology on which they are based, David P. Gauthier celebrates Hobbes's "concept of authorization" as his "enduring contribution to political thought," and one that can be made quite compatible with limited and responsible government. Taking Hobbes's account of man entire, however, without modification, Gauthier concludes that Hobbes "is not really able to offer any alternative to anarchy—not even what his critics consider tyranny," *The Logic of Leviathan: The Moral and Political Theory of Thomas Hobbes* (Oxford: Clarendon Press, 1969), 170, 171, 173, 177.

The writings of Locke also display an ambivalence about force and freedom. The most commonly accepted view of both his sympathizers and his antagonists is that Locke was an individualist.[11] Vaughan called him "the prince of individualists," which puts Locke at the "freedom" pole of the spectrum, albeit a kind of freedom is involved of which Vaughan does not approve.[12] Yet Willmoore Kendall, who is also critical, says that Locke's solution to the leading problems of political theory is "at every point except one, that of the majority-rule democrat." "Locke did *not* begin," he writes, "with individuals in a state of nature, but with a definition of political power so authoritarian and collectivist in its bearing that no genuine individualist . . . could conceivably accept it." For him Locke belongs at the "force" pole; his theories raise the specter of tyrannical majorities.[13] In my own reading of Locke, I find a paradox in his tacit assertion that the absolute sovereignty of a social majority (which Locke calls "the greater force") is necessary to secure the liberty of the individual. This reading will be expounded and justified in an appropriate place.

Political philosophy since Rousseau, as well as before him, wears a Janus face. This is probably least true of Immanuel Kant, Rousseau's great admirer, who has usually been accorded a respected place as a philosopher of freedom in the annals of political thought. Thus Lewis White Beck calls him "a republican and a humanitarian, as deeply committed to a defense of the rights and interests of mankind as any French or American revolutionary."[14] Similarly John Ladd writes that "the key to Kant's moral and political philosophy is his conception of the dignity of the indi-

11. See J. W. Gough, *John Locke's Political Philosophy* (Oxford: Clarendon Press, 1973), 27–28. Geraint Perry, *John Locke* (London: George Allen and Unwin, 1978), presents a good, brief, up-to-date statement of the individualist view. See especially 152.

12. Vaughan, *Studies in the History of Political Philosophy*, 156.

13. Willmoore Kendall, *John Locke and the Doctrine of Majority Rule* (Urbana, Ill.: Univ. of Illinois Press, 1959), 66–67. This view is rejected out of hand by John Dunn, *The Political Thought of John Locke* (Cambridge: Cambridge Univ. Press, 1968), 129. A more measured criticism of Kendall's view is found in Perry, *John Locke*, 100.

14. Introduction to Immanuel Kant, *Perpetual Peace* (New York: Liberal Arts Press, 1957), viii.

vidual. . . . Kant may be regarded as the philosophical defender par excellence of the rights of man."[15]

Yet even with regard to Kant there is dissent. He can be read another way, and Isaiah Berlin has so read him and moved him into the ranks of the authoritarians. In his well-known inaugural lecture, "Two Concepts of Liberty," Berlin asks what there might have been about Kant's philosophy that allowed his "severe individualism" to be transformed into "something close to a pure totalitarian doctrine" by later writers in the idealist tradition who claimed intellectual descent from Kant.[16] He finds the answer in Kant's philosophy of law, which was based on the concept of objective ethical reason rather than on utilitarian interest, Berlin's own point of departure. Since some people do not listen to the voice of reason speaking in them, the ruler must assume that if the law he imposes is a rational law "it will automatically be approved by all the members of . . . society so far as they are rational beings. For if they disapprove, they must, *pro tanto*, be irrational; then they will need to be repressed by reason."[17] Thus Berlin has found in Kant a version of Rousseau's conception of being "forced to be free." Though he educates people to rationality, the legislator cannot rely wholly on persuasion. He must enforce rational law objectively for the public good. Though Berlin grants that Kant came near to asserting the "'negative' ideal of liberty" in his concern to guarantee individual autonomy within structures of impersonal law, he believes that Kant did not, like the utilitarian upholders of that ideal, regard all ends as equal. For Kant, he believes, "'reason' . . . is a faculty that creates or reveals a purpose identical in, and for, all men. In the name of reason anything that is non-rational may be condemned, so that the various personal aims which their individual imagination and idiosyncrasies lead men to pursue . . . may, at least in theory, be ruthlessly suppressed to make way for the demands of reason."[18]

Georges Vlachos finds contradiction and paradox in a rather different interpretation of Kant's idea of law. Vlachos points to

15. Translator's introduction to Immanuel Kant, *The Metaphysical Elements of Justice* (Indianapolis: Bobbs-Merrill Co., Library of the Liberal Arts, 1965), ix.

16. Isaiah Berlin, *Two Concepts of Liberty* (Oxford: Clarendon Press, 1958), 37.

17. Ibid.

18. Ibid., 38, fn. 1.

"the separation between law and morals" made by Kant, which
makes Kant on the one hand a partisan of established centralized
power and on the other a philosopher who reasons "in terms of
the rights of man." The first leads him to develop an unconditional metaphysics of order which is "as incredibly static as is the
rational mechanism of the Hobbesian state." "The dialectic of
progress is reduced to a legalism which is flatly contradictory to
the dynamic aspects of universal history." In summary, "the contradiction is ultimately reflected in the uncertain dualism of natural law and positivism." Though originally considered by Kant to
be complementary elements in a fundamental dialectical synthesis, liberty and power become separated and opposed to one
another along the way. The result is a radical cutting apart of the
destiny of the individual from that of the state, which leaves the
individual isolated. And from isolation to "the total effacement of
the individual there is but a single step." Juridically considered,
the individual becomes "a mere aspect of the state, pure and
simple." Thus, according to Vlachos, there remains an unbridge-
able gulf and a contradiction between positivist legality and the
legitimacy of individual freedom in Kant's thought. Personalism
becomes a mere pretext for justifying a positivistic formalism.
The human person becomes swallowed up in the abyss which
separates forever "liberty and power."[19]

Hans Saner has yet another way of understanding the paradoxical relationship of force to freedom in Kant's political thought.
For him it takes the form of freedom-producing conflict. For
Saner, the laws by which historical struggle takes place are
ontologically more significant than the positive laws of political
society that obtain at any particular time. "Lawful struggle," he
writes, "for the rule of law will go on until the idea of a state with
the greatest possible freedom for all has been realized." "The laws
eliminate the function of the struggle; but struggle as such does
not become superfluous, for the law can be broken. Even when it
holds sway, it has to fight for its rule." Though peace and freedom are necessarily ultimately congruent, as political goals, they
do not go together in the historical process. "War itself, if it is

19. Georges Vlachos, *La Pensee Politique de Kant* (Paris: Presses Universitaires
de France, 1962), 584–86, my translation.

waged for freedom or the right, can be the beginning of a lawful struggle."[20]

About Georg Friedrich Hegel as about Rousseau, there has been long-standing prolific, and very acrimonious controversy. There are commentators who call him an apostle of liberalism; others see him as a conservative; still others have dubbed him a proto-fascist. Among the commentators in English, debate about Hegel's position on the force–freedom spectrum has centered symbolically not so much on paradoxical expressions as on ambiguous German sentences, which can be rendered into English in remarkably different ways.[21] A special bone of contention has been the sentence, "Es ist der Gang Gottes in der Welt, dass der Staat ist," an editorial emendation based on lecture notes that appears in a posthumous edition of *The Philosophy of Right* and therefore not even Hegel's own words for certain. Those who construe Hegel as an authoritarian favor the Loewenberg translation of 1929, in which the sentence reads, "The State is the march of God through the world." Those who class him with the philosophers of freedom prefer, "It is the way of God with the world that there should be the state."[22] Many other passages which are certainly Hegel's own work furnish fuel for the polemical fires, for example, the assertion that "the real (*wirklich*) is rational."

T. M. Knox points up the problems of Hegel's thought by restating the philosopher's central theoretical concern as a hard question, which looks like a Sphinxian riddle: "How is it possible to combine the individual Greek's complete devotion to his city with the modern emphasis on the paramount importance of individual freedom?"[23] Knox resolves the problem by arguing

20. Hans Saner, *Kant's Political Thought: Its Origin and Development*, E. B. Ashton, trans. (Chicago: Univ. of Chicago Press, 1973), 310, 312.

21. A paradox is nevertheless found in Hegel's famous description of the culmination of history as the world spirit's recognition of its freedom in the contemplation of necessity.

22. See Walter Kaufmann's discussion of this matter in Walter Kaufmann, ed., *Hegel's Political Philosophy* (New York: Atherton Press, 1970), 4–5. Kaufmann puts Hegel in the liberal camp and calls Loewenberg's work a mistranslation. Kaufmann's volume appears in the "Atherton Controversy" series and organizes leading examples of the polemical exegesis of Hegel as two "debates."

23. Ibid., 16.

that Hegel "tried to find a place in the State *both* for individual liberty *and* for strong government." And he argues that Hegel "rejects the doctrine that might is right, allows freedom of conscience, and does not make the individual a mere means to the ends of the State."[24] He seems to make Hegel a liberal conservative (or conservative liberal), perhaps à la Constant or Alexis de Tocqueville, without expressly labeling him so.

Z. A. Pelczynski wishes to place Hegel squarely within the liberal tradition. While "neither Hegel nor Paine were prophets of liberalism, . . . the one and the other shared its fundamental assumptions," he writes. "They belonged . . . to the right and the left of liberalism."[25] Shlomo Avineri, John Plamenatz, and Herbert Marcuse also put Hegel in the liberal camp.[26] Charles Taylor does so also, but as someone who understood and criticized middle-class, individualist liberalism and who also understood well the problems of the utopian revolutionary's quest for freedom.[27] Sidney Hook, by contrast, argues that Hegel "cannot be legitimately regarded as a liberal, . . . his social and political philosophy is closer to Edmund Burke than to Tom Paine."[28] In other words, for Hook he is a pure conservative. In a polemical article Pelczynski claims, however, that Hook has used the harsher appellations of "authoritarian thinker, a supporter of absolutism and fellow-traveller of reaction."[29] Karl R. Popper has gone to the extreme of depicting Hegel as a chief precursor of totalitarianism. "Nearly all the more important ideas of modern totalitarianism," he believes, "are directly inherited from Hegel,

24. Ibid., 25.
25. Ibid., 85. See also Z. A. Pelczynski, "The Hegelian Conception of the State," in Z. A. Pelczynski, ed., *Hegel's Political Philosophy: Problems and Perspectives* (Cambridge: Cambridge Univ. Press, 1971), 1–29.
26. Pelczynski, ed., *Hegel's Political Philosophy*, chaps. 6, 9; John P. Plamenatz, *Man and Society*, vol. 2 (New York: McGraw-Hill 1963), chaps. 3, 4; and "History as the Realization of Freedom," in Pelczynski, ed., *Hegel's Political Philosophy*, 30–51; Herbert Marcuse, *Reason and Revolution*, 2nd ed. (New York: Humanities Press, 1954).
27. *Hegel* (Cambridge: Cambridge Univ. Press, 1975).
28 In Kaufmann, *Hegel's Political Philosophy*, 88.
29. Ibid., 82.

who collected and preserved what A. Zimmern calls the 'armoury of weapons for authoritarian movements.'"[30]

The ambivalent character of Hegel's thought is revealed not only in the polemics of his interpreters and commentators but also in the diverse and even contradictory character of his influence. Thus, while it is the case that T. H. Green, a father of neo-Liberalism (the liberalism of the modern democratic welfare state), was an avowed Hegelian, so too were the conservative philosopher Bernard Bosanquet and the philosopher of Italian fascism Giovanni Gentile.[31]

The work of the most prominent Hegelian of our time, Karl Marx, also points in opposite directions of force and freedom. In this case, there has been a great, ongoing debate as to whether Marx was a humanist, and fundamentally a liberal democrat, or an authoritarian "scientist" whose preoccupation was coercion and manipulation. The humanists usually focus attention on the early writings of Marx, with their Hegelian concern to understand the spiritually crippling alienation of capitalist society and their dream of overcoming alienation and the renewal of the human spirit under communism. "Marx held that free and independent man could exist only in a social and economic system that, by its rationality and abundance, brought to an end the epoch of 'pre-history' and opened the epoch of 'human history,' which would make the full development of the individual the condition for the full development of society, and vice versa." Thus Erich Fromm states the humanist thesis about how Marx is

30. K. R. Popper, *The Open Society and Its Enemies*, vol. 2 (London: George Routledge and Sons, 1945), 58–59.

31. See V. R. Mehta, *Hegel and the Modern State: An Introduction to Hegel's Political Thought* (New Delhi: Associated Publishing House, 1968), 137. Kelly expressed well the multifaceted character of Hegel's thought and its controversiality as well when he wrote that "liberalism snipes at its ambiguous authoritarianism and its quaint notion of liberty . . . Jacobinism dislikes its moderated pluralism and anti-populism; Marxism derides its pretensions toward impartiality and justice, given the social system out of which it had been confected. To some it has seemed a monster, to others a pedantic irrelevancy." George Armstrong Kelly, *Hegel's Retreat from Eleusis: Studies in Political Thought* (Princeton, N.J.: Princeton Univ. Press, 1978), 230.

to be read. Leszek Kolakowski and Shlomo Avineri are two other prominent scholars who agree.[32]

The interpretation of Marx as scientist underlies the official Marxism of Soviet ideology. In this version, Marx is seen as the discoverer of the laws of dialectical development and the formulator of a predictive social and political science. The categories of Marxist analysis in this view are preeminently those of necessity and of scientific prediction and control, not alienation and freedom. This reading of the doctrine posits the need for a scientific elite, the leadership of the Communist party, who know better than the average person how to comprehend dialectical development and how to maneuver strategically on the basis of such knowledge. In this way Marxism becomes a logic of power rather than of freedom.[33] Western scholars such as A. James Gregor and Karl R. Popper have also emphasized Marx's interest in developing a science of total social control but have concentrated on showing that Marxism really is not a science at all but rather a scientistic hocus-pocus. The authoritarian and totalitarian implications of dialectical history have been pointed up by Nikolai A. Berdyaev and Sidney Hook, who read Marx as profoundly anti-humanist. Hook thinks that Marx moved from a truly humanist standpoint in his early writings to determinism and authoritarianism in his collaboration with Engels, a collaboration that produced the canon of "scientific Marxism" of which Lenin and his successors made practical political use.[34] Humanist Marxism has become in the last few years an ideology of liberal dissent within the Soviet Union and within the Communist satellite societies of Eastern Europe, where it does battle with the Marxist "science" of officialdom.

32. The quotation from Fromm appears in V. Stanley Vardys, ed., *Karl Marx: Scientist? Revolutionary? Humanist?* (Lexington, Mass.: D. C. Heath & Co., 1971), 55. See also Leszek Kolakowski, *Toward A Marxist Humanism: Essays On The Left Today*, J. Z. Peel, trans. (New York: Grove Press, 1968); and Shlomo Avineri, *The Social and Political Thought of Karl Marx* (Cambridge: Cambridge Univ. Press, 1968). The Vardys volume contains a selection from writers on both sides of the interpretive controversy.

33. See the excerpt from O. V. Kuusinen, *Fundamentals of Marxism–Leninism*, 2nd ed. (Moscow: Foreign Languages Publishing House, 1963), in Vardys, *Karl Marx*, 1–5.

34. See excerpts from all these writers in Vardys, ed., *Karl Marx*.

In the case of Nietzsche, paradox plays a more salient role than with any of the other philosophers discussed here. It seems, in fact, to be a central principle of his method. A hundred contradictions mark Nietzsche's work, and the antinomies of force and freedom find a prominent place among them. Karl Jaspers writes that "each one of [Nietzsche's] affirmations appears to be cancelled out by another. For every judgment in Nietzsche's work one can almost always find an opposite conclusion as well." Thus everyone can cite Nietzsche as authority, "believers as well as the godless, conservatives and revolutionaries, socialists and individualists, . . . the free spirit and the fanatic."[35] Jaspers sees the paradoxes as dictated by Nietzsche's conception of truth. "The conspicuous contradiction must be seen," he writes, "as necessary, as implicit in reality, not as a sign of poor thinking, but of truthfulness."[36]

The political philosophy of Nietzsche is, therefore, especially prone to contradictory interpretations. And they have been written in abundance. Though aware of the paradoxical and many-sided character of Nietzsche's thought, Jaspers himself has singled out one aspect of it as dominant. Jaspers's Nietzsche is a humanist. Thus the overman is taken as a symbol of what man may become if he learns to conquer and overcome himself.[37] Instead of the

35. Karl Jaspers, *Nietzsche: Einfuehrung In Das Verstaendnis Seines Philosophierens* (Berlin: Verlag Walter de Gruyter & Co., 1936), 8. See also Walter Kaufmann, *Nietzsche: Philosopher, Psychologist, Anti-Christ* (New York: Random House, Vintage Books, 1968), 16ff. Kaufmann treats the judgment that Nietzsche's work is rife with contradictions as an aspect of the Nietzsche "legend" and insists that ambiguity and paradox are merely superficial.

36. Jaspers, *Nietzsche*, 8.

37. Ibid., 107. Rudolf Steiner, an early German interpreter of Nietzsche (1895) held a similar view. See his *Friedrich Nietzsche: Fighter for Freedom*, M. I. deRis, trans. (Englewood, N.J.: Rudolf Steiner Publications, 1960), 126. "This person dependent only upon himself, this possessor of creativity out of himself *alone*" is Nietzsche's Superman. See also Bernd Magnus, *Nietzsche's Existential Imperative* (Bloomington & London: Indiana University Press, 1978), who treats Nietzsche's Superman idea as an "eternalistic countermyth" to the Judeo-Christian world myth, which "attempts to retrieve the dignity of man and world by eternalizing each moment, without contamination from a 'beyond' " (159). Cf. Bernard Den Ouden, *Essays on Reason, Will, Creativity, and Time: Studies in the Philosophy of Friedrich Nietzsche* (Washington, D.C.: University Press of America, 1982), 100.

prophet of nihilism, Nietzsche becomes for Jaspers one of the "radical awakeners" of philosophy, whose function is to compel us to find and fulfill the truth in our own existence. He becomes a humanist existentialist.[38] It is certainly the case that Nietzsche led Jaspers himself along the path to liberal humanism. Walter Kaufmann is another leading interpreter of Nietzsche as humanist.

For Crane Brinton, the true Nietzsche leads down a very different path. Brinton tells us that Hitler's *Mein Kampf* could not have been written "without the aid of Friedrich Nietzsche."[39] Like Jaspers, however, Brinton recognizes that Nietzsche's work is paradoxical and at least appears to point in opposite directions. Brinton reads Nietzsche primarily as a *politique et moraliste*, that is, as someone especially interested in society and politics. "Throughout his work," Brinton writes, Nietzsche "seems torn between the contrary ideals of anarchy and authority; rarely, if ever, does he solve the conflict with the common play on words, the assertion that true liberty is true obedience. He certainly is not fairly labeled *either* as anarchist *or* as authoritarian. . . . Perhaps he believed in the anarchical solution for an elite, the Supermen, in the authoritarian solution for the many, the herd men?"[40] This citation shows how Brinton himself resolved Nietzsche's paradox, as does his account of the "Superman" of the future. Nietzsche, he tells us, plays the role of the "preacher, urging masters to be bold, active, brave, cruel, hard, voluptuous, manly, and to keep the slaves in their places."[41] J. P. Stern, while he treats Nietzsche's work as "experiment and hypothesis, not precept" remarks that

---

Den Ouden reads the "will to power" as "the will to dynamic self-energization. Thus *Macht*, rather than meaning power over other individuals, would suggest the release of individual energies which are vital to self-actualization and self-transformation."

38. Leonard Ehrlich, *Karl Jaspers: Philosophy as Faith* (Amherst: Univ. of Massachusetts Press, 1975), 28, 220.

39. Crane Brinton, *Nietzsche* (Cambridge, Mass.: Harvard Univ. Press, 1941), xv. There is no evidence that Hitler ever read Nietzsche.

40. Ibid., 118.

41. Ibid., 120.

42. J. P. Stern, *Nietzsche* (Hassocks, England: Harvester Press, 1978), 148–49. Tracy Strong, who reads Nietzsche with more subtlety than Brinton, in interpreting Nietzsche's doctrines of "the will to power," "nihilism," and "the eternal return" and who seems less willing than Brinton to take Nietzsche's violent

"the totalitarian ideologists were only too willing to take his experiments for precepts."[42]

The Case of J. S. Mill

The problem of overcoming the tensions between anarchical freedom and authority, defined only as power, is clearest in the work of the theorists just reviewed. These are the philosophers about whom there has been most debate. But it can also be found in the work of much less controversial thinkers, such as John Stuart Mill, who is generally regarded as the most simon-pure of liberals and individualists.

A study by Gertrude Himmelfarb has revealed an important ambivalence at the heart of Mill's political philosophy. Himmelfarb distinguishes between the John Stuart Mill of *On Liberty* and an "other" Mill. While the Mill of *On Liberty* is a dyed-in-the-wool philosophical radical who exalts the absolute autonomy of the individual in all things, especially in thought, expression, and life-style, the "other" Mill is a social conservative. The "other" Mill invokes authority and finds it important for society to mold and shape the opinions and feelings of individuals. "What is generally ignored," Himmelfarb writes, "by both the partisans and the critics of *On Liberty*, is that Mill himself did not always subscribe to the idea of liberty presented in that work."[43] In fact, she finds that only Mill's writings on women have a genuine affinity to *On Liberty*, which are the only ones "indeed, which do not actually conflict with it."[44]

---

language at face value, writes that "there is no doubt that Nietzsche thinks that the function of [a dominating and legislative] political class will be to reshape what it means to be human." The new politics will not be for the purpose of dividing up what there is to get; "the new idea of politics must be war to *say what will count*, what the standards by which men will measure themselves shall be. This is politics to *define* the world, not to gain control of a portion of it." But what this morality is to be is not yet known. And "Nietzsche finds that at this time in history, the conjoining of morality and war . . . is not only dangerous, but leads nowhere except to insanity." Tracy Strong, *Friedrich Nietzsche and the Politics of Transfiguration* (Berkeley: Univ. of California Press, 1975), 290–91.

43. Gertrude Himmelfarb, *On Liberty and Liberalism: The Case of John Stuart Mill* (New York: Alfred A. Knopf, 1974), xiii.

44. Ibid., xx.

The "other" Mill, according to Himmelfarb, "belongs to an older liberal tradition, the tradition of Montesquieu, Burke, the Founding Fathers, and Tocqueville. It is a tradition that is essentially modern and yet resonant of classical thought."[45] Though Himmelfarb insists that this is a "genuinely liberal tradition," the more appropriate term for the reality she wishes to represent is surely conservatism. I know of no one else who is ready to call Burke a liberal, or to identify traditionalism as liberal. Himmelfarb says that the liberalism of the "other" Mill embraces such values as "justice, virtue, community, tradition, prudence, and moderation."[46] While these are hardly words that stand for mere force or power, it is significant that in Himmelfarb's view their acceptance by Mill contradicts his view on liberty. The disciplinary character of this second Mill, which Himmelfarb finds attractive, stands in clear and unreconcilable tension with the ideas of the libertarian Mill.

Although for the Mill of *On Liberty* the greatest civilizer and educator of mankind was the free individual, especially the experimenter with new ideas and life-styles, the "other" Mill believed

> that an essential ingredient of civilization was an education in discipline to inculcate in each person the habit of "subordinating his personal impulses and aims, to what were considered the ends of society"; that civilized society also presupposed the existence of some "fundamental principles" which men . . . placed "*above* discussion"; that morality . . . could best be promoted by "laws and social arrangements," . . . that the moral defect of Fourierism was its reliance . . . on the notion that "nobody is ever to be made to do anything but act as they like."[47]

Himmelfarb does not feel at all uncomfortable in having discovered the "other" Mill. Indeed, she seems relieved to have been able to do so. She does not call Mill's invocation of authority a kind of force or manipulative enterprise. Rather, for her, it is an important antidote for the fevers brought on by a too single-minded cleaving by modern liberal society to the "one very simple

45. Ibid., xxi.
46. Ibid., xxii.
47. Ibid., 338, citing "Coleridge," "Utilitarianism," and a letter of March 31, 1849, to Harriet Taylor.

principle" of *On Liberty*.[48] Yet neither she nor Mill has pointed out or justified a philosophical ground for the moral ideals they have invoked against the abstract and universal application of the "one very simple principle." Within Mill's metaphysics and theory of knowledge those ideals would have to have the status of a mere myth. And the gentlemanly elite, the clerisy who are to be the manipulators of the myth, become ipso facto authoritarians who discipline society according to norms that are philosophically arbitrary.

Another writer, less intellectually and emotionally tied to Mill, has pointed out "the hidden and at times overt class bias of his warnings and recommendations" and the "hostile relationships between the political virtue defined and discerned by Mill, and the actual or likely class interests of those whom he wished to see in authority."[49] The conflict to which Graeme Duncan is alluding in this passage, of which, he believed, Mill himself was aware, might well be identified as a conflict between the Mill of *On Liberty* and the "other" Mill. It must have made Mill uneasy about invoking authority. "To elevate [Mill's dream of an ultimate homogeneous community], along with scattered statements in support of a clerisy or a rational dominant group, and his justifications of a unifying educational system and a religion of humanity, into the central theme in his writings," writes Duncan, "does violence to his continuing and powerful espousal of liberal values of free discussion and argument."[50] To point it out, however, is to point out the existence in Mill's thought of a significant tension between his ideas of individual liberty and his principle of social authority—a principle that in Mill's epistemology must require psychological coercion.

Outline and Argument of the Book

Of obvious importance in explaining the diversity, indeed polarity, of interpretation that runs throughout the commentary literature on the modern classics are the differing ideological commitments

48. Ibid., chap. 1.
49. Graeme Duncan, *Marx and Mill: Two Views of Social Conflict and Social Harmony* (Cambridge: Cambridge Univ. Press, 1973), 280.
50. Ibid.

of the commentators. The utility of manipulating the reputation of the "greats" for polemical purposes is plain. But if there were not real ambiguities, tensions, and contradictions in the classic texts, persuasive "proof-texting" by the controversialists would not be possible. Three chapters of the book (3, 4, and 5) will be devoted to documenting the existence of these ambiguities and tensions and to an argument that they root in the metaphysical and epistemological assumptions these writers, despite their great diversity, hold in common. These are the assumptions that "doing" metaphysics and "doing" epistemology consists in showing how Descartes's dual categories of mind and body are related to one another in the singleness of human experience and that from such a showing one can self-consistently proceed to explain the structure of political reality. If no noncontradictory or nonproblematical account can in fact be given of the relationship of body to mind, one would expect that the metaphysical contradictions into which these writers consequently fell would produce precisely the tensions and contradictions found in the political theories built on such faulty metaphysics. To lay a groundwork for these three chapters requires detailed examination (chapter 2) of the exact character of the dualistic system of reality and of knowledge that Descartes developed and bequeathed to his philosophical posterity, of the circumstances under which that system of thought came into being, and of the political questions that arise from the various possible ways of relating mind to body.

The last section of each of the three central chapters will add to the philosophical analysis a reflection on the paradoxes of force and freedom in the world of political action that mirror those in the world of political thought. Chapter 6 looks at some recent efforts by students of political philosophy to replace the dualistic world of Descartes with a holistic mode of understanding of political reality that might eliminate tension and paradox. In my view, however, these efforts have not succeeded, because they have been unable to break clear of the fundamental categories of body and mind as the starting points of their argument. They have taken the problem too much on Descartes's terms.

In a final chapter I shall first speak briefly of the work of Alasdair MacIntyre, who has begun to move successfully beyond

Descartes but in reacting to the problems of universalistic scientism has problematically broken also with the idea of universal moral norms. The bulk of the chapter will be devoted to working out a theory of existential universal principles of right that may form the foundation of an unparadoxical way of ideas. They establish a consensual moral link, a principle of legitimacy, that will allow us to remove existing tensions in our present way of relating force to freedom.[51]

51. For a different but related treatment of the problem of irony and paradox in modern political thought, see Thomas Spragens, *The Irony of Liberal Reason*, (Chicago: Univ. of Chicago Press, 1981).

2

Cartesian Dualism and Political Paradox

Force and Necessary Law:
The Historical Background of Cartesian Thought

Modernity does not begin with freedom or with law but with force—the sovereign state as it emerged from the wars of the Reformation. "Law is nothing else than the command of the sovereign in the exercise of his sovereign power," wrote Jean Bodin.[1] Medieval theology and the Scholastic philosophy of natural law, which from the days of Aquinas had, at least in idea, knit together the *Respublica Christiana* of Europe, were both in disarray. Like our own time, the sixteenth and seventeenth centuries were a period of existential and ideological incoherence, a time that demanded a new way of ideas to frame a new way of life. And the starting point was force.

When Jean Bodin, writing in the midst of the religious wars in France, sought in his *Six Books of the Republic* to establish the ground of right for the political community on the basis of physical force—on the mere fact of subjection of the citizen to the ruler—he was attempting to find a *raison d'être* for the state other than the human common good which had traditionally been its *raison d'être*. He was trying to explore and understand the way which Machiavelli had opened to the modern mind. The attainment of this objective called for an intellectual position lying altogether outside the moral orbit

1. Jean Bodin, *Six Books of the Commonwealth*, abridged ed., M. J. Tooley, trans. (Oxford: Basil Blackwell, 1955), 35.

of good and evil. . . . What had to be overcome was the whole traditional notion of an end to be pursued for the perfection of man.[2]

The medieval concept of law had been intimately tied to the idea of perfection, both in the human and in the nonhuman sphere. Natural law described the tendencies in all natural beings to fulfill specific functions or ends legislated for them, as their essences, by God. It was knowable by human reason, conceived as an impression in human beings of Divine Reason, and it was identified with the reason of God. Nature was conceived as a moral reality, to be understood under the categories "good" and "bad." "Good" is that existent particular that fulfills its function or end; "bad" the one that fails adequately to realize its essential end. Reason, shared by man and God, pronounces the judgment of good and bad both on things and people. It also joins mind and body as a single organic whole.

The Reformation of the sixteenth century brought a sudden end to this Gothic music, reducing it to the blaring cacophony of theological dissonance and war drums. Until the middle of the seventeenth century, law was effectively suspended. Mutilation, murder, and massacre were the order of the day as Protestants and Catholics mutually sought to impose by will and force what rational debate could not accomplish by persuasion— a new religious and political unity in Europe. It was probable that the concept of law ultimately to emerge from the political and military standoff in which this chaos culminated would bear the marks of willfulness and violence. A third of the population of Germany was destroyed in the Thirty Years' War by military action and by famine produced by widespread desolation of the land. Two other things made a coercive concept of law inevitable—characteristics of the newly authoritative theologies and the language of the natural science that was coming into its own during the same period.

Both Lutheranism and Calvinism downgraded the role of reason in moral questions. Obsessed by an overwhelming sense of

2. Charles N. R. McCoy, *The Structure of Political Thought: A Study in the History of Political Ideas* (New York: McGraw-Hill, 1963), 187–88.

human sinfulness and depravity, both theologies dubbed faith the sole basis of knowledge, and grace the sole instrument of decent behavior. Scandalized by the human irrelevance of the intricacies of late Scholastic reasoning and by the excesses of the Renaissance clergy, the authors of both theologies declared the world of essences and Divine intentions closed to the human mind. In place of a humanistic God, who shared his plans for the world with reasonable and worldly prelates such as Aeneas Silvius, they worshipped a stern and punishing Jehovah of holy but inscrutable will, whose commands and dire penalties were thought an adequate motive for pious behavior. Even in the portions of Europe that remained Catholic, the outworn reign of Scholastic reason came to an end as pietistic reformers cleansed the Augean stables of the traditional church. Especially in Jansenism, a Catholic counterpart to Calvinist reform, a wrathful and willful God replaced the reasonable deity of the High Middle Ages. Its stern spirit continued to pervade the life of the Tridentine church down to our own time.

When in 1648 the Peace of Westphalia wrote a definitive end to the religious struggles of more than a hundred years, and the modern state in unstable equilibrium replaced the shadowy *Respublica Christiana* of the Middle Ages as the legal form of Europe, a whole new intellectual system was required to explain and legitimate the new political order. Teleological natural law was in general disrepute, and, in place of a single authoritative theological system, a number of adamant and hostile faiths had established stable political bases.

A new consensual world view was to grow out of the new reality that had emerged from the lengthy period of unmitigated force and from the categories of the new science that postulated the world as a field of forces. In the new science, nature and law meant something quite different from their signification in the romantic teleology of Scholasticism. Nature had become an observable process of bodies in motion, and law a pattern of necessary and recurrent relationships amongst these bodies, discovered by empirical measurement. Giordano Bruno stated the new conception succinctly when he wrote that "Nature is nothing but a force implanted in things and the law by which all entities proceed along their proper paths."[3] *Physis*, the broad and frequently ambiguous concept of "nature" in classical teleology, had been narrowed down to the precise notions of "physics." The necessity imputed to the new natural law derived from the fact that the instrument of scientific calculation and prediction was mathematics, whose clear and distinct ideas were assumed to be a perfect representation of the reality they measured. Gottfried Wilhelm Leibniz justified this assumption by saying that "all things are governed by reason and because otherwise there would be no knowledge, which would be contrary to the nature of the sovereign principle."[4]

Before Descartes and others sought to clear the away the rubble of a now functionless and apparently irrelevant tradition and to fashion a new canon of knowledge, experimenters working with pragmatic and ad hoc procedures had piled up an impressive collection of new information about the world and invented scores of ingenious machines to control it. They had also prepared the way for theoretical synthesis of the new body of useful knowledge. Here is J. H. Randall's list of the achievements of the experimenters:

> To the original minds who shared Galileo's emphasis on experiment . . . were due the discoveries that made Newton's work possible. Especially successful were the triumphs of mathematics in the field of fluids and gases. Torricelli, Galileo's pupil, in 1643 invented the barometer and weighed the atmosphere, and Pascal confirmed his measurements four years later by his famous experiment of carrying a barometer up a mountain and observing the diminishing atmospheric pressure. To Pascal, too, is due the formulation of the laws of pressure in liquids, while Robert Boyle, who had studied under Galileo, discovered the law of pressure in gases. It is significant that within twenty years these facts had been used in machines for raising water, and that by the end of the century Newcomen's steam engine had begun the application of steam power to industry. . . . To light, too, mathematics was outstandingly applied,

3. Giordano Bruno, *De Immenso*, book 8, chap. 9, cited in Ernst Cassirer, *The Philosophy of the Enlightenment* (Boston: Beacon Press, 1951), 44.

4. Letter to Varignon, Feb. 2, 1702, cited in Cassirer, *Philosophy of the Enlightenment*, 58.

and the science of optics . . . [developed] in 1695 . . . critically measured the speed of light.[5]

The one tool on which the entire work of these men depended was mathematics, which would soon become not only the language of Newton's synthesis, but also the chief element in a new conception of reason. As Hiram Caton has succinctly phrased it, "the dependence of certainty on the mathematical paradigm in effect equates the reasonable with the mathematical."[6] Mathematics has been put to work to discover invariable laws by which to describe and predict the movement of empirical forces.

From the Reformation and the scientific revolution of the Renaissance there thus emerged two worlds. On the one hand, there was an infinitely plural world of value and moral purpose. Divorced from the concept of public reason, it was presided over by a variety of warring faiths, each with its special conception of divine guidance and of human goodness. On the other was the world of technical rationality, the world of science, knit together as a public reality by its adherence to a single concept of method. René Descartes was to transmute that fruitful instrument of empirical prediction and control into a comprehensive standard of public truth, moral as well as physical, one that would furnish the basic categories of philosophy and *Weltanschauung* for the next three hundred years. It would enshrine a mechanistic and necessitarian concept of law that would make it impossible to establish a workable relationship between force and freedom.

The Authority of Cartesianism

By the end of the seventeenth century, Cartesianism was accounted "the new philosophy" and was identified with science. The writings of the schools, by contrast, had been dubbed "ancient philosophy." And there was a Cartesianism for the many as well as for the few. "All over Europe Descartes's work had been taken over by popularizers and teachers," writes Jonathan Rée.

5. J. H. Randall, Jr., *The Making of the Modern Mind*, rev. ed. (Boston: Houghton Mifflin Co., 1940), 256.

6. Hiram Caton, *The Origin of Subjectivity: An Essay on Descartes* (New Haven & London: Yale Univ. Press, 1973), 35.

"In 1625 . . . a disciple of Descartes gave a series of popular lectures on Cartesian physics in Toulouse, and the lectures achieved a level of popularity normally reserved for great preachers."[7]

While Cartesianism carried out its most sweeping revolution in philosophy and physics, its influence is found even in areas about which the philosopher had written nothing. Thus the author of the preface to Sir Dudley North's *Discourses Upon Trade* (1691) tells us that North's attempt to explain economics on the basis of a few first principles was due to the influence of Descartes's new method.[8] Though for a while Newton came to eclipse Descartes, it has since been recognized again that it was Descartes who established the major categories of modern thought. As Rée puts it, "It is the old view which is closest to the truth. The principles of the 'new philosophy,' and the theory of knowledge and the theory of human nature which go with it; the concepts of an idea, of mathematical laws of nature, and of a world which is not supervised by a personal God, are so fundamental to modern consciousness that it is hard not to regard them as part of the natural property of the human mind."[9] Jacques Maritain also writes that "the figure of Descartes dominates all philosophy of the past three centuries, his historical significance is inexhaustible."[10] Even Hegel and Marx, whose dialectical holism repudiates Cartesian dualism, show the influence of Descartes in their starting point—the assumption that there are two polar points of reality that must be sewn together by historical process.

It is from the puzzles, tensions, and ambiguities of Cartesian philosophy, I shall argue, that the ambivalences, tensions, and paradoxes of modern political thought, described in the last chapter, have arisen. The common currency of the diverse modern conceptions of individual freedom is found in the autonomy of Descartes's lone thinker, while the notion of force they share derives from the Cartesian view of body as mathematically structured matter whose motions are governed by necessary laws. Just

7. Jonathan Rée, *Descartes* (New York: Pica Press, 1974), 151–52.

8. Ibid., 152.

9. Ibid., 157.

10. Jacques Maritain, *The Dream of Descartes*, M. L. Andison, trans., (New York: Philosophical Library, 1949), 9.

as Cartesian dualism contains a fundamental ambiguity about the precise relationship between the free determinations of mind and will of the observer and political actor and the necessary movements of observed body (political behavior), so is there an ambiguity about how subjective freedom of individual political choice can intelligibly be related to the objective necessities of a manipulable body politic.

The Character of Cartesian Dualism

The following is an exegesis of Descartes's *Discourse on Method* and of the parts of the *Meditations* that flesh out the metaphysical and epistemological position developed in outline in the *Discourse*. I intend to show that the metaphysical grounding of Descartes's view of scientific method is much more modern than most scholars have realized and sheds much more of the author's medieval background than is generally supposed. It is my view that Descartes was doing more in the *Discourse* than adumbrating and justifying a certain method of empirical investigation. I shall try to show that his intention was to destroy, root and branch, every element of the already dissolving traditional *Weltanschauung* made up of Christian theology and Aristotelian philosophy. The thoroughly revolutionary character of his thought is attested by Descartes's insertion, tacitly, into the structure of the *Discourse* of an ironic metaphor of creation. The six parts of the *Discourse* can be understood as six days of creation, a new creation that was to supplant the story of Genesis. In place of a "living soul" fashioned in the "image of God," Descartes created for a new age a "thinking thing."

Many scholars hold that in his *Discourse on Method* Descartes proved the existence of an autonomous, nonmaterial self, characterized by the activity of thinking. In this reading, Cartesian dualism signifies a nonmaterial thinker and material body, which are ontologically disjoined from one another. Each thinker is a world unto himself, free to follow his own will and the dictates of his creative imagination, at least in thought. He stands wholly outside the world of body, or extension, but is capable of observing and of scientifically measuring and manipulating it, to serve the purposes that are given by his free will. Since so radical a dualism is ontologically implausible, Descartes sews his centrifugal whole together by the public demonstration of a perfect God, who fashioned both thinker and body (imperfect beings), and whose existence must be proven in order to guarantee the reality of both mind and body.

Among recent commentators, Albert G. A. Balz, Bernard Williams, Edward A. Ballard, and Norman Kemp Smith all hold for an interpretation similar to the one just outlined. Others, such as A. Boyce Gibson, A. K. Stout, Anthony Kenny, and S. V. Keeling point up numerous difficulties in Descartes's proofs of God's existence and even reduce them to nonsense. But they do not suggest that Descartes may have deliberately employed weak or false arguments.[11] Kenny, for example, remarks that for all that Descartes's argument shows, "the idea of a being possessing every perfection may be as nonsensical as the idea of a being possessing every possible shape." He also finds a fundamental incompatibility between the cogito and the ontological argument.[12] And S. V. Keeling concludes that "Descartes seems mistaken in supposing he has proved God to exist. What he *does* prove is, that *if* there exists anything having the defining attribute of 'God,' then its existence would be a *necessary* . . . and not merely a contingent existence."[13] Leon Pearl presents a similar review of Descartes's theology and a conclusion about the ontological argument identical to that of Keeling.[14]

11. See Albert G. A. Balz, *Descartes and the Modern Mind* (New Haven: Yale Univ. Press, 1952), Chaps. 9–18; Bernard Williams, "René Descartes," in *Encyclopedia of Philosophy*, vol. 2 (New York: Macmillan and The Free Press, 1967), 348–50; Edward G. Ballard, *Philosophy at the Crossroads* (Baton Rouge: Louisiana State Univ. Press, 1971), 58–61; S. V. Keeling, *Descartes* (London: Oxford Univ. Press, 1968), chap. 4; Norman Kemp Smith, *New Studies in the Philosophy of Descartes* (London: Macmillan, 1952), chaps. 10, 11. The following commentators point out numerous difficulties in Descartes's proofs of God's existence but do not suggest that Descartes might have been playing with his readers: A. Boyce Gibson, *The Philosophy of Descartes* (London: Methuen, 1932), chaps. 3, 4; A. K. Stout, "The Basis of Knowledge in Descartes," in Willis Doney, ed., *Descartes: A Collection of Critical Essays* (Garden City, N.Y.: Doubleday, 1967); Anthony Kenny, *Descartes: A Study of His Philosophy* (New York: Random House, 1968), chaps. 6, 7.

12. Kenny, *Descartes*, 130–31, 170–71.

13. Keeling, *Descartes*, 106–130, 166–78.

14. Leon Pearl, *Descartes* (Boston: Twayne Publishers, 1977), 117–48. See especially 145.

Another school of thought, of which Hiram Caton is the most articulate spokesman, holds a very different interpretation of Descartes's ontology. In this view, the thinking self is a consciousness that depends radically on the world of body for existence and is not a fully autonomous "self." Its being is the direct result of sensations emanating from body, and, without these sensations, there would be no thinking activity. Nevertheless, Descartes believed that the thinker is somehow very different from the bodies that give rise to his thought, according to Caton. The mind must, by powers of its own, judge and sort the data of the senses. Descartes was also aware of the freedom of his will to determine his purposes and to manipulate and control body to serve them. But all this is known directly, by the "good sense" of the thinker, through the clarity and distinctness of his ideas as he formulates them in the presence of sense data. Or else it is willed into being by the thinker. None of it requires a proof of the thinking self or, indeed, permits a claim of such perfect autonomy. Nor does it in any way rely upon a notion of God, a problematical concept. It is also a dualism replete with ambiguity which in my view gives rise to the tensions of force and freedom in modern political thought.[15]

Caton arrived at his view of Descartes's dualistic system by reviewing the entire corpus of Descartes's thought, relying as much on the implications of the scientific essays, such as the *Optics*, as on the explicitly philosophical works. Caton also documented in detail his belief that Descartes deliberately veiled his meaning using evidence partly internal and partly external to the Cartesian texts. I shall attempt to verify Caton's thesis with detailed internal evidence through a close reading of the *Discourse on Method* and to explain the importance of this view of Descartes's ontology as a source of political paradox. (See appendix A for a note on the method I have employed in interpreting Descartes.)

The First Day

The first paragraph of Part 1 of the *Discourse on Method* opens with the words "*Le bon sens*" (good sense). This is a synonym for "*la raison*," the faculty of judging, which is also rendered as "*la lumière*

15. See Caton, *Origin of Subjectivity.*

naturelle" (the light of nature). "Good sense," Descartes tells us, "the ability to judge correctly, and to distinguish the true from the false . . . is the same by nature in all men."[16] It is not a difference in intellectual capacity that accounts for different opinions but rather differences in approach or methodology.

Descartes's starting point in constructing his method is a recognition that all received ideas are suspect. From his Scholastic education he was able to salvage only a few tools of learning, such as language and mathematics. But all supposed substantive knowledge, such as that found in treatises of philosophy, had to be put aside as lacking any certain foundation. Leaving all this behind, together with the teachings of custom and lore, he has set out to learn empirically and experimentally. His data are the "great book of nature" *(le grand livre du monde)* and the interior world of his own self—his mind and will *(en [soi]-même)* (8). And his motive is practical knowledge for which judgment is sharpened by interest. Thus Descartes pronounces his new "*Fiat lux!*" and with his new method divides the day from the night.

God said, "Let there be light," and there was light.
God saw that light was good, and God divided light from darkness.
God called light "day" and darkness he called "night."
Evening came and morning came: the first day.[17]

The Second Day

Descartes next sets forth the principal rules of his method— an analytic logic. It was to be philosophy of a new sort—not a medieval reflection on being but a modern analysis of making,

16. See Etienne Gilson's commentary in René Descartes, *Discours de la Méthode*, Texte et Commentaire par Etienne Gilson (Paris: Librairie Philosophique J. Vrin, 1962), 81–82. Quotations from *The Discourse* and *Meditations* are from René Descartes, *Discourse on Method and Meditations*, L. J. Lafleur, trans. (Indianapolis & New York: Bobbs-Merrill Co., Library of Liberal Arts, 1960). This quotation is from pages 3 and 4. Other quotations are parenthetically identified by their page numbers in the Lafleur translation. With permission of Bobbs-Merrill Co., Inc., copyright ©, 1960 by the Liberal Arts Press, Inc., a division of the Bobbs-Merrill Co., Inc.

17. Genesis 1:3–5, in Alexander James, ed., *The Jerusalem Bible* (Garden City, N.Y.: Doubleday, 1966), 15.

creating. Descartes's reflection is value-free, impersonal, dispassionate—"untroubled by any cares or passions."

In Part 2 Descartes employs an elaborate architectural metaphor. He writes of the construction of buildings, of city streets, of towns; he considers problems of renovation—of individual houses and of whole cities. And he contrasts the rational order of the modern city with the rambling planlessness of "those ancient towns which were originally nothing but hamlets, and in the course of time have become great cities" (10). Chance, not rational planning, governed their construction. But we soon realize that this is but a metaphor for psychic and social order—the world views of individuals and societies, the revolution of reason versus the traditionalism of custom. From buildings to ideas—and the building of ideas, both individual and social. On the second day of Genesis God is an architect who constructs the arching vault of heaven to separate the waters above from those below the earth. In the second part of his *Discourse* Descartes, the new master builder, replaces the old vault of ideas with one of his own construction.

The discussion of architecture appears at first to approve the rationalist and holistic approach of the town planner who blueprints an entire city. But we are soon given to understand that Descartes wants to proceed to social reform in a gradualistic manner. "We never tear down all the houses in a city just to rebuild them in a different way to make the streets more beautiful," he writes, "but we do see that individual owners often have theirs torn down and rebuilt. . . . By this example I was convinced that a private individual should not seek to reform a nation by changing all its customs and destroying it to construct it anew, nor to reform the body of knowledge or the system of education" (11). But for himself, he "could not do better than to reject . . . completely" the opinions he had received since birth and then "to resume them afterwards, or perhaps to accept better ones in their place, when I had determined how they fitted into a rational scheme" (11). The rule here seems to be free thought for the individual but tradition for society.

But if the outlook of individuals changes radically, does this not ipso facto spell ideological revolution for society? Descartes attempts to forestall such a conclusion with an explicit disclaimer of revolutionary intent: "I cannot at all approve those mischievous spirits who, not being called either by birth or by attainments to a position of political power, are nevertheless constantly proposing some new reform. If I thought the slightest basis could be found in this *Discourse* for a suspicion that I was guilty of this folly, I would be loath to permit it to be published" (11). His intention, he claimed, was solely to "reform [his] own ideas, and rebuild them on foundations that would be wholly [his]" (12–13). But then he goes on to write, improbably, that if his "building has pleased [him] sufficiently to display a model of it to the public, it is not because [he advised] anyone to copy it" (13). But surely this must have been his ultimate decision—to change the world; for why else would he have made his *Discourse* public, if he did not expect others to learn from him? In Part 1 he had written openly of his work as a subject for imitation. The expectation, however, could not appear to ruling authority as an invitation to wholesale and sudden reform. Hence we are told that he did not believe that many could understand and profit from the knowledge of his method. In readying himself for the great adventure in rational revolution Descartes writes:

> Like a man who walks alone in the darkness, I resolved to go slowly and circumspectly that if I did not get ahead very rapidly I was at least safe from falling. Also, just as the occupants of an old house do not destroy it before a plan for a new one has been thought out, I did not want to reject all the opinions which had slipped irrationally into my consciousness since birth, until I had first spent enough time planning how to accomplish the task which I was then undertaking, and seeking the true method of obtaining knowledge of everything which my mind was capable of understanding. (14)

Descartes's new vault of heaven would have to be constructed and installed slowly and with great care.

With this lengthy introduction Descartes prefaces his presentation of "The Principal Rules of the Method," which turns out to be a mathematical system modeled on geometry and logic. The first rule is to accept nothing as true that does not present itself "clearly and distinctly" to one's mind.

The second [rule] was to divide each of the difficulties which I encountered into as many parts as possible, and as might be required for an easier solution.

The third was to think in an orderly fashion, when concerned with the search for truth beginning with the things which were simplest and easiest to understand, and gradually and by degrees reaching toward more complex knowledge, even treating, as though ordered, materials which were not necessarily so.

The last was, both in the process of searching and in reviewing when in difficulty, always to make enumerations so complete, and reviews so general, that I would be certain that nothing was omitted.

These long chains of reasoning, so simple and easy, which enabled the geometricians to reach the most difficult demonstrations, had made me wonder whether all things knowable to men might not fall into a similar logical sequence. (14)

Descartes thus expounds a method which leads him to search for knowledge of the world as a logical structure governed by mathematical necessity—a world of necessary law.

In Part 2 of the *Discourse* Descartes has nothing to say about the application of his new method to specific problems. We are in this part moving beyond the empirical world. Our attention is confined exclusively to the world of clear and distinct ideas. Here we have laid out before us a sturdy new "vault of heaven"; he has furnished us with a practical system for laying bare the abstract order that lies within the "great book of nature" *(le grand livre du monde)*, the regularity in all things that, as perfect mathematical order, radically transcends while it gives structure to and supports all things.

God said, "Let there be a vault in the waters to divide
the waters in two." And so it was.
God made the vault, and it divided the waters above
the vault from the waters under the vault.
God called the vault—"heaven."
Evening came and morning came: the second day.[18]

18. Genesis 1:6–8.

The Third Day

In Part 2 Descartes has given us a system of mind. We have not been shown how it is to be used. The arch of heaven has separated the superior from the inferior waters, but it has not given us dry land to walk on. We do not know yet how to act. It is on the third day that dry land appears. In Part 3 Descartes tells how we are to proceed to the reform he has heralded. "In planning to rebuild one's house it is not enough to draw up plans for the new building, tear down the old one, and provide . . . materials . . . and obtain workmen for the task. We must see that we are provided with a comfortable place to stay while the work of rebuilding is going on" (18). In other words, we must develop a rule that can establish a workable connection between the city framed by the new way of ideas and the present city, between the new vault of heaven and the old earth of Genesis. That Descartes thinks he has made such a connection is signified by the title of this part: "Some Moral Rules Derived from the Method"—principles of practical procedure.

Descartes's practical method, or provisional code of moral behavior, consists of four maxims. The first is to obey all the laws and customs of present society, "constantly retaining the religion . . . in which by God's grace, I had been brought up since childhood, and in all other matters to follow the most moderate and least excessive opinions to be found in the practices of the more judicious part of the community" (18).

In spelling out this rule, Descartes copies Machiavelli in urging that attention should be paid to the conduct rather than the words of the members of the community. By implication one would believe what one wished, and the followers of the new method would of course subscribe to the theoretical truths that it laid bare. But in acting, it would be prudent to follow the practical norms one observed in the behavior of one's society. Since this behavior will be various, one is advised to follow the rule of moderation and avoid copying excessive behavior. Another maxim can be summed up as firmness or resoluteness in action, according to the principle of probability. And a third calls for independence combined with self-control. In the midst of the old order, one remains free of it, for one's thoughts may remain "wholly under our control" (20).

Descartes's last maxim was to review all the occupations possible in this life, "in order to choose the best" (22). He decided for himself that he could not do better than continue in the work in which he was engaged, which was the pursuit of truth, according to the principles of his new method, plus the three practical maxims just surveyed. Thus, when imitated by others, his method becomes a *modus vivendi* for all free thinkers who are engaged in the search for truth. Walking still on the old earth, one could take comfort in gazing up at the new vault of heaven.

In Part 3 Descartes has created the new land of the free thinker and ordered it under his new vault of heaven. He makes us aware of his new creation by closing this part with a reminiscence of his travels: "I wandered here and there throughout the world, trying everywhere to be spectator rather than actor in all the comedies that go on" (22). The reminiscence seems to imply another maxim—that the seeker after truth will not be a person who is active in the social and political life of his own society but rather an observer of the passing scene who lives apart. In this way he calls up before us the image of the value-free scientist who lives apart from the world he studies—passive and detached, autonomous mind looking in on an alien world of body, whose motions he observes and charts.

---

*God said, "Let the waters under heaven come together
into a single mass, and let dry land appear." And
it was so.
God called the dry land "earth" and the mass of waters
"seas," and God saw that it was good.
Evening came and morning came: the third day.*[19]

The Fourth Day

Descartes has willed that a new light be shed on reality; he has fashioned a new heaven of theoretical inquiry; and he has produced dry land to walk on as we prudently build up the knowl-

19. Genesis 1:9–13.

edge required to renovate the earth. He must now hang lights in his heaven to illuminate the way.

He proceeds to doubt away "as absolutely false," everything that is in the least uncertain. This requires that he reject everything received through the senses, "as our senses deceive us at times" (24). With this accomplished, the certain truth of Descartes's famous cogito remains.

> While I thus wished to think everything false, it was necessarily true that I who thought so was something. Since this truth, *I think, therefore, I am,* . . . was so firm and assured that all the most extravagant suppositions of the sceptics were unable to shake it, I judged that I could safely accept it as the first principle of the philosophy I was seeking. (24)

The "I" whose reality he thus established is the thinking self, the mind that thinks, "entirely distinct from the body and . . . easier to know than the latter" (25). And it was the clarity of his thought of the thinking self that guaranteed its existence—"I saw very clearly that to think one must exist. So I judged that I could accept as a general rule that the things we conceive very clearly and . . . distinctly are always true" (25). As for his ideas "about the many things outside" him, he was not "troubled to discover where they came from," because he could find nothing in these ideas superior to himself. If it turned out that they actually existed, he could explain their perfection as a derivation from his own nature. "If they did not exist, I could believe that they were derived from nothingness, . . . that they were derived from my own defects" (26). He thus appears to make the world of body radically dependent on the world of the self, conceived as mind, and specifically on the world constituted by *his* mind. Body becomes a function of the individual's mind.

Two lights have been hung in Descartes's heaven. Clear and distinct ideas radiate the guarantee of Cartesian truth. The abstract light of the first day becomes concrete in the sun of the mind's clear concepts. The body, as a moon, reflects them back. But Descartes discovers a problem in his formula and voices it: "There may well be some difficulty in deciding which are those [ideas] we conceive distinctly" (25).

Apparently to answer this question Descartes inserts at this point two conventional proofs of the existence of God, following a reflection on the idea that his doubting showed his spirit was not wholly perfect and that it is "a greater perfection to know than to doubt" (25). He then decides to find out from what source he had learned to think of something more perfect than himself, and it "appeared evident that it must have been from some nature which was in fact more perfect" (25). He decides to have recourse to the hypothesis that a perfect being, God, put the idea of a more perfect being than himself in his mind, since to derive it from nothingness "was manifestly impossible" and to derive it from himself "no less repugnant to good sense than it is to assume that something comes from nothing." But how could the hypothesis be proven? Descartes writes: "Since I knew some perfections which I did not possess, I was not the only being in existence—I will here use freely, if you will pardon me, the terms of the school—and that it followed of necessity that there was someone else more perfect upon whom I depended and from whom I had acquired all that I possessed" (26).

The existence of God "follows of necessity" from my knowledge of perfections that I do not possess. We marvel that so large a question should be dealt with so summarily! And we notice that the proof does not settle the question that inaugurated it—how one distinguishes a clear from an unclear idea. But the careful reader recognizes that Descartes is speaking conventional theological language to the conventional-minded for the sake of his freedom, in keeping with the first maxim of his "provisional code of morality." The unconventional free thinker recognizes that Descartes did not mean *him* to take the argument seriously. For Descartes has already asked his pardon for making free use of "the terms of the school," terms that had already been rejected in Part 1 with all the ragtag baggage of traditional lore.

At the end of a long paragraph detailing the qualities and attributes of God, which follows upon the capsule proof, Descartes asserts a new proof of the existence of the thinking self. In it the power of God takes the place of the clear idea as the explanatory ground of the thinker's existence. "If there were in the world bodies, or even intelligences or other natures that were not wholly perfect, their being must depend on God's power in such a way that they could not subsist without him for a single moment" (27).

The language fits perfectly the implicit metaphor of sun and moon. For the light of the moon cannot subsist for one moment without the light of the sun. But we realize that Descartes is still speaking within the tradition to traditionalists. For he here once more answers a question that he had not raised. The discussion of the deity presumably was undertaken to distinguish clear from unclear ideas, not to ground the existence of the thinking self. But no criterion of distinction is presented. Instead Descartes gives us an example of a clear idea. He directs us to the world of mathematics. We are shown that the validity of geometrical propositions, "the great certainty which everyone attributes to them," rests solely on the ground "that they are clearly and evidently conceived." But we are cautioned that there is "nothing at all in them to assure me of the existence of their object; it was clear, for example, that if we posit a triangle, its three angles must be equal to two right angles, but there was nothing in that to assure me that there was a single triangle in the world" (27). Then, with the *apparent* object of showing us that this observation does not adversely affect his conventional proof of the existence of God Descartes remarks:

> When I turned back to my idea of a perfect Being, on the other hand, I . . . discovered that existence was included in that idea in the same way that the idea of a triangle contains the equality of its angles to two right angles, or that the idea of a . . . circle includes the equidistance of all its parts from its center. Perhaps, in fact, the existence of the perfect Being is even more evident. Consequently, it is at least as certain that God, who is this perfect Being, exists, as any theorem of geometry could possibly be. (27, 28)

But this is double talk. For if existence is included in the idea of God in the same way that the idea of a triangle includes the equality of its angles to two right angles, it is included only definitionally as a statement about attributes. Elsewhere Descartes "emphasizes that mathematical entities are not substances or independent of physical substances but are rather modes or attributes of substances. For example, he writes: 'geometrical figures are considered not as substances but as the limits [*termini*] within which substance is contained,' and that 'order and number are not something different from the things which are ordered and numbered, but they are only the modes under which one considers them.'"[20] Thus, if the existence of God is as certain "as any theorem of geometry could possibly be," it is uncertain, for the theorems of geometry refer to modes of existence, not to existence itself.[21]

While the free thinker understands that Descartes sees conventional proofs of the existence of God as logical games, he is troubled by the fact that Descartes's criterion of truth—clear and distinct ideas—in fact is inadequate to establish any kind of existence, including the existence of the self. It is rather a guarantee of logical coherence. Can he therefore have been serious in defining the thinking self as "entirely distinct from the body"? We seem to have lost our sun and are back at the point at which we started. But Descartes soon restores it to us—by hanging a moon back in the sky, the moon he had started with—body. We are shown *how* this moon reflects the light of its Cartesian sun and thereby guarantees its existence.

The final argument of Part 4 of the *Discourse* begins with a rumination on "corporeal objects" and on the human habit of supposing that only those things are intelligible that can be pictured.

> Even philosophers hold it as a maxim in the schools that there is nothing in the understanding which was not first in the senses, a location where it is clearly evident that the ideas of God and of the soul have never been. It seems to me that those who wish to use imagery to understand these matters are doing precisely the same

20. Charles Adam and Paul Tannery, eds., *Oeuvres de Descartes*, vol. 7 (London: Macmillan, 1952), 381; vol. 8, 26; E. S. Haldane and G.R.T. Ross, *The Philosophical Works of Descartes*, vol. 2. (Cambridge: Cambridge Univ. Press, 1965), 227; vol. 1, 241, cited in Alan Gewirth, "Descartes: Two Disputed Questions," *Journal of Philosophy* 68 (May 6, 1971): 289–90.

21. In *Meditations* Descartes presents three more proofs of God's existence, at greater length than in the *Discourse*. Two are found in the Third Meditation (cosmological proofs) and one in the Fifth (an ontological proof). Elsewhere I have presented a detailed analysis of these as deliberately spurious efforts. See William T. Bluhm, "Descartes's Six Days of Creation: An Interpretation of the *Discourse on Method*" (Talk delivered at the Medieval House, University of Rochester, February 9, 1983), 46–54.

thing that they would be doing if they tried to use their eyes to hear sound or smell odors. There is even this difference: that the sense of sight gives us no less certainty of the truth of objects than do those of smell and hearing, while neither our imagery nor our senses could assure us of anything without the cooperation of our understanding or reason. (28)

In this marvelous paragraph Descartes aims another blow at the Scholastics by pointing up the discrepancy between their affirmation that the basis of all knowledge is sense and the entirely abstract character of their metaphysical proofs. At the same time he supplies an empirical ground for his rational principle of certainty. In effect, he is telling us that if clear and distinct ideas of purely abstract objects do not guarantee their existence, clear and distinct ideas conjoined with the data of the senses do. Nevertheless, in his tacit metaphor, reason remains the greater light, the sun, and sensation the lesser, the moon. Descartes concludes that

> We should never be convinced except on the evidence of our reason. Note the I say of our *reason*, and not of our imagination or of our senses; for even though we see the sun very clearly, we must not judge thereby that its size is such as we see it . . . For reason does not insist that all we see or visualize in this way is true, but it does insist that all our ideas or notions must have some foundation in truth. (30)

In the penultimate paragraph of Part 4 Descartes speaks once more to the conventionalists, telling them that the way to be sure that their waking thoughts are true and their dreams false is to "presuppose the existence of God," since the criterion of clarity with which he started "is known to be true only because God exists" (29). (It is interesting that even in this conventional statement, God has been reduced from a proven existent to a presupposition.) But in the last paragraph he returns to his true criterion of validity, the clear and distinct idea. It is by virtue of the clarity and distinctness of our waking ideas, he tells us, that we can affirm their truth and distinguish them from the fictions of our dreams, "since our reasonings or judgments are never as clear and distinct in sleep as in waking life, although our imaginations are then lively and detailed" (30).

We now have Descartes's complete argument about certainty before us, for we have learned in what sense "clarity and distinctness of idea" remains a criterion of truth. In this final paragraph Descartes is talking neither about the clarity and distinctness of our idea of God or of ourselves but rather about the clarity and distinctness of our reasonings about corporeal entities—some ostensibly real, some imagined. And we discern the one from the other by the greater clarity and distinctness with which we reason about the experience of sense when awake than we do about the fantasy dream world when we are asleep.

But how can we be sure that the whole corporeal world which we *think* we discern is not an illusion? For the answer to this we must go back to the fourth paragraph of the part. There we were told that if the things of the corporeal world "really existed," we could "believe that whatever perfections they possessed might be derived from my own nature; it they did not exist, I could believe that they were derived from nothingness, that is, that they were derived from my own defects" (26). The statement is enormously pregnant, for, taken together with the message of the last paragraph, it reduces the question of certainty to a question of clear reasoning about the manifold of mutually implicative mind and body. Explicitly, Descartes tells us that what we can know about body is radically dependent on our minds, either on their perfections or imperfections. Body is mind-dependent for its existence. But conversely, by inference, we should be able to say nothing about our minds or selves unless there were a world of body, or rather sensations of such a world, to think and reason about.[22]

Perhaps this is the complete significance of the expression *bon sens* (good sense) with which the *Discourse* opens. For sense alone signifies the faculty of perceiving external objects, the corporeal world, while good sense means the ability to judge well or accurately, to distinguish the true from the false in our judgments about the corporeal world.[23] Thus Descartes fashions the two

22. Once more, Descartes's *Meditations* give us assurance that this was his intention. In the Sixth Meditation he sets forth a dualism of mind and body, albeit one very different from the duality of the surface argument, in which two absolutely heterogeneous and independent principles are ranged side by side. The reality of mind and body, as Descartes presents it, is one of complex interdependence and ambiguity. And the statement describing it is practical rather than theoretical. For an analysis of this argument see Bluhm, "Descartes's Six Days of Creation," 57–62.

23. See Caton, *Origin of Subjectivity*, 32–33, 108.

lights that are to enlighten his new creation by day and by night and to give validity to the findings of his method—the interdependent lights of reason and of the senses—*bon sens*.

―――――――――

God said, "Let there be lights in the vault of heaven to divide day from night, and let them indicate festivals, days and years. Let there be lights in the vault of heaven to shine on the earth." And so it was. God made the two great lights: the greater light to govern the day, the smaller light to govern the night, and the stars

. . .

God saw that it was good.
Evening came and morning came: the fourth day.[24]

The Fifth Day

We have now arrived at Part 5 of the *Discourse* that Descartes entitles "Some Questions of Physics." Having established his method as a system of reasoning about the motions of the corporeal world, rather than about elusive abstract ideas like self and God, Descartes is now equipped to understand and measure, to give intelligible form to sensible reality. He is ready on his fifth day to create earth's living creatures. The material of this part is presented as a summary of an earlier treatise "which certain considerations" prevented him from publishing when he wrote it. This was a volume entitled *The World, or A Treatise on Knowledge*, (*Traité de la Lumière*), which he withheld from publication from fear of official persecution because of the condemnation of Galileo.[25] His intention was to include in it "all that [he] thought and knew . . . concerning the nature of material things" (31).

The theme of the part is mechanics. There are "certain laws which God has so established in nature, and the notion of which has so fixed in our minds, that after sufficient reflection we cannot doubt that they are exactly as observed in all which exists or which happens in the world" (31). To demonstrate the universality and inexorability of these laws, the laws of physical motion,

24. Genesis 1:14–19.
25. It received posthumous publication.

Descartes tells us that he "resolved to leave this world for [the learned] to dispute about, and to speak only of what would happen in a new one, if God should now create, somewhere in imaginary space, enough matter to make one" (32). He goes on to argue that "even if God had created several worlds, there would have been none where these laws are not observed" (32). And in time, because of these laws, the chaos would have fashioned itself into "an earth, some planets and comets, . . . a sun and fixed stars" (32). Here Descartes speaks almost expressly the latent intention of his *Discourse*—to create a new heaven and a new earth as a system of impersonal and necessary law.

This general cosmological statement is followed by a brief paragraph accounting for the surface features of the earth, both land and water, and then by a discussion of the nature of fire. We understand this section's brevity, for Descartes had already on the "third day" (in Part 3) created the dry land and the seas. He makes it clear that this is a review by telling us at the outset that he is summarizing in Part 5 what he had earlier treated *in extenso* in another book. But passing from "the description of inanimate objects and plants" to that of "animals, and particularly of man," he points out to us that he is now dealing with new material. The fifth day begins. Referring to his earlier unpublished treatise on *The World*, Descartes writes that at the time he "did not yet know enough to speak of these [animals and men] in the same style as of the rest *(du même style que du reste)*, in showing the causes of their existence and showing from what origins and in what manner nature must have produced them" (34). In this single isolated sentence Descartes tells us that animal and human reality are no different in their fundamental processes from nonhuman reality. All things consist simply of matter and motion. But the thought receives no development, and much of the sequel seems to deny it.

The free thinker also finds a signal in the fact that Descartes has placed his discussion of human creation (focusing on the supposed uniqueness of an autonomous rational faculty) in the fifth day, which in Genesis was devoted only to the creation of the denizens of the sea and of the air. On his own sixth day we shall see that Descartes fashions a very different image of the specifically human from the view presented in Part 5, that is, different from the conventional view that "the rational soul . . . could not possibly be derived from the power of matter . . . but must have been specially created" (43).

But if in Part 5 Descartes's true intention is to say that man is a machine, is not the independent thinker of Parts 3 and 4 a mirage? We have already seen in Part 4 that this independence does not extend to disembodied existence and that mind is intimately connected with body. And this theme is developed in detail in the *Meditations*—that the human person is a complex reality composed of mutually implicative body and mind; without body, mind would have nothing to think about. Yet he also maintains, in the *Meditations*, the separateness of mind from body, the autonomy of the judgmental function. But that autonomy is not a perfect one. Descartes makes it clear in his essay on the passions that human values are given by body and that the function of mind is rationally to order and discipline these passionate values to optimize their satisfaction, not to replace them. Only judgment is uniquely characteristic of mind.

God said "Let the waters teem with living creatures,
and let the birds fly above the earth within the
vault of heaven." And so it was.
God created great sea-serpents and every kind of winged
creature. God saw that it was good. . . .
Evening came and morning came: the fifth day.[26]

The Sixth Day

Descartes entitles Part 6 of his *Discourse* "Some Prerequisites for Further Advances in the Study of Nature." Its theme is the promise that experimental natural science holds for the future benefit of mankind. Descartes is pragmatic not apocalyptic in his expectations. "Truth can be discovered only little by little, and in a few subjects," he writes, "so that he who pursues truth is often obliged to admit his ignorance when discussing a subject which he has not investigated" (52). And he understands that natural sci-

26. Genesis 1:20–25.

ence will be built up only gradually and by painstaking, laborious experiment. He offers his own work on optics and meteorology (two treatises that were originally published together with the *Discourse*) as a contribution to the effort. He is modest about what he has done, yet he is ambitious for the future. "I want it to be understood," he writes, "that the little I have learned thus far is a mere nothing compared to what I do not know, and yet do not despair of learning" (48–49). He understands that the construction of science must be a cooperative effort by many scholars and by many generations of scholars through thousands of careful experiments.

Despite his personal modesty and his gradualist view of the progress of science, Descartes's ultimate hopes are large ones. He is satisfied "that it is possible to reach knowledge that will be of much utility in this life," via the methods of scientific analysis he has used and that he has summarized in the *Discourse on Method*.

> And that instead of speculative philosophy now taught in the schools we can find a practical one, by which, knowing the nature and behavior of fire, water, air, stars, and heavens, and all the other bodies which surround us, as well as we now understand the different skills of our workers, we can employ these entities for all the purposes for which they are suited, and so make ourselves masters and possessors of nature. (45)

He looks forward to "the invention of an infinity of devices" to improve the fruitfulness of agriculture and that will enable mankind to enjoy "all the wealth of the earth without labor." He envisages great improvements in medicine that will conserve the principal and basic good of health. He even believes that medicine may one day "make men in general wiser and more clever than they have been so far" (46). And ways may be found to ward off "the enfeeblement of old age" (46).

On his sixth day, therefore, Descartes has fashioned in his own image a new man—a "thinking thing"—to take the place of the "living soul" of Genesis who was created in the image of God. He is a scientist-pragmatist who keeps his clear analytical mind trained on the "Great Book of Nature." He is daily at work in his laboratory, busily unlocking the powerful secrets contained in that book with which he brings under control and shapes to his fancy the raw materials that Descartes has supplied for his creative talent. He does not merely "fill the earth and conquer it." He refashions the whole of reality to suit his will.

═══════════════

> God said, "Let the earth produce every kind of
> living creature: cattle, reptiles, and every kind
> of wild beast." And so it was . . .
> God said, "Let us make man in our own image, in the
> likeness of ourselves, and let them be masters of
> the fish of the sea, the birds of heaven, the
> cattle, all the wild beasts and all the reptiles
> that crawl upon the earth." God created man in
> the image of himself, in the image of God created
> he him, male and female he created them.
> God blessed them, saying to them, "Be fruitful,
> multiply, fill the earth and conquer it. Be masters
> of the fish of the sea, the birds of heaven and all
> living animals on earth." . . . And so it was.
> God saw all he had made, and indeed it was very good.
> Evening came and morning came: the sixth day.[27]

The Seventh Day

On the seventh day, Genesis tells us that God rested. It is significant that Descartes did not follow his example; the *Discourse* has no seventh part. The utilitarian technologist does not passively contemplate his work in serenity. For contemplation represents to him the failed way of tradition. Utilitarian progress demands ceaseless activity.[28]

27. Genesis 1:24–31.

28. This reading together with my more extensive unpublished paper, "Descartes's Six Days of Creation," complements and completes that given the *Discourse* by Joseph Cropsey in *Interpretation* I/2 (Winter 1970): 130–43. Cropsey there noted the incongruence between the new method of reasoning proposed by Descartes and the metaphysics of Part 4 in which the existence of God and the immortal soul are expounded but left the problem unanalyzed (134). Cropsey also noted the parallel in Part 5 to the biblical account of creation but did not notice the overall comparability of the six parts to the six biblical days of creation. My reading agrees with and substantiates the interpretation of Descartes's metaphysics made by Caton in *Origin of Subjectivity*. Caton writes:

The two simple natures [mind and body] are related by the necessity of

The Boundary Problem in Cartesian Dualism
and the Question of Freedom versus Determinism

Descartes's new work of creation has replaced the outworn metaphysics of transcendent teleology with a useful methodology of scientific cognition and control. The new man that takes form in the *Discourse* and *Meditations* has overthrown the priestly myth of divine ordination of all things and has taken to himself the attributes of ethical freedom and technical power. He has also laid the groundwork for the ambivalence of modern political culture.

We seem firmly to have established two ultimate, though mutually dependent, principles of reality—body and mind. Yet how and where shall we place the boundary that divides them in order properly to discriminate the role and function of each? On the one hand, reality is a world of corporeal extension, which is known to us through a sensorium that is itself extended and through ideas fashioned by this sensorium that are also corporeal. On the other hand, there is the judging mind that discriminates the true from the false among the ideas that the sensorium produces; body, acting on its own, deceives and gives rise to fantasy as well as truth. It must be corrected. But reason or judgment, in processing the materials of sense to get at the truth, transcends the reality of sense to accomplish this. The truth that it knows is a purely abstract, nonempirical order whose mathematical clarity, distinctness, and coherence are its guarantee.

Ironically, in pursuit of certainty, the judging mind finds truth and knowledge not in the world of sense, which it set out to measure and comprehend, but in the mirror of its own logical

---

mutual implication both in the *ordo essendi* and the *ordo cognoscendi*; in the former, because mind is an "effect" of extension, an effect which is not an extended thing but cognitions; in the latter because all that the mind is able to know clearly is extension. Mind and body are therefore the coordinate first principle of science. This interlocking relationship and reciprocal determination is the true "guarantee" of the correspondence between the world *(ordo essendi)* and the clear ideas of reason *(ordo cognoscendi)*. (108)

Caton does not present a systematic, part-by-part reading of the *Discourse* but bases this judgment on both direct and indirect evidence from the entire corpus of Descartes's work.

self—in its own ideas. Though the concepts of the understanding, according to Descartes, do not proceed from itself but from imagination—from mind working on sense data within the sensorium—it is clear that their creation is not wholly, or perhaps principally, a physical process. Caton puts the matter succinctly when he writes:

> If the mind does not passively receive ideas but must work them up from sensibility—then the "synthetic" or creative function of the mind becomes a matter of first importance. If we consider that the known real is always a mathematical structure "worked up" by the mind in the way just described, we begin to approach the view that the mind knows only so much of the world as it puts into it.[29]

If we pursue this line of analysis, all of Descartes's doubts about the corporeal world rise up once more before us, and we are at a loss to resolve them. The dualism of body and mind passes over into a monistic idealism. As Caton notes, this takes us beyond Cartesian thought "into the terrain of transcendental philosophy," but it proceeds with perfect logic out of Descartes's principles.[30] It produces the paradoxical thought that when body takes the form of consciousness it ceases to be body and passes over into mind. In the terminology of the subject–object dichotomy, the subjective self swallows up the objective world.

Our reflection on Cartesian dualism may produce the opposite result of a reduction to body if we examine the implications of saying that the movements of matter in the sensorium produce ideas that are corporeal. If matter can form the conceptual world, as Descartes thought it could, why cannot it also arrange and correct the application of concepts?[31] The idea of a self-correcting mechanism that behaves analogously to Descartes's faculty of reason or judgment is both theoretically and practically feasible since the advent of computer technology. In Skinnerian psychology it constitutes a fully mechanistic epistemology. In this case, object devours subject in the act of producing it. Or as Caton puts it, "at the apex of objectivity the subject is least conspicuous; he

29. Caton, *Origin of Subjectivity*, 170. See also 163.
30. Ibid.
31. See *Meditations*, 133.

tends to disappear into the object. For that reason the vision of mind and body may deteriorate into materialism."[32]

If we consider the Cartesian criterion of certainty, we get still a different paradoxical result. When the myth of God has been thought away in the subterranean argument, only "clarity and distinctness of idea" are left as marks of truth. And these concepts are epitomized by mathematical order. But as Caton points out, "the truths of mathematics and logic are not more evident and certain to Descartes than they were to other philosophers; his method adds nothing to their indubitability."[33] On what, then, does Descartes's certainty rest? Our answer is found in an act of will—resolute affirmation of the whole body of evidence. A new dimension of reality is added. The self is not mind alone but mind and will. Or is it perhaps will alone? "Just as it was by an act of will that assent to truths above reason was made, now, thanks to the consciousness that freedom of will is the 'only thing that truly pertains to us,' Descartes exercises the virtue of generosity to affirm that alone which is truly his own."[34]

We learn from the Fourth Meditation the importance that Descartes gave to free will in his schema. He tells us that its amplitude is at least subjectively as great as the free will of God. "I experience it to be so ample and extended that there are no limits which restrict it."[35] Do we not then, by our fiat, create the world in which we live? Are we not then the authors of all things? We were told in that meditation that our mistakes must be attributed to the disproportion between our understanding (which is limited) and our will (which is unlimited) but that the will can get its bearings by objective reality if it hews to the criterion of clarity and distinctness in judging the true and the false.[36] But if that criterion is itself the product of an act of will, all objective standards are lost. We are afloat on a sea that is entirely the product of our freedom. Once again, objective order disappears into subjectivity in the very act of our search for objectivity. The dualism now becomes one of body and will, of which will is the major term.

32. Caton, *Origin of Subjectivity*, 181.
33. Ibid., 125.
34. Ibid.
35. *Meditations*, 112, 113.
36. Ibid., 115.

Since Descartes never writes about mind and will as such, in the abstract, but takes his bearing toward the truth from the individual's mind and will, we confront still another paradox. In the pursuit of the objective order of truth and existence, we end up with a subjective truth about the world—a mere reflection of our individual existence. I make up the world—each of us lives in a solipsistic universe. For Descartes has given us no intersubjective principle of judgment.

Contemplation of Descartes's untidy and ambiguous dualism has thus called up for us two possibilities for its clarification— reduction to a pattern of public force and reduction to a pattern of private freedom. We may understand the world as a predictable field of meaningless forces in motion, a field that includes our own "free" selves. On the other hand, our minds may solipsistically absorb the world into ourselves. Or one may try to understand one pole of the duality as a condition of the realization of values inherent in the other—force as the ground of freedom or freedom as an entree into determinate force. If we demand logical consistency of reality, any one of these reductions of incoherent dualism is as plausible as the other. At the political level, as we shall see, all of them are problematical.

We have been dealing to this point with truths as a matter for contemplation rather than for action. This has been so, even in our discussion of will, which we examined as the creator of a truth to be known in a contemplative way. This was Descartes's chief theoretical concern; his habit of mind was that of the spectator, the detached scientist.[37] But we must also address the question of truth in action, which brings us to the subject of values and goals. Once more we find ourselves in the midst of paradox.

The idea of human action implies a certain autonomy in the actor, an intention; otherwise he is merely an event in the chain of causality—an effect or a transmitter of causes external to himself in a mechanical series. But if we begin the analysis of action from the material pole, we do not seem able to get beyond mechanical concepts and necessary law. In the Sixth Meditation, for example, Descartes tried to establish the reality of corporeal beings by reflecting on the experience of sensation. It is in these paragraphs

37. See *Discourse*, 22.

that he takes up, for the first time, the subject of goal-seeking under the rubric of "advantages and disadvantages." He writes that he felt that the body that he sensed as his own "was one of a world of bodies, from which it was capable of receiving various advantages and disadvantages." He identified the one by a "certain feeling of pleasure" and the other "by a feeling of pain."[38] In the Fourth Meditation Descartes seems at one point to be concerned with action in an ethical frame of reference. This is in the section that deals with the disproportion between unlimited will and limited understanding. The disproportionate relationship, he writes, makes it happen that the will is "very easily turned aside from the true and the good and chooses the false and the evil. And thus it happens that I make mistakes and that I sin."[39] This reminds us of the biblical account of the original sin of Adam, which resulted from abuse of free will. But it is merely window dressing for the surface argument. For in the same meditation, Descartes has made it clear that we have no insight into God's plan for us; that is, we have no conception of our perfection as a guide to the proper ethical use of our free will.[40] There is no ethical understanding to guide action, only theoretical reason or judgment, which guides the conception of reality not of moral truth.

Another indication that we are to disregard this passage as mere surface argument is found in the synopsis of the *Meditations*, which appears at the beginning of the treatise. There Descartes says clearly that in the Fourth Meditation he does "not in any way treat . . . of sin—that is, of error committed in the pursuit of good and evil—but only of that which occurs in the judgment and discernment of the true and the false."[41] Pleasure and pain thus become the touchstones of action, but they both represent passive sufferance, not action. The values whose pursuit brings us pleasure or pain are not chosen by us but are given by body as desires or appetites. They are, so to speak, programmed into us. Goal-seeking behavior is a Skinnerian pursuit of pleasure and avoid-

38. *Meditations*, 128–29.
39. Ibid., 114.
40. Ibid., 111.
41. Ibid., 73–74.

ance of pain, and all the ideas involved occur "without the necessity of my consent."[42] In this model, will seems ruled out as
a concept of choice behavior. Thus Descartes's explanation of
choice, which is normally a concept of free action, eventuates in a
description of determinate mechanical behavior.

Nowhere in the *Discourse* or in the *Meditations* does Descartes
approach theoretically the question of choice or value from the
voluntarist pole. We have only the mechanistic discussion of
goal-seeking and the provisional morality for living the life of
reason in the traditional city that appear in the *Discourse*. A
starting point for such a theory is found in the *Discourse*, however.
And it is restated in a later treatise, *On the Passions of the Soul*
(1649), in which Descartes presents his "most perfect morality."
The third maxim of the *Discourse* is to accustom oneself "to believe
that nothing except our thoughts is wholly under our control."[43]
In the *Passions* the same thought appears as the idea "that there is
nothing that truly pertains to [one] but the free disposition of his
will."[44] This appears to be a restatement of an idea popular
among the Stoics, who sought to accommodate their conception
of individual free will to the necessary order of the cosmos. On
the one hand, it is an expression of resignation to determination
by the objective order. But on the other, it is an expression of
freedom and power, which takes the form of self-conquest or
self-mastery. In the *Discourse* Descartes had written that his freedom was secure if he learned to "conquer [himself] rather than
fortune, and to alter [his] desires rather than change the order of
the world."[45] What is involved seems to be a limitation of the
thrust of personal desire by the dispassionate (scientific?) assess-
ment of possibilities. What is significant here is that the good or
the valuable is defined simply by the empirically possible rather
than by any intrinsic standard of the good. Or we may say that the
idea of value as appetitively given carries over from the assess-
ment done at the material pole. The voluntarist perspective is
confined to reordering appetitive drive to tune it to rational

42. Ibid., 129.
43. *Discourse*, 20.
44. Cited in Caton, *Origin of Subjectivity*, 57.
45. *Discourse*, 20.

possibility, that is, to conformity with the harmony of the whole. Free will then becomes the master engineer whose work is to fashion a logical structure out of the disorderly motions presented by nature. Free will does not extend to the free fashioning of goal values but only to our instrumental behavior. Yet a voluntarist paradox appears. In the exercise of our freedom we fit ourselves into a determinate mechanical order.

The recipe for freedom in the *Passions* in the form of Stoic resignation does not seem to conform to the activist, reform notions of the *Discourse*, which envisioned a whole new world of human utility. The spirit there was Promethean not fatalist. Since the maxims of "provisional morality" given there (and repeated in the *Passions*) envisioned the eventual supersession of tradition by science, the reader's mind is open to the idea of a "perfect morality" for the time when all things will be made new. But all that Descartes gives us of the final morality, as we have seen, is the injunction to treasure our thoughts as the only things that are truly ours. Perhaps what he means to tell us is that whether we succeed, individually or collectively, in the conquest of physical nature envisioned in the *Discourse* or partially fail (at least individually) in that conquest, our freedom will in *both* cases consist in the recognition of objective necessity. For it is objective necessity that determines what we want and how much of it we can get.[46] In such a situation freedom could be no other than a clear recognition of the facts. Thus the paradox—we find our freedom in the "clear and distinct idea" of objective necessity.

In seeking to understand reality, we proceed phenomenologically. That is, we start with the self-evidence of consciousness and attempt to work our way out to the world. This leads us to conceive reality as an interlocking manifold of body and mind. If it were not for the motions of body in the sensorium, no ideas would be generated to make us aware of the existence of the self as mind and will. And if it were not for the self-consciousness of mind, we would not be aware of the existence of body or be capable of judging its true manifestations from appearance. But since there is no third reality against which we may measure mind and body, we are unable to establish boundaries between the two

46. See Caton, *Origin of Subjectivity*, 57, 190.

provinces. An intense analytical effort designed to accomplish this may result in reducing mind to an epiphenomenon of bodily motion, if we start our analysis with the sensorium. Or it may result in reducing body to a fiction of mind, if we begin with the phenomenon of consciousness. What seemed at the outset of our reflection a relation of mutual support between mind and body turns out to be one of mutual contradiction. Is one principle after all the truth of the matter and the other an illusion? If so, by what procedures can we reduce illusory appearance to theoretical truth? Or will we find the truth of the matter only in an entirely different way, by abandoning the dichotomy as our point of departure?

And here the matter stands. All modern philosophy from Descartes to our time is marked by dualistic paradox.

> Everywhere we find the objectivity of science in collision with the subjectivity of thinking. Man is a reflex automaton, yet a proud, ambitious automaton who rebels against necessity—a spiritual automaton. . . . He is yoked to the serfdom of passive perception, but he is also the sovereign knowing subject. He is an insignificant part of nature, yet a point outside it. He yearns for security, but would realize it by audacious and haphazard enterprises. He seeks to master the passions, yet his whole good is to enjoy them. These and other oppositions grow from Cartesian dualism. . . . The greatness of Descartes's philosophy is due less to the problems it solves or to the certainties it produces than to the depth of its contradictions. Their depth may be appreciated by observing that although nearly every significant thinker of the past century was a critic of dualism, none surmounted it.[47]

From Metaphysical Paradox to Political Paradox

Ontological paradox leads readily into political puzzlement. First a question arises as to whether the freedom of the individual can

---

47. Caton, *Origin of Subjectivity*, 202. The importance of Descartes for a writer with as different a metaphysic as Hegel's is evident in Hegel's exclamation in his lectures on the history of philosophy that the journeying mind will cry: "'Land!' when he sights the writings of Descartes, and will at last feel at home." Cited in James Collins, *Interpreting Modern Philosophy* (Princeton, N.J.: Princeton Univ. Press, 1972), 54.

be made compatible with the demands of public order. If there is no model of human perfection given to the self (as mind and will) by nature, the self is free to choose its own ends in absolute autonomy. And all individuals have an equal right to pursue private values. But if individual ends clash, how can mutual frustration be prevented in the competition for preferred position in the public world of body? What kind of objective authority will be accepted as legitimate by freedom-loving individuals to produce a peaceful and orderly society? Would the existence of any public authority at all be legitimate? Can any notion of lawful authority be established and on what basis, if there are no natural norms of moral order?

If value is given by body, and my freedom extends only to implementing the needs of body, efficiency seems to replace autonomy as preeminent in the hierarchy of public goods. For the needs of body can be generalized and quantified. Social and political manipulation by a master engineer might produce the greatest sum possible of material values and would, therefore, have the highest place. But if this is the case, what is the value of individual freedom?

If to me the most real experience is of myself and of the values I legislate for myself, and the rest of the world appears as an aggregate of bodies in motion, how can the principle of community be established? Is it possible to communicate between free minds and wills through the medium of objective sense? How do we know whether we have attained our goal, since we cannot establish a boundary between mind and body? In any given instance, am I communicating with another person, or am I being confronted by an automaton? If communication turns out to be possible, what might serve as a principle of consensus? How can the equal community of minds and wills be translated into equal objective laws? And in a regime of even equal laws, what happens to my freedom? If a community of values *must* be established, if a political system cannot function without a general will, what kinds of manipulation are required to form a common cognition of the whole? And who is capable of such manipulation?

The history of modern political philosophy constitutes a continuing discourse on themes such as these—a continuing effort to solve the knotty contradictions they embody.

3

Reduction to Body and Uncertain Dualism:
Hobbes, Locke, and Rousseau

Hobbes: The Cycle of Anarchy and Absolutism

The modern liberal state was born in England out of the civil conflicts of the seventeenth century. With it was conceived the first political theory based on the counterpoint of force and freedom. We find it in the political philosophy of Thomas Hobbes (1588–1679) who, despite differences with Descartes, carried forward and developed the Cartesian way of thinking about the world. "Bodily sensations along with their mental correlates . . . give the central principles in this philosophy," as for Descartes.[1] The clear, distinct, and logically conjoined ideas of deductive explanation are authoritative for Hobbes as for Descartes. In his *Principles of Philosophy* Descartes developed the concept of motion as a link between exterior and interior phenomena—an idea that was to be central in Hobbes's system. And an analysis of the passions was for each of them the doorway to systematic ethics.[2]

In 1637 Hobbes received a copy of Descartes's *Discourse on Method* from Sir Kenelm Digby, a few months after its first publication and three years before Hobbes's publication of his first work on politics, *The Elements of Law*.[3] William Cavendish, a

1. W. Cunningham, *The Influence of Descartes on Metaphysical Speculation in England* (London: Macmillan, 1876), 70.

2. Ibid., 66–74.

3. Samuel I. Mintz, *The Hunting of Leviathan* (Cambridge: Cambridge Univ. Press, 1962), 10. Hobbes's only earlier publication was a translation of Thucydides's *Peloponnesian War*, which was brought out in 1628.

leading member of the noble English house that patronized
Hobbes, was also a patron of Descartes and of Pierre Gassendi,
the French Epicurean philosopher, while Charles Cavendish
sought favors of the English king for Descartes and attempted to
bring him over to England.[4] Both Descartes and Hobbes engaged
in the study of sense experience and worked in optics and in
geometry. And a controversy developed between them about
which had arrived first at the idea of the subjectivity of secondary
qualities, an important notion in optics, which "allowed natural
phenomena to be reduced to quantitative problems, and for
Hobbes . . . provided a basis for his more general mechanical
view of nature."[5] (Actually, Galileo had worked it out before
either of them, as early as 1623.)[6]

The interesting possibility that Hobbes's scientific researches
might have led him to dualism or, more likely, into an idealistic
solipsism is found in the problem of relating Hobbes's way of
thinking about exterior reality to the scientific operations of the
mind. As Miriam Reik points out, "since accidents are only appearances and experientially without connection, those propositions which make up science (the causes of which are ultimately
accidents) threaten to lose their reference to anything beyond the

4. Miriam M. Reik, *The Golden Lands of Thomas Hobbes* (Detroit: Wayne State
Univ. Press, 1977), 68. Reik rejects the periodization of Hobbes's work into two
parts—a humanist period lasting through his translation of Thucydides and a
scientific period from then on. Indeed, she thinks the humanist–scientific dichotomy is unrealistic for the century as such. She writes that
   the scholar "who wishes to relate Hobbes's thought to the advances of early
   modern science will find that Hobbes's infancy was concurrent with Galileo's
   earliest lectures at Pisa and the experiments at the Leaning Tower; he will
   see Hobbes at middle age pondering the Cartesian method and reading the
   De Motu Cordis by his friend William Harvey. In his old age, the philosopher
   may have read the issue of the Philosophical Transactions of the Royal
   Society that printed the first paper submitted by Sir Isaac Newton." (15)
For an interpretation of Hobbes that stresses the importance of transformed
Aristotelian ideas in his political theory, see Thomas A. Spragens, *The Politics of
Motion: The World of Thomas Hobbes* (Lexington, Ky.: University Press of Ken-
tucky, 1973).
   5. Reik, *Golden Lands*, 71.
   6. Ibid.

phantasms they signify. With the connection to the ontological realm . . . almost wholly cut off as a source of truth, Hobbes's interest is thrust back onto the realm of words themselves." It was only Hobbes's notion of "evidence" (that we have an image correlative to words) that provided him with a link between words and the nonlinguistic world that rescued him "from lapsing into a total subjectivism."[7] Though at one time Hobbes stood thus on the verge of solipsism, we know that his firm and final choice was for a thoroughgoing materialism.[8] While "Descartes sturdily defended his dualistic universe, . . . Hobbes implacably went about absorbing *res cogitans* into a scheme of matter in motion."[9] Nevertheless, we know that the long dispute between Descartes and Hobbes, most notable in the acid contribution of Hobbes to the *Objections* to Descartes's *Meditations*, was at least partly grounded on common ideas. Both were early exponents of a purely mechanical conception of nature.[10]

Hobbes took his stand at the material pole of the Cartesian dichotomy of mind and body, though there is a question as to whether he was able to maintain it with perfect logical consistency. In his effort at materialist explanation, Hobbes conceived life as "but a motion of Limbs." Thoughts were "every one a *Representation* or *Apparence* of some quality, or other accident of a body without us; which is commonly called an *Object*." All of them had their origin in "Sense."[11]

In expressing his materialist metaphysics and his sensationalist psychology, Hobbes made liberal use of the necessitarian concept of law that had been found operationally useful by the new science in describing and predicting the motions of physical bodies. We note the similarity of Hobbes's first law of motion to that later developed by Newton. Hobbes states the law in these words as he introduces the subject of imagination in chapter 2 of *Leviathan*: "When a Body is once in motion, it moveth (unless

7. Ibid., 73.
8. Ibid.
9. Ibid., 77.
10. Ibid., 78.
11. Thomas Hobbes, *Leviathan* (London: Penguin Books, 1968), 81, 85. Parenthetical page references are to this edition.

something else hinder it) eternally; and whatsoever hindreth it, cannot in an instant, but in time, and by degrees quite extinguish it" (88).[12] Hobbes makes use of the law to connect body to mind and to reduce the second to the first.

Hobbes uses the first law of motion to account for what goes on in the mind when the object that was the original cause of sensation is removed. The motions that it originally set up continue indefinitely, until obliterated or altered by other motions, and become the elements of our imagination, or memory. (He calls memory "nothing but decaying sense" [88].) From here Hobbes goes on in chapter 3 to the "Trayne of Imagination," or *Mentall Discourse*, both unguided and guided by some motive desire, and thence in chapters 4 and 5 to speech, reason, and science. In this way, all mental activities, including the highest mental functions, are explained as the result of moving matter operating according to the first law of motion. The processes are necessary, logical, and impersonal. Value—as motive goal—is supplied by passion, which produces either desire for or aversion to things in the outer world. Voluntary motion, either toward or away from these objects, begins in the imagination, which furnishes a thought of "*whither, which way,* and *what*" (118–19). In this description of human action (or reaction) in the world of sense, we find a moral counterpart to the law of gravitation.

"Whatsoever is the object of man's Appetite or Desire," Hobbes wrote, "that is it, which he for his part called *Good*: and the object of his Hate, and Aversion, *Evill*" (120). Hobbes even managed to fit the concept of will into his necessitarian schema, calling it "in *Deliberation*, the last Appetite, or Aversion," immediately preceding action.[13] In its exercise man could not be distinguished

12. Cf. Newton's phraseology: "A body undisturbed by force will continue indefinitely at a constant speed and in a straight line." Quoted in Edgar N. Johnson, *An Introduction to the History of the Western Tradition*, vol. 2 (Boston: Ginn and Co., 1959), 159.

13. For an interpretation of the concepts of will and voluntarism and of their roles in modern social contract theory, which is very different from the one presented in this book, see Patrick Riley, *Will and Political Legitimacy: A Critical Exposition of Social Contract Theory in Hobbes, Locke, Rousseau, Kant, and Hegel* (Cambridge, Mass.: Harvard Univ. Press, 1982).

from the lower animals. For "Beasts that have *Deliberation*," wrote Hobbes, "must necessarily also have Will" (127).

How could freedom be defined within such a system? In reducing the subjective pole of Descartes's dualism to objective order, Hobbes was prepared to proceed ruthlessly. He presents his definition of "Liberty, or Freedom" in chapter 21, which he entitled "Of the Liberty of Subjects," where he tells us that the term *freedom* means absence of external impediments to motion. It might be applied to inanimate and irrational as well as to rational creatures. "A Free-Man, is he, that is in those things, which by his strength and wit he is able to do, is not hindred to doe what he has a will to" (262). Since, however, each of us is determined in our behavior by our passionate desires, the definition must be made consistent with necessity. He therefore writes,

> As in the water, that hath not only *liberty*, but a *necessity* of descending by the Channel: so likewise in the Actions which men voluntarily doe; which (because they proceed from their will) proceed from *liberty*; and yet because every act of mans will, and every desire, and inclination proceedeth from some cause, and that from another cause, which causes in a continuall chaine . . . proceed from *necessity*. (263)

From this general definition, in which freedom is seen only as an aspect of necessity, Hobbes moves on to the liberties of subjects, which consist only in those things against which the Sovereign has erected no impediments to action. The necessity of our wills is bounded by the necessity of the Sovereign's will.

> The Liberty of a Subject, lyeth therefore only in those things, which in regulating their actions, the Sovereign hath praetermitted: such is the Liberty to buy, and sell, and otherwise contract with one another; to choose their own aboad, their own diet, their own trade of life, and institute their children as they themselves think fit; & the like. (264)

But here we are in the midst of the construction of the commonwealth. Much earlier, Hobbes had presented a different definition of liberty as he discovered it in the state of Nature. It was "the Liberty each man hath, to use his own power, as he will

himselfe, for the preservation of his own Nature, that is to say of
his own life" (189). And to this psycho-political phenomenon
Hobbes attached a name of the highest value. He called it the
fundamental "Right of Nature" and identified it with the traditional concept of *Jus Naturale*. In this fashion the divinely mandated obligation of medieval man to realize his natural perfection
passed over into the observed passion of modern man for individual preservation—a passion discoverable in the liberty of the
individual to act or move at will in the absence of external restraints.

Hobbesian value is mandated by desire. Norms flow no longer
from natural obligation but from what we naturally desire to
do.[14] But it is significant that Hobbes does not baptize *whatever* we
wish to do as the Right of Nature. In a state of Nature many
drives, such as those for glory and for the joys of conquest, are
operative. But only the passion for preservation, manifest in the
liberty we have to pursue it, is called by the name of "Right." It is
mentioned for the first time at the outset of chapter 14, in book 1
immediately following the description in chapter 13 of the chaotic
"war of all against all of the state of Nature," in which the ideas of
public "Right" and "Wrong" have no place at all.

The public concept of "Right" for Hobbes, as for traditional
man, is equivalent to the "rational" or "reasonable." But Hobbesian reason is wholly instrumental, not teleological, and is directed to the realization of ends set by desire not by a purposive
God. Of all the desires pursued by men in the state of nature, only
preservation is rational, for it is the only value by which the
conflictual behavior of men can be harmonized. It is the only

14. I reject the view expressed by Taylor and Warrender that Hobbes sets
forth a deontological ethics in which duty to perform the norms of the law of
nature and the will of God has primary value in favor of the position that
Hobbes's ethics are purely egoistic. See A. E. Taylor, "The Ethical Doctrine
of Hobbes," *Philosophy* (1938), reprinted in K. C. Brown, ed., *Hobbes Studies*
(Oxford: Clarendon Press, 1965), and Howard Warrender, *The Political Philosophy
of Hobbes: His Theory of Obligation* (Oxford: Clarendon Press, 1957). See also
Michael J. Oakeshott, "Moral Life in the Writings of Thomas Hobbes" in *Rationalism
in Politics and Other Essays* (New York: Basic Books, 1962), 264–83, as well as
Oakeshott's introduction to *Leviathan* (Oxford: Clarendon Press, 1947). F. C.
Hood, *The Divine Politics of Thomas Hobbes* (Oxford: Clarendon Press, 1964),
has Hobbes appear as a Christian moralist.

value that can be enjoyed by all in equal measure. (Glory and conquest demand a fight to the death, since not all can enjoy them.) In this way, in his definition of fundamental right, Hobbes brings liberty and law together within the concept of rational decision; and we seem to have laid the foundation for a political theory in which the Cartesian poles of impersonal force and personal freedom can be combined within a monistic and unproblematical metaphysics. Let us see what in fact emerges.

Hobbes's strategy is to proceed with an analysis of the dictates of reason. After announcing the "Right of Nature," reason declares the correlative "Laws of Nature"—precepts "by which a man is forbidden to do, that, which is destructive of his life, or taketh away the means of pursuing the same: and to omit, that, by which he thinketh it may be best preserved" (189). We have an image of free-moving political bodies, each rationally determined in its course of movement toward the goal of self-preservation (for "Law determineth, and bindeth" [189]). Here we have moved from a psychological to a political version of the first law of motion. But when we have advanced just so far in reason, Hobbes makes it clear that we have not yet escaped the war of all against all for in deciding on his means to preservation, "every man has a Right to every thing," even "to one another's body" (190).

No particular system of political bodies is fully rationalized; that is, it is not a harmonious system like that of the heavenly bodies until its members are cognizant of the "first, and Fundamental Law of Nature; which is, *to seek Peace, and follow it,*" a very specific precept of reason (190). But even this is insufficient to perfect harmony, because its injunction is conditional on other men being willing to do the same. When they are not, the second branch of the rule comes into force, which is, "By all means we can, to defend our selves." And we are enjoined "to seek, and use, all helps and advantages of Warre" (190). Therefore, another law is required which decrees that when all are willing, men should lay down their right to all things and be contented with a narrower scope of liberty. Thus reason tells us that we must renounce the exercise of our full Right of Nature to make its rational object obtainable—the preservation of existence.

The injunctions of the laws of nature culminate in a mutual consent to renounce the full use of the Right of Nature and to authorize a third person, who stands outside the agreement, to act as sovereign enforcer of the contract.[15] By the act of authorization this Leviathan is empowered to use his Right of Nature to compel each of the contractants to abide by his agreement and to enforce the "first, and Fundamental Law of Nature." At this point the system becomes perfectly operative as a harmonious, rational order. In the model world, Hobbes's system of natural law, in its political as well as in its psychological embodiment, is perfectly determinate.

By the time the argument has arrived at this point, we no longer have a regime of liberty under law, which seemed implicit in Hobbes's definition of the Right of Nature. Instead we have a liberty that is effectively limited only by fear of the coercive use of force. In Hobbes's understanding, men are not rational by nature but are made so only by the experience of fear. It was fear of violent death that produced the recognition of the Right of Nature and that brought them to covenant with one another to abate and curtail its use. And it is through fear and force that the Leviathan keeps the contractants obedient to their own rational desire. He himself stands apart from the rational agreement, in no wise limited to rational (lawful) behavior, but rather its source and guarantor. Hobbesian law is not prior to force. It emerges from force, which is its author. For force and fear are the authors of reasonable behavior. In this way, force emerges as superior to, and in tension with, individual freedom.

If we follow the logic of Hobbes's argument in a different direction, we discover that freedom, the other pole of the force–freedom dichotomy, emerges supreme. And we discover that unlike a model of the physical world, Hobbes's political model fails to predict. In chapter 8 of the first part of *Leviathan*, Hobbes discusses madness. In the preceding chapters he has already given an exhaustive account of Reason, Science, the passions, and the nature of good and evil. The treatment of madness occurs in the context of a discussion of the intellectual virtues and their

15. For an excellent treatment of Hobbes's use of the concept of authorization and of its development and role in Hobbes's theory of representation see Hannah F. Pitkin, "Hobbes's Concept of Representation—I," *American Political Science Review* 58 (December 1964): 902–18.

defects. "The Passion, whose violence, or continuance maketh Madness," he tells us, "is either great *Vaine-Glory* which is commonly called *Pride*, and *self-conceit*; or great *Dejection* of mind" (140). *Vaine-Glory* he had already defined in treating of the passions in chapter 6 as a kind of wishful thinking. We might today call it delusions of grandeur—being caught up in a "Walter Mitty" fantasy of power and glory. Its chief characteristic is divorce from reality, that is, from the chain of causes and effects. It is pure fantasy. As such, *Vaine-Glory* is passive, a mere daydreaming (125). But it may give rise to anger, "the excess whereof, is the Madnesse called Rage and Fury." And this in turn will result in irrational behavior in the real world. In chapter 11, whose central theme is the "perpetuall and restlesse desire" of all men for "power after power, that ceaseth only in Death," we learn that some vainglorious men "are enclined to rash engaging" (164). And in chapter 13 we are told that no bounds can be placed on what a man may claim as necessary for his safety, since "there be some, that taking pleasure in contemplating their own power in the acts of conquest, . . . pursue [conquest] further than their security requires." These seem to be vainglorious men, whose dreams of grandeur lead them into ever new adventures, make them forget the simple dictates of security, and thereby expand the security requirements of all other men (185). This leads directly to a review of three chief causes of quarrel—gain, safety, and reputation, the first two of which appear as substantial and rational values, and the third, as fantasy. The pursuit of reputation, says Hobbes, leads men to use violence "for trifles, as a word, a smile, a different opinion, and any other sign of undervalue" (185). The result is the war of all against all.

Competition for honor and status Hobbes treats as a distinctly human trait, which sharply distinguishes the human being from other social animals such as bees and ants. He tells us that "amongst men there ariseth on that ground, Envy and Hatred, and finally Warre; but amongst [ants and bees] not so" (226). Here he seems to single out vainglory as the distinctly human cause of conflict. In fact, he goes so far as to present pride as the distinctly human trait; he tells us that "man, whose Joy consisteth in comparing himself with other men, can relish nothing but what is eminent" (226). This passage is followed almost immediately by a description of the contract that authorizes the creation of sovereignty, "that by terror [of the Sovereign's power and strength] he is inabled to forme the wills of them all to peace at home, and mutual ayd against their enemies abroad" (227–28). Thus at two climactic points in the drama of *Leviathan*, we find vanity intimately associated with the problem of peace and its solution.

The concepts glory, vainglory, and pride are well known in the common sense, and they have a long history in the moral tradition. The actions with which they are identified do not have their origin in motions of the external world, impinging upon the organs of sense, which stimulate appetite or aversion. They are, on one reading, self-operative and arise from the profound depths of the human soul. They are quite cut off from the mechanical chain of causes and effects. As Leo Strauss has put it, "the [mechanistic] view of human appetite, which at first sight seems to be the specifically Hobbesian view, is, however, contradicted . . . by his repeated and emphatic statement that human appetite is infinite in itself and not as a result of the infinite number of external impressions."[16] In key passages of *Leviathan*, *The Elements of Law, De Homine*, and other works, Strauss points out, Hobbes "bases the proposition that life is limitless appetite mechanistically on the assumption that appetite is only an automatic consequence of perception, but also on the incompatible assumption that appetite is essentially spontaneous."[17] "The origin of man's natural appetite is . . . not perception but vanity."[18] Especially revealing of this vitalistic strand in Hobbes's psychology is the passage in which he writes that "men from their very birth, and naturally, scramble for everything they covet, and would have all the world, if they could, to fear and obey them."[19] Significant also is the closing paragraph of chapter 28 of part 2 of

16. Leo Strauss, *The Political Philosophy of Hobbes* (Oxford: Clarendon Press, 1936), 9. I develop in this section Strauss's reading of the place of vanity in Hobbes's moral philosophy. For a critique of this approach see Raymond Polin, *Politique et Philosophie Chez Thomas Hobbes* (Paris: Presses Universitaires, 1953).

17. Strauss, *Political Philosophy of Hobbes*, 9.

18. Ibid., 11.

19. *Decameron Physiologicum*, in Sir W. Molesworth, ed., *The English Works of Thomas Hobbes*, vol. 7 (London: Longman, Brown, Green, & Longmans, 1845), 73.

Leviathan in which Hobbes tells us that he took the title of his work from a comparison of his model Sovereign with the creature mentioned in "the last two verses of the one and fortieth of Job; where God having set forth the great power of *Leviathan,* called him King of the Proud" (362).

Hobbes had been able to reduce Descartes's mind (as will and reasoned judgment) to a function of body. But in human vanity he discovered another sort of mind and will that proved recalcitrant. He was either less able than Descartes to shake himself loose from the hold of tradition or else felt compelled to take account of a leading aspect of the human psyche of which Descartes was either obtusely unaware or which he deliberately ignored. Whatever the reason, here was a kind of free will that would play havoc with the rational fear that Hobbes made the linchpin of his political order.

Appetite that is stimulated by motions external to the psyche can also be controlled by counterstimuli that are external. Thus, if sight of another man's property produces in me a desire to seize it, sight of the policeman will produce a sensation of fear that counterbalances the antisocial appetite and cancels it out. In the world of the model, it was fear of violent death in the war of all against all that triggered the rational recognition of need for sovereign power, that is, for a constantly operative repressant of antisocial acts that lead to conflict and insecurity. When individual reason momentarily deserts us in the face of overwhelming passion, the public reason, in the form of the sovereign's agent, takes control of my behavior because his presence produces the fear of punishment. In this fashion, fear becomes the trigger of Hobbes's rational mechanism, and natural freedom is contracted away. But if my appetite does not arise from an external cause but is self-operative and limitless, how can I be sure that it will be controlled by any counterstimulus coming from the world of sense? Might I not be so caught up in my delusions of grandeur and spontaneous desire for power after power as to block out sensations coming from the public world of reason? Perhaps this is why Hobbes labeled vainglory a "madnesse," because it was not amenable to control by a rational passion such as fear of public chastisement. It produces behavior as an autonomous cause, quite cut off from the mechanical chain of causes and effects in the public world of moving bodies. For its nature is radically different from that of body, and we have no inkling as to how such a free will can be coordinated with the rational movements of Hobbesian body. Read this way, the problem of Hobbes's political theory is not induction of rational action by fear and force but rather the elimination of the possibility of all legitimate and effective authority by an irrational and anarchic freedom. Autonomous Cartesian will emerges to swallow up and destroy the rational movements of body.

That Hobbes himself saw the implications of this sort of human freedom—the freedom to defy all law and rational direction—is clear from his discussion of the dissolution of the commonwealth. In a chapter devoted to the liberty of subjects, Hobbes remarks that "the Obligation of Subjects to the Sovereign is understood to last as long, and no longer, than the power lasteth, by which he is able to protect them. For the right men have by Nature to protect themselves, when none else can protect them, can by no Covenant be relinquished" (272). But why should the Sovereign be unable to furnish the protection for which he was instituted, if we imagine individual acts of sovereign authority resulting in the healthy fear of punishment intended by the political covenant? His powerlessness would have to result from the ultimate ineffectiveness of this fear or from his inability to produce it because of the insulation from public order implicit in Hobbesian vainglory.

The free will of Hobbesian man is essentially a freedom to do limitless evil in the form of prideful aggression. But persons engaging in such aggression are unaware of the true nature of their behavior—being mad. To them, in their private delusions, their actions would be the epitome of justice. It is for this reason—fear that individual freedom to set one's own moral standards leads to dangerous illusion and limitless villainy—that Hobbes refuses to leave the individual conscience the choice of moral principles. "That every private man is Judge of Good and Evill actions" was therefore to him a poisonous doctrine, which produced a diseased commonwealth (365). With faith shattered in the ability of man to know and be guided by a divinely ordained code of right, how could the individual be left on his own to work out moral principles? With conscience gone, only solipsistic vanity remained. If society was to be ordered and peaceful, "Right" would have to be artificially constructed. To construct it required the rationalization, the remaking of human nature by public authority. For freedom to be effectively defined as security of person and property, as freedom to trade and to raise one's children as one wished, the terrible freedom of moral choice had to be forcibly removed by public authority. The new man would have to be forced to be free.

Could this be fully accomplished? While "potent men, digest hardly any thing that setteth up a Power to bridle their affections," Hobbes thought that the "Common-peoples minds" were "like clean paper, fit to receive whatsoever by Publique Authority shall be imprinted in them" (379). Thus Hobbes was sanguine that an able Sovereign, by the teaching of his doctrine, might "convert his Truth of Speculation into the Utility of Practice" (408). Out of the common man might be created a race of utilitarian liberals. Yet, a theoretical flaw remained in the scheme. For how could a quality like Hobbesian free will, understood as vainglory, different from and somehow lying beyond the measurable world of body and motion, be governed by the causal laws of that world?

We must grant, however, that there are problems with the Straussian reading of the character and significance of Hobbesian vanity and vainglory. In chapter 11 of *Leviathan*, for example, where Hobbes writes of a general human inclination as a "perpetual and restlesse desire of power after power, that ceaseth only in Death," he does not attribute restlessness to a vainglory that lies beyond the world of empirical causes and effects. It arises rather from uncertainty; no one can "assure the power and means to live well, which he hath present without the acquisition of more" (161). Hobbes also writes that the motives in the background of the restless pursuit of power may be various; some seek fame, others pleasures of the senses. It is also the case that Hobbes does not claim that all vainglorious men are daredevils. Some are quite the opposite. In one passage he tells us that some vainglorious men are "enclined only to ostentation; but not to attempt. Because when danger or difficulty appear, they look for nothing but to have their insufficiency discovered" (123). And in listing the leading causes of conflict, it may be significant that Hobbes places "Glory" only third, after "Competition" and "Diffidence" (185). So the evidence about vanity, the key concept of the Straussian reading, is mixed.

Despite these ambiguities, and even if we discount the Straussian reading altogether, the government of fear and force and the Hobbesian formulation of the Right of Nature by their own logic, dissolve public authority and return us to the state of nature in which anarchic freedom reigns. We note, for example, that since the purpose of the basic Right of Nature is the security of a man's person and life, he can never covenant away his right to defend that security.

> Therefore there be some Rights, which no man can be understood by any words, or other signes, to have abandoned or transferred. As first a man cannot lay down the right of resisting them, that assault him by force, to take away his life; he cannot be understood to ayme thereby, at any Good to himselfe. The same may be sayd of Wounds, and Chains, and Imprisonment. (192)

The individual thus makes no unqualified submission to authority. He remains the ultimate judge of his own security. He is pledged by nature to resist authority when it approaches to seize and punish him. "No man is supposed bound by Covenant, not to resist violence; and consequently it cannot be intended, that he gave any right to another to lay violent hands upon his person" (353). By his covenant he gave away only the right to defend another person. And since it is a fundamental Hobbesian assumption that the individual is ever ready to kick over the traces of reason, so that threat of punishment must be ever present to him to keep him rational, that very threat of Leviathan is likely to trigger resistance.

Recognizing the vulnerability of his sovereign authority because of the individual's reserved right of resistance, Hobbes sought to build up the instrumentalities of his police power. The Sovereign is placed entirely beyond the law, as its author. He cannot ever be charged with breach of the covenant, since he is not a party to it. He is authorized to act by the covenant but not limited in his actions by it. The king can do no wrong. The Sovereign is empowered to do whatever he thinks necessary to be done, "both before hand, . . . and, when Peace and Security are lost, for the recovery of the same" (232–33). To do this he is empowered "to be Judge, or constitute all Judges of Opinions and Doctrines, as a thing necessary to Peace" (233). Parties are forbidden, as equivalent to factions and conspiracy, "a fraudulent seducing of the [Sovereign] Assembly for . . . particular interest" (286).

Yet the more centralized the sovereign power and the more threatening its weapons, the greater the likelihood that the fear so engendered will not redound to preserve the submission of the subjects but rather will result in the resistance whose right one can never cede. Therefore Hobbes grants that "in case a great many men together, have already resisted the Sovereign Power unjustly, or committed some capital crime, for which every one of them expecteth death, whether have they not the Liberty to joyn together, and assist and defend one another? Certainly they have" (270).

Thus when lawbreaking is widespread enough, the former prohibition by the covenant of assisting another is raised, and it becomes lawful to do so. "The Obligation of Subjects to the Sovereign, is understood to last as long, and no longer, than the power lasteth, by which he is able to protect them. For the right men have by Nature to protect themselves, when none else can protect them, can by no Covenant be relinquished" (272). As the number of rebels under threat of punishment (and therefore not protected) grows, the power of the Sovereign, and with it his legal authority, wanes and is finally dissolved. Hobbes might well have gone further—to note that the logic of his own conception of natural liberty implies the dissolution of sovereign power and, hence, anarchy. Not only ignorant and passionate men but rational men, who remember their right of resistance, will turn upon a Sovereign who threatens them and thus return to the state of nature. Rational natural liberty implies anarchy, which implies sovereignty, which in turn implies rational natural liberty, which implies anarchy. Hobbes presents us a logic of perfect instability.

From freedom to force and back again is the natural cycle.[20]

Locke: The Social Engineering of Middle-Class Freedom

A subtler version of utilitarian politics than Hobbes's and one that moderated the role of central authority was required for a liberalizing England that was still searching for divine warrants for political truth and for English Puritans who had set out to build an individualistic New Jerusalem in America. John Locke (1632–1704) saw the need and met it in full.

Just as for Hobbes, Locke's point of departure in philosophical analysis was the work of René Descartes. Though Locke's *tabula rasa* theory is often held up as a critique of the Cartesian doctrine of innate ideas in surveys of seventeenth-century thought, more astute scholarship has emphasized the affinity of Locke's work to that of Descartes. It was the simplistic innatism of the Cambridge Platonists and of the university teachers of his time in general rather than that of Descartes that Locke principally addressed in his refutation of "innate ideas."[21] One writer notes that in proving his own existence, Locke "affirms that 'in every act of sensation, reasoning, and thinking we are conscious to ourselves of our own being.'"[22] One can in fact view Locke's *Essay Concerning Human Understanding* as an elaborate effort to work out systematically the detailed relationships that exist between sensations and ideas—relationships whose centrality for our understanding of being and thinking Descartes had merely sketched.

In his political writings, Locke's affinity for Descartes is not apparent. In the *Two Treatises* and *Letter Concerning Toleration* Locke eschews the technical language and scientific method of exposition that he employs so carefully in the *Essay*. The vo-

---

20. For other treatments of Hobbes's political thought see M. M. Goldsmith, *Hobbes's Science of Politics* (New York: Columbia Univ. Press, 1966); Michael J. Oakeshott, *Hobbes on Civil Association* (Berkeley: Univ. of California Press, 1975); W. von Leyden, *Hobbes and Locke: The Politics of Freedom and Obligation* (New York: St. Martin's Press, 1982).

21. Cf. John W. Yolton, *John Locke and the New Way of Ideas* (London: Oxford Univ. Press, 1956), 29.

22. Cunningham, *Influence of Descartes*, 97, citing *Essay*, book IV, chap. 9, sec. 3.

cabulary is popular, and the texts are larded with references to Scripture and natural law. Traditional commentary on Locke's politics holds that there is little connection between these works and the *Essay* and claims that there are, in fact, a number of philosophical inconsistencies between them.[23] More recent scholarship, however, has argued for a fundamental consistency throughout Locke's work and has explained the difference in tone and language as strategic rather than philosophical. Like Descartes, Locke understood well the utility of prudent disguise.[24]

The dualism of the *Essay* appears, on the surface, to be more thoroughgoing than in the philosophy of Hobbes. Locke presents sensation and reflection as two sources of ideas. The first involves the observation of "external sensible objects," the second, "the internal operation of our mind perceived and reflected on by ourselves."[25] Our knowledge he describes as the product of understanding or reason observing the agreement or disagreement of our ideas. Mind seems therefore to have more independence for Locke that it did for Hobbes. There is also a self that is not merely the sum of its sensations (and does not clearly appear in Hobbes). The judgmental function of the mind is not radically subordinated to desire and choice. Even "sense per-

23. William A. Dunning, *A History of Political Theories* (New York: Macmillan, 1921), 345; George Sabine, *A History of Political Theory* (New York: Henry Holt, 1950), 523–26; Charles A. Vaughan, *Studies in the History of Political Philosophy*, vol. 1 (Manchester: Manchester Univ. Press, 1925), 158–61, 165–66, 201.

24. See Leo Strauss, *Natural Right and History* (Chicago: Univ. of Chicago Press, 1953), 206–09; Richard Cox, *Locke on War and Peace* (Oxford: Clarendon Press, 1960). The Strauss–Cox reading of Locke has stirred considerable controversy. See especially Hans Aarsleff, "The State of Nature and the Nature of Man in Locke," in John W. Yolton, ed., *John Locke: Problems and Perspectives* (London: Cambridge Univ. Press, 1969): 99–136. The work of Richard Ashcraft, John Dunn, Martin Seliger, John W. Yolton, and many others also takes issue with the Strauss–Cox interpretation. For an effort to define a third position that embraces elements both of the Strauss–Cox reading of Locke and of the interpretations by Ashcraft, Aarsleff, and Seliger, see William T. Bluhm, Neil Wintfeld, and Stuart Teger, "Locke's Idea of God: Rational Truth or Political Myth?" *The Journal of Politics* 42 (May 1980): 414–38. For a detailed review of much of this literature of controversy see Michael Zuckert, "The Recent Literature on Locke's Political Philosophy," *The Political Science Reviewer* 5 (Fall 1975): 271–304.

25. John Locke, *An Essay Concerning Human Understanding*, A. C. Fraser, ed. (New York: Dover Publications, 1959), vol. I, book II, chap. i, sec. 2, 122.

ception . . . is an act. It does not proceed mechanically."[26] Nor is memory reduced to "decaying the sense" as it is for Hobbes. Locke also does not assign the process of thinking to a function of body but explains it by supposing it to be an action of "some other *substance*, which we call *spirit.*" This is not to say that we have a clear idea *either* of body *or* of spirit but simply that we think they are two substances "the one being supposed to be (without knowing what it is) the *substratum* to those simple ideas we have from without; and the other supposed (with a like ignorance of what it is) to be the *substratum* to those operations we experiment in ourselves within."[27]

On the other hand, there are passages in the *Essay* in which Locke gives to spirit spatial referents and one in which he supposes it is possible that thinking is an attribute of matter. The mystery of dualism obviously did not suit his empirical cut of mind. Thus in section 19 of the same chapter of book 2 from which the last quotation derives, Locke says that he finds "no reason why it should be thought strange, [to] make mobility belong to the spirit; for having no other idea of motion, but change of distance with other beings that are considered as at rest; and finding that spirits, as well as bodies, cannot operate but where they are; and that spirits do operate at several times in several places, I cannot but attribute change of place to all finite spirits."[28] But place can refer only to extension, by definition. Is Locke therefore subtly reducing mind to matter in this passage?

More important is the passage of book 4 in which Locke suggests that it is possible that thinking should be a faculty of matter. There is no way to demonstrate either that we are both material and immaterial substance or that we are matter that thinks, and perhaps we shall never know what the truth is. Nevertheless, he believes we should not deny the possibility that "God can, if he pleases, superadd to matter a *faculty of thinking*" just as well as to suppose that he has superadded to it "*another substance with* a faculty of thinking."[29] If such a possibility were real, it would of

26. Richard Aaron, *John Locke* (Oxford: Clarendon Press, 1965), 133.
27. *Essay*, vol. I, book II, chap. xxiii, sec. 5, 395.
28. Ibid., sec. 19, 408.
29. *Essay*, vol. II, book IV, chap. iii, sec. 6, 193.

course rule out the immortality of the soul—a conclusion that was immediately perceived by Edward Stillingfleet, the Bishop of Worcester, with whom Locke exchanged a voluminous correspondence. Here, Stillingfleet thought, was a dangerous break with tradition, which might well threaten both religion and morality. Aaron remarks that some of Locke's language "savoured of the materialism of Hobbes."[30] It certainly echoes the problematical language of Descartes.

Like Hobbes, Locke makes a state of nature the starting point of his political philosophy. But his language contains no overt hint of materialism. Nature is not a field of free-moving bodies, each at liberty to do anything whatsoever to preserve itself. For Locke it is rather "a state of perfect freedom" that all men are naturally in "to order their actions . . . within the bounds of the law of nature."[31] The basic human condition is therefore not one of unimpeded physical movement but rather one of moral restraint. For the law of nature "obliges every one, and reason, which is that law, teaches all mankind who will but consult it, that being all equal and independent, no one ought to harm another in his life, health, liberty or possessions."[32] Thus the moral determinations of mind rather than the passionate movements of body appear as the fundamental human reality.

There are, nevertheless, transgressors of the law of nature to be reckoned with: "degenerate" men, "noxious creatures" who are not readily controlled by the decentralized execution of the law of nature that the state of nature implies. They produce great "inconveniences" in the state of nature and make of it a state of war characterized by "force without right." To remedy the defect, men contract with one another to establish civil society for which a public authority is brought into being to enforce the law of nature.[33]

The fact that Locke began the story of human politics with moral community rather than with atomic clusters of clashing individuals

30. Aaron, *Locke*, 147 (ref. book IV, chap. iii, sec. 6).

31. John Locke, *Second Treatise on Civil Government*, in Sir Ernest Barker, ed., *Social Contract* (London: Oxford Univ. Press, 1947), chap. ii, sec. 4, 5.

32. Ibid., chap. ii, sec. 6, 7.

33. Ibid., chap. ii, sec. 10, 10; chap. ii, sec. 13, 13; chap. iii, sec. 19, 18.

allows him realistically to prescribe responsible government controlled by the community from below, in place of Hobbes's irresponsible and authoritarian Sovereign. It also guarantees the continued viability of that government through arrangements that supply executive vigor in combination with institutionalized restraints on the use of power, providing that the underlying moral community remains intact. This community is embodied in the social majority to which Locke's individual contractants yield up their executive power of the law of nature and which operates on the basis of majority rule.

But in discussing the principle of majority decision, Locke interjects a mechanical metaphor: "That which acts any community, being only the consent of the individuals of it, and it being one body, must move one way, it is necessary the body should move that way whither the greater force carries it, which is the consent of the majority, or else it is impossible it should act or continue one body, one community."[34] Implicit in the necessitarian physical metaphor Locke chooses here is a callousness to the rights of an individual, which surfaces only in a later chapter (18).

Analysis shows that Locke's community is not spontaneous but must be formed by social processes that involve learning. For in Locke's epistemology there are no innate ideas. In the first instance, only a few men know the law of nature with which they have become acquainted through painful experience and through the activity of their reason. As Hans Aarsleff summarizes Locke's argument, "many men will not come by their moral rules by their own efforts. They will absorb them from the general tenor of society, even in pre-political society . . . or they will learn them from superior individuals and assent to them once they are pointed out."[35] Locke never says that the law of nature is known to all individuals. It is indeed "intelligible and plain to a rational creature, and a studier of that law."[36] But these may be only a few, an elite. The many are "ignorant for want of study of it."[37] They

34. Ibid., chap. viii, sec. 96, 81.
35. Hans Aarsleff, "The State of Nature and the Nature of Man in Locke," in Yolton, ed., *John Locke*, 133.
36. *Second Treatise*, chap. ii, sec. 12, 12.
37. Ibid., chap. ix, sec. 124, 105–06.

must be taught. In *The Reasonableness of Christianity* Locke makes it clear that this is the business of the social elite. In the teaching of religion, in particular, the law of nature should be stressed, for its precepts, according to Locke, are the same as those of the gospels.

> The greatest part of mankind want leisure or capacity for demonstration; nor can carry a train of proofs, which in that way they must always depend upon for conviction, and cannot be required to assent to, until they see the demonstration. . . . The greatest part cannot know and therefore they must believe. . . . The instruction of the people were best still to be left to the precepts and principles of the gospel.[38]

Locke's law of nature is an artificial affair in yet another sense. For in his subterranean argument Locke shows that it is not in a strict sense law at all but rather, à la Hobbes, a set of precepts of enlightened self-interest.

Locke nowhere sets forth in detail his moral theory. His most extensive treatment of the subject is found in some brief *Essays on the Laws of Nature* and in the *Essay*. In both he gives an extremely hedonistic account. "Good and evil," he writes

> are nothing but pleasure or pain, or that which occasions or procures pleasure or pain to us. Moral good and evil, then, is only the conformity or disagreement of our voluntary actions to some law, whereby good or evil is drawn on us, from the will and power of the lawmaker; which good and evil, pleasure or pain, attending our observance or breach of the law by the decree of the law-maker, is that we call reward and punishment.[39]

This might have been written by Hobbes, except that in the context in which he presents this description of moral behavior, the legislator in view is the Diety. It is the divine law that "is the only touchstone of moral rectitude; and by comparing them to this law, it is that men judge of the most considerable moral good or evil of their actions; that is, whether, as duties or sins, they are like to procure them happiness or misery from the hands of the Almighty."[40] This is a divine law that is far removed from the

---

38. *Works*, vi. 146, cited in Aarsleff, "The State of Nature," 132.
39. *Essay*, vol. I, book II, chap. xxvii, sec. 5, 474.
40. Ibid., sec. 8, 475.

traditional conception in which good and evil referred to inherently right actions rather than to the pleasure or pain that result from our acting. For Lockean man no other motive than self-interest can make man moral, a term which itself has no substantive meaning.

Fear of the pains of hell is the ultimate sanction of Locke's law of nature. And for this reason men must be taught that there is such a place and that there is a God who decrees it as a punishment for those who violate the rules that he has arbitrarily willed. Yet we have grounds to suppose that Locke did not believe that the existence of such a God could be demonstrated by reason, though he made good use of him as a social myth, which served as the foundation for the legitimacy of his moral code. A nineteenth-century commentator noted that in Locke's time one "heard the opinion mooted that . . . in the various passages in which Locke refers to the existence of a Deity, he is merely . . . endeavoring . . . to take away any grounds for invoking against him an *odium theologicum*."[41] And in the recent leading scholarship on Locke, Leo Strauss and Richard Cox assume that Locke wrote as a skeptic. My own investigations lead to the same conclusion and to the judgment that the elaborate proofs of the existence of God in the *Essay* were mere window dressing. (Indeed, I have attempted to show, in another place, that in a subterranean argument Locke asserts the opposite of his apparent intention, namely, that no proof of the existence of God can be given on the basis of sensation or reflection—his two sources of knowledge. The idea of God can never be more than a "presupposition.")[42] Locke here follows closely Descartes's lead. Both men agreed that the idea of God has vast social utility, whether demonstrable or not. And in his letter on toleration Locke writes emphatically that "the taking away of God, though but even in thought, dissolves all."[43]

The upshot of all this is the conclusion that Lockean individualists can be made moral, that is, be taught to conform to social rules

41. Cunningham, *Influence of Descartes*, 111.
42. See Bluhm et al., "Locke's Idea of God," 414–38.
43. John Locke, *A Letter Concerning Toleration* (New York: Liberal Arts Press, 1950), 52.

of comity on the basis of their own self-interest, which the elite will
understand by reason alone and which the common man can be
taught in the form of religion. It is possible in a state of nature for
an enlightened elite to form a social majority around the salutary
myth of the law of nature and therefore to give the keeping of
that law into the hands of the majority. As long as the myth is
taught and accepted, the social bond holds up. Peace, order, and
liberty, defined as the security of persons and property, can be
guaranteed by a strictly limited constitutional system of government. In this way, most of Hobbes's irrational egoists can be made
to modify their libertarian impulses by deft processes of socialization. Incorrigible vainglory does not figure as a difficulty in
Locke's theory. The problem of liberal society is solved by the
subtle reduction to body that Locke has accomplished.

As it did for Hobbes, Locke's "mind" loses autonomy as a
conceiver of value and as a guide of action. It becomes instead the
rational order of matter in motion, harmonizing the passionate
demands of body, but never legislating goals or ends for body. So
defined, mind is operative from the beginning only in a few.
These must act as sociopsychological engineers to bring the majority to rational behavior by subtle manipulation of their ideas.

But the rational order of body, as I have defined it, is a peculiarly class affair. It is not a universal psychic pattern but a
middle-class pattern. It was a conception of reason carried by the
middle-class social elite that Locke saw rising to eminence and
prosperity and of which he was a member. But Locke was confi-
dent that with the help of his political science these men could
universalize their values. Nonconformists did not concern Locke,
who thought them powerless to disturb the stability of his system.
"The right of resisting, even in . . . manifest acts of tyranny," he
wrote,

> will not suddenly, or on slight occasions, disturb the government.
> For if it reach no farther than some private men's cases, though
> they have a right to defend themselves, and to recover by force what
> by unlawful force is taken from them, yet the right to do so will not
> easily engage them in a contest wherein they are sure to perish: it
> being as impossible for one or a few oppressed men to disturb the
> government where the body of the people do not think themselves

concerned in it, as for a raving madman or heady malcontent to overturn a well-settled state, the people being as little apt to follow the one as the other.[44]

Locke thinks that such "heady malcontents" will be few and that most men's "wheels" will mesh well with one another in his fine-tooled machine, operated on the basis of necessary law.

In his *Letter Concerning Toleration* Locke, unlike Hobbes, argues for liberty of conscience and of religion—an area of individual autonomy and indeterminacy. But the right obtains only as long as conscience confines itself to private acts that have no bearing on the public order of property and preservation. When it does have a bearing, restrictive laws are made. These are considered to be "not made about a religious, but about a political matter."[45] The boundary of the things of God is determined by the judgment of Caesar. Thus for Locke as well as for Hobbes, compulsive and determinate law ultimately overrides the claims of freedom. The two may, if not must, be mutually exclusive. And when they are, private freedom must give way to the rational order of public law. The device of political socialization, indoctrination of a population in the Natural Law myth, is available to Locke's rational elite to insure that the collision of individual freedom with law is averted to the greatest extent possible. Thus in a variety of ways, Locke, like Hobbes, swallows up freedom in the determining force of necessary law.

In this fashion, the freedom of Locke's natural man is formed to a middle-class pattern by Locke's engineering elite. Those who accept the Lockean myth are not aware of what is happening to them. But those "madmen" and "noxious creatures" who stand outside the social agreement of Locke's law of nature will not recognize the legitimacy of the social machinations of the elite. To those few who insist on their natural freedom to act, these machinations are arbitrary force, designed to deprive them of their birthright; for Locke's law of nature is only a myth, which the middle class find salutary for their interests, not a divine promulgation. Thus in Locke's reductionist system, as in Hobbes's, freedom gives way to force or remains in permanent tension with it.

44. *Second Treatise*, chap. xviii, sec. 208, 174.
45. *Letter Concerning Toleration*, 42.

By nature there is no way of bringing liberty into congruence with law; this can be done only by convention—middle-class convention.[46] Now that the values of his middle class and especially their definition of freedom have come under heavy fire, however, by large numbers—indeed, by whole social classes of alienated "madmen"—Locke's assumptions about human nature and about the relationship of mind to body and of force to freedom are called in question.

Legitimate Chains and Solipsistic Freedom: Rousseau

Man was/is born free, and everywhere he is in chains. One who believes himself the master of others is nonetheless a greater slave than they. How did this change occur? I do not know. What can make it legitimate? I believe I can answer this question.

> J. J. Rousseau, *On the Social Contract*,
> book 1, chapter 1, "Subject of this
> First Book"

Interpreters of the *Social Contract* are divided on whether the book is best understood as a theory of freedom or as a theory of authoritarian control.[47] But few would be ready to argue that Rousseau (1712–1778) himself did not conceive his book as a treatise on freedom. Thus the passage from the first chapter that I have quoted above, which states Rousseau's intention quite plainly (to describe a regime of "legitimate chains"), is frequently interpreted by commentators to make it conform to the language of the rest of the book. Annie Osborn, for example, in her insightful comparison of Rousseau and Burke, writes: "'Man is born free,' Rousseau has asserted in the famous opening words of his treatise. Freedom was man's birthright. It was force, not nature, that had made the 'first' slave."[48]

46. I follow here C. B. Macpherson's analysis of Locke's theory as an example of "possessive individualism." See *The Theory of Possessive Individualism: Hobbes to Locke* (London: Oxford Univ. Press, 1962).

47. For a bibliography of the interpretive literature and excerpts from leading books in the Rousseau controversy, see Guy H. Dodge, ed., *Jean-Jacques Rousseau: Authoritarian Libertarian?* (Lexington, Mass.: D. C. Heath, 1971).

48. Annie M. Osborn, *Rousseau and Burke* (London: Oxford Univ. Press, 1940), 10.

She then goes on to develop the concept of freedom and entirely ignores the statement about legitimate chains. John Charvet, in his more recent work on Rousseau similarly insists that the theme announced in the opening paragraph of the book is freedom, though he takes more careful account than Osborn of Rousseau's actual language:

> Rousseau's aim . . . is not to show how the chains can be abolished and natural freedom recovered in society, for political society requires constraints and natural freedom consists in the absence of all such constraints. His aim is rather to show how the necessary constraints of political society can be legitimate and thereby compatible with, if not natural freedom, then an essential human freedom nevertheless.[49]

It seems important, however, that Rousseau himself does not say that his intention is to show how a regime compatible with "an essential human freedom" can be established. He does not talk of constraints but says quite clearly that he will describe "legitimate chains." And this is entirely consonant with the flat statement he makes in *Emile* that

49. John Charvet, *The Social Problem in the Philosophy of Rousseau*, (Cambridge: Cambridge Univ. Press, 1974), 120. I have found four writers who seem ready to take Rousseau's statement of his theme pretty much at face value, though they do not offer an explanation of the disciplinarian character of Rousseau's best society in terms of the logic of his metaphysics, nor do they show why Rousseau transmutes the language of constraint and force into the language of freedom. J. Manners, in his inaugural lecture as professor of history at the University of Leicester, writes that Rousseau wished "to remind us that our freedom is not his freedom, our choice is not his choice. Our way may be nobler than his, but it must be more costly. We are warned in the opening sentences: 'Chains' can be made 'legitimate.'" *The Social Contract and Rousseau's Revolt Against Society* (Leicester: Leicester Univ. Press, 1968), 16. Judith Shklar in *Men and Citizens: A Study of Rousseau's Social Theory* (Cambridge: Cambridge Univ. Press, 1969) writes that for Rousseau only justice, defined as civil equality, "makes the social contract a plausible justification for the 'chains' of civil society," (179). Lester G. Crocker speaks of Rousseau's "chains" as "social and governmental restrictions" and says that the author's emphasis is on how they may be legitimated. He approves of the exegesis of the passage given by Albert Schinz, who wrote that "far from denying the necessity of 'chains,' Rousseau was only proposing the substitution of another kind." *Etat présent des travaux sur Jean-Jacques Rousseau* (New York, 1941), 398, cited in *Rousseau's Social Contract* (Cleveland: Western Reserve Univ. Press, 1968), 55–56.

it is necessary to choose between making a man or a citizen; for one cannot do both at the same time . . .

Natural man exists entirely for himself, he is the numerical unit, the absolute whole, who relates to no one but himself, or to one like him. Civic man is only a fraction, which depends on the denominator, and whose value lies in its relationship to the whole, which is the social body. Good social institutions are those which are best suited to denature man, to deprive him of his absolute existence in order to give him a relative one, and to transport the *self (moi)* into the communal unity, in such a fashion that each particular no longer believes himself to be one, but rather part of the unity, and is no longer perceptible except in the whole.[50]

On the other hand, we know that by the time we get to chapter 4 of book 1 of the *Social Contract*, Rousseau is ready to tell us that the contract is designed to solve the problem of how to establish a mutual defense system in which "each one, uniting with all, nevertheless obeys only himself and remains as free as before."[51] And in chapter 8 we learn that "To the . . . acquisitions of the civil state could be added moral freedom, which alone makes man truly master of himself. For the impulse of appetite alone is slavery, and obedience to the law one has prescribed for oneself is freedom."[52] Here obviously are the words that led Osborn and Charvet to modify Rousseau's statement of his intention in their paraphrases of the book's initial lines. But would they receive warrant from Rousseau to do so? For in the sentence subsequent to this passage, the philosopher tells us that he has "already said too much about this topic, and the philosophic meaning of the word *freedom* is not my subject here."[53] He has already written at the outset that the question he intends to answer concerns "legitimate chains."

What are we to make of all this? J. McManners, in his inaugural lecture as professor of history at the University of Leicester,

50. Jean-Jacques Rousseau, *Emile* (Paris: Editions Garnier Frères, 1961), 9. My translation.

51. Jean-Jacques Rousseau, *On the Social Contract*, R. D. Masters, ed., J. R. Masters, trans. (New York: St. Martin's Press, 1978), 53. All references to the *Social Contract* are to this edition.

52. Ibid., 56.

53. Ibid.

points out that Rousseau in his *Confessions* "tells us how his imagination loved to work by contraries; to depict spring, he must be in
winter, to describe a rustic scene, he must be indoors, 'if I were
put in the Bastille, I should paint a picture of liberty.' [But] when
he wrote *The Social Contract*, he was not in the Bastille; he was at
the freest time of his life. . . . Free, living near to nature, he
depicted the opposite."[54] McManners argues that the explanation for the play of contraries in the *Social Contract* and for the fact
that Rousseau's "'totalitarian passages' are so grim, and, by contrast, his love of freedom . . . so intense" is to be found "in the
context of his passionate, intensely personal revolt against society."[55] A loner and a rootless person, Rousseau hated the social
order in which he spent his life. He would have been alienated
from any social order.[56] Hence, social order, as such, constituted
"chains." Even that just social order that will "abolish great
evils, . . . bring true equality, . . . make every man feel he 'belongs', . . . give us a new kind of liberty, through community with
our fellows" must be seen as "chains."[57]

McManners presents a plausible psychological explanation of
the contradiction we have found in Rousseau's formulation of the
problem of the *Social Contract*, though it tends, like the explanations of Osborn and Charvet, to do away with the contradiction by
making Rousseau view his system of the General Will as offering
"a new kind of liberty," which is in some sense truly liberty. It is
superior, however, to Charvet's resolution of the problem, a
resolution that frames the problem as a paradox that requires
that "the good society . . . both denature man and yet be founded
upon man's nature."[58] For Charvet argues that Rousseau tried to
resolve (or rather "dissolve") the paradox but that its "dissolution
involves the dissolution of Rousseau's whole enterprise."[59] My
own view is that the *Social Contract* is indeed fraught with paradox
but that Rousseau did not feel required to resolve it. He did

54. McManners, *Social Contract*, 16. See also B. Munteano, *Solitude et Contradictions de J.-J. Rousseau* (Paris: Nizet, 1975).
55. McManners, *Social Contract*, 6.
56. Ibid., 8–9.
57. Ibid., 14–15.
58. Charvet, *Social Problem in the Philosophy of Rousseau*, 3.
59. Ibid.

denature man, and yet he did found his state on human nature.[60]

Still other interpreters of the "chains" passages have emphasized the rigors of life in Rousseau's best policy, but they have tried to show that these are required to insure the realization of a conception of human freedom different from that of natural man.[61] Like those just reviewed, these writers hold that Rousseau himself judged this new sort of freedom to be genuine and, according to some, to be a higher kind of freedom, while granting Rousseau's nostalgia for the freedom of nature. No one has entertained the possibility that Rousseau himself may have used the language of freedom in a purely mythical sense, for popular consumption, and that the values that he found in the patriotic society of the *Social Contract* might have nothing to do with freedom in the only sense of that term meaningful to Rousseau.

In the following pages I have tried to place my own interpretation of Rousseau's "chains" in the context of his own version of Cartesianism. In this framework we are able to see that Rousseau could properly use the word *freedom* only for the life of the individual in a state of nature and that the artificial state of society is incompatible with any version of the concept of freedom. It is

60. Cf. J. L. Talmon, *The Origins of Totalitarian Democracy* (New York: Praeger, 1960), 38–40.

61. John B. Noone, Jr., in interpreting the passage in question, softens Rousseau's language and says that in view of the impossibility of a return to nature by most men, Rousseau asks "whether there is a legitimate way of circumscribing man's natural freedom. He thinks there is." *Rousseau's Social Contract: A Conceptual Analysis* (Athens, Ga.: Univ. of Georgia Press, 1980), 9. Ramon N. Lemos gives Rousseau's expression a positive connotation, in the light of later passages, and interprets the "chains" as "the bonds of moral law and moral obligation" that are necessary "for the attainment of moral freedom." He adds that "given the superiority of moral freedom to other forms of freedom, the transition from the freedom from moral obligation with which man is born to the acquisition of the bonds of moral obligation is a change to be welcomed rather than lamented." *Rousseau's Political Philosophy* (Athens, Ga.: Univ. of Georgia Press, 1977), 104. Stephen Ellenburg interprets Rousseau's "chains" as the condition of citizen independence. "The social contract establishes the legitimacy of some 'chains' of common life, specifically those bonds which make citizens self-governing." True citizens remain "perfectly independent of all [their] fellow citizens." *Rousseau's Political Philosophy* (Ithaca, N.Y.: Cornell Univ. Press, 1976), 241. Note how far apart these two interpretations of Rousseau's idea of "true" freedom are.

governed by force. Vis-à-vis freedom, Rousseau has denatured social man in the fullest sense. Yet he also builds on nature.

Rousseau did not employ the language of natural law in his theorizing, because he believed it had been abused by earlier philosophers. In the preface to the *Second Discourse* he criticized the rationalist assumptions of natural law theory, which confined to man "the competency of the natural law," as the "only animal endowed with reason." Furthermore, the natural law authors could not agree on the content of the law. Also, as Rousseau saw it, the idea of the law of nature served each of them only as a convenient myth for legitimating a particular view of the common interest—the use of the concept we earlier attributed to Locke. "The writers of these books," he says, "set out by examining what rules it would be proper for men to agree to among themselves for their common interest, and then they proceed to give the name of natural law to a collection of these rules, without any other proof than the advantage they find would result from a universal compliance with it."[62]

If the natural law language of rationalist moral theory did not appeal to Rousseau, the physicalist world view of the new natural sciences certainly did. In the preface to the *Second Discourse*, Rousseau refers to original man, man of the state of nature, prior to his corruption by social convention, as a "being always acting from certain and invariable principles." The necessitarian and mathematical character of the concept is evident. The method of analysis used in his *Discourse* Rousseau also expressly modeled on that of the natural scientists: "The researches, in which we may engage on this occasion, are not to be taken for historical truths, but merely as hypothetical and conditional reasonings, fitter to illustrate the nature of things, than to show their true origin, like those systems, which our naturalists daily make of the formation of the world."[63] In short, he employed a naturalist's nomological model in expounding his views about human development—one based on the concept of necessary law.

62. *Discourse on the Origin and Foundation of Inequality* in Jean-Jacques Rousseau, *The Social Contract* and *Discourse on the Origin and Foundation of Inequality*, L. F. Crocker, ed. (New York: Washington Square Press, 1967), 171.

63. *Discourse on the Origin and Foundation of Inequality*, 177.

In the *First Discourse* Rousseau appeals for support to "the illustrious philosophers" whom he calls "preceptors of the human race"—namely, Newton, Descartes, and Bacon.[64] And of the three, Descartes was peculiarly salient for the outlook that Rousseau developed. Harold Höffding, in writing of Rousseau's years of study at Les Charmettes, notes that it was his physician there, Dr. Salomon, who "initiated [Rousseau] into the study of philosophy and other sciences," and that this man was a "zealous Cartesian." He goes on to say that "with all his study of Locke besides Malebranche and Fenelon, the Cartesian thinkers exercised the greatest influence on both the content and direction of [Rousseau's] ideas."[65]

Rousseau devoted no single book to the systematic exposition of a metaphysics and theory of knowledge. His work is that of a moralist, educator, and political theorist. A metaphysical position is indeed implicit in all his works and is spelled out in part in the *Second Discourse* and in the "Creed of the Savoyard Vicar," a central section of *Emile*. And all its terms of reference are Cartesian. This is especially evident in the mode of exposition that Rousseau chooses for the argument of the Savoyard Vicar and for the starting point of self-identification he employs there. There are, of course, differences from the full Cartesian position noticeable throughout. But they are all variations on a theme by Descartes.

After finding himself in the condition of "uncertainty and doubt, which Descartes requires to search for the truth," the Savoyard Vicar consults his "inner light" for inspiration. Like Descartes, he looks within himself for the beginning of certain truth. "Who am I? What right have I to judge of things? And what is it that determines my judgments?" he asks himself. "I exist and have senses by which I am affected," he replies. "This is the first

64. Cited in Roger D. Masters, *The Political Philosophy of Rousseau* (Princeton: Princeton Univ. Press, 1968), 228, n. 78.

65. Harold Höffding, *Jean-Jacques Rousseau and His Philosophy* (New Haven: Yale Univ. Press, 1930), 35. For a detailed study of the influence on Rousseau's thought of modern natural law theorists such as Grotius, Pufendorf, Hobbes, and Locke, see Robert Derathé, *Jean-Jacques Rousseau et la Science Politique de Son Temps* (Paris: Presses Universitaires, 1950).

truth that strikes me, and to which I am compelled to assent."[66]
Thus Rousseau writes clearly and in public view what Descartes
had been compelled to say only covertly—that sensation rather
than abstract thought is the guarantee of the thinker's existence.

In the preface to his *Discourse on the Origin of Inequality* Rousseau
argued that

> man's obligations are not dictated to him merely by the slow voice of
> wisdom; and as long as he does not resist the internal impulses of
> compassion, he never will do any harm to another man, nor even to
> any sentient being, except in those lawful cases where his own
> preservation happens to come in question, and it is of course his
> duty to give himself the preference. . . . If I am obliged not to injure
> any being like myself, it is not so much because he is a reasonable
> being, as because he is a sensible being.[67]

This statement, which makes feeling the basis of political right, is
a logical extrapolation from Descartes's rejection of the concept
of rational man in his search for clear and distinct ideas of
fundamental reality. In the *Meditations* Descartes had written

> What then have I previously believed myself to be? Clearly, I be-
> lieved that I was a man. But what is a man? Shall I say a rational
> animal? Certainly not, for I would have to determine what an
> "animal" is and what is meant by "rational," and so, from a single
> question, I would find myself gradually enmeshed in an infinity of
> others more difficult and more inconvenient, and I would not care
> to waste the little time and leisure remaining to me in disentangling
> such difficulties.[68]

After this ejaculation, Descartes went on to list the ideas "which
arose naturally and of themselves" in his mind, whenever he
considered what he was. They all referred to sense experience—
to the sensed movements of the body such as "consuming nour-
ishment," "walking," "perceiving and thinking." And he concluded that "As for what body was, I did not realize that there
could be any doubt about it, for I thought I recognized its nature
very distinctly."[69] He then went on to give an operational defini-

66. *Emile*, 325 [my translation].
67. *Discourse on the Origin and Foundation of Inequality*, 172.
68. Lafleur, ed., *Discourse and Meditations*, 82–83.
69. Ibid., 83.

tion of body in terms of repeatable experimental processes. Thus, while thinking is something radically different from body itself, it comes into being only in the presence of and as a function of the movements of body, which are the first things of which I am clearly aware when I reflect on the question, "What am I?" Rousseau followed up this Cartesian judgment in the fashion I have reviewed. Feeling thus replaces reason as the basic concept of political science. For Hobbes and Locke the problem of good political order had been one of organizing rationality—establishing a harmony of reason. For Rousseau it became first one of organizing community—by weaving together individual feelings into fellow feeling.

The primacy of sensation in our knowledge of existence did not imply a monistic materialism for Descartes, nor did it for Rousseau. In analyzing his own behavior in *Emile*, Rousseau's Savoyard Vicar was convinced that his will, not some property of matter, was its cause. "I wish to act and I act; I wish to move my body and my body moves; but that an inanimate body at rest begins to move by itself or produces movement is incomprehensible and unexampled. The will is known to me by its action, not by its nature."[70]

In the *Discourse on Inequality* Rousseau wrote that "in the power of willing, or rather of choosing, and in the consciousness of this power, nothing can be discovered but acts, that are purely spiritual, and can not be accounted for by the laws of mechanics."[71] Animals are only ingenious machines "to which nature has given senses to wind [them] up."[72] It is in his consciousness of his liberty "that the spirituality of [man's] soul chiefly appears."[73] Just as our sensations originate with the movements of our body, so our sentiments are the product of our wills. Both have the status of feelings. Our will determines as well our judgments about reality, so far as we act to mold and change that reality.[74]

Like Descartes, Rousseau affirmed a dual metaphysics of body

70. *Emile*, 330 [my translation].
71. *Discourse on the Origin and Foundation of Inequality*, 187.
72. Ibid., 186.
73. Ibid., 187.
74. Ibid., 62.

and spirit—the one a realm of mechanical force and the other a realm of originating freedom. But could he erect a self-consistent social and political theory on such a foundation? For how can a metaphysics of private *sentiment* be demonstrated to be a public *cognitive* reality, a rational truth? Descartes never faced this challenge.

As Roger Masters has shown, Rousseau was well aware of the difficulty. In *Emile* he affirmed freedom of the human will as his metaphysical "first principle" on the ground that, unlike the assumption of the materialists that motion inheres in matter as a primary property, the sentiment of free will is based on our immediate experience. He also argued in *Emile* that the concept of substance logically implies duality when referred to human nature. As Masters sums the matter: "metaphysical dualism is prior to the idea of God." "Whereas belief or disbelief in the incomprehensible idea of God [set forth as religious dogma in the Profession of Faith of the Savoyard Vicar] is a purely personal matter, the philosophical doctrine that matter moves by itself depends on concepts which other men should be able to understand."[75] On the other hand, as Masters notes, in the Profession of Faith Rousseau granted that all metaphysical doctrines are weak.[76] And if we look at the *Second Discourse*, we find that Rousseau was not unqualifiedly willing to urge his metaphysical "first principle" in the context of a sociopolitical investigation. In his description of the state of nature, Rousseau tentatively assigns free will as the distinctly human characteristic (in comparison with other animals) but then "immediately withdraws this argument in favor of perfectibility as the distinct quality of man."[77] Following Strauss, Masters concludes that Rousseau did this to free his "analysis of the state of nature from any metaphysical objections which might have been raised by materialists; perfectibility is an observable phenomenon which, unlike the spirituality of man's soul, is subject to empirical or scientific proof."[78]

In order to save freedom as the basis of Rousseau's political

75. Masters, *Political Philosophy of Rousseau*, 67.
76. Ibid., 72.
77. Ibid., 69.
78. Ibid., 71 and notes 59, 60.

theory, Masters contends that Rousseau's weakly argued dualism is detachable from his politics. "Although Rousseau was hardly a modern positivist," Masters writes, "he comes close to what is now called a 'value-free' approach within the realm of metaphysics; one can reject Rousseau's conception of moral freedom based as it is on metaphysical dualism, without undermining his notions of natural freedom and civil freedom."[79] Masters attempts to justify this assertion by arguing that Rousseau's "natural freedom" has empirical reference and is not a transcendental metaphysical concept. He also believes that "civil freedom" as well can be observed. "If the criteria for civic freedom have been properly defined, as presumably Rousseau himself does in the *Social Contract*, any competent observer, regardless of his metaphysical beliefs, should be capable of discovering whether a given society has legitimate laws and is therefore free."[80]

I cannot agree with the last part of Masters's analysis. In view of the devastating argument mounted against the fact–value dichotomy in recent years within the literature of the philosophy of science by writers such as Thomas Kuhn, Charles Taylor, and John Gunnell, it is not credible to say that one's metaphysics (translate as "ideological position") is irrelevant for judging the legitimacy or freedom of a given political order. It is through the reader's own world view that Rousseau's criteria of civic freedom are filtered. How otherwise could it be affirmed by some writers that Rousseau's principles of democratic freedom furnish a description of totalitarian societies such as Nazi Germany (J. L. Talmon) and by others that these same principles constitute the basic assumptions of Western liberal democracies (Frederick Watkins)? Rousseau's criteria of freedom can be *variously* defined. Masters's argument also contradicts his earlier assertion that "the freedom of man's will as distinct from physical matter is in a sense the root of Rousseau's political thought."[81]

A close look at the passage of the *Second Discourse* in which Rousseau affirms free will as the decisively human characteristic reveals that he recognized even there the philosophical untena-

79. Ibid., 73.
80. Ibid.
81. Ibid., 69.

bility of his assertion—its mythical character as a public concept.

> I can discover nothing in any animal but an ingenious machine, to
> which nature has given senses to wind itself up, and guard, to a
> certain degree, against everything that might destroy or disorder it.
> I perceive the very same things in the human machine, with this
> difference, that nature alone operates in all the operations of the
> beast, whereas man, as a free agent, has a share in his. One chooses
> by instinct; the other by an act of liberty; for which reason the beast
> cannot deviate from the rules that have been prescribed to it, even
> in cases where such deviation might be useful, and man often
> deviates from the rules laid down for him to his prejudice. Thus a
> pigeon would starve near a dish of the best meat, and a cat on a heap
> of fruit or corn, though both might very well support life with the
> food which they thus disdain, did they but bethink themselves to
> make a trial of it. It is in this manner that dissolute men run into
> excesses, which bring on fevers and death itself; because the mind
> depraves the senses, and when nature ceases to speak, the will still
> continues to dictate.[82]

The example of free behavior Rousseau offers here involves
the human ability to learn, through experimentation, new ways of
satisfying instinctive desires. A pigeon will starve beside the dish
of meat and a cat on a heap of fruit, for neither is "free" to
experiment with this unaccustomed sort of food. But a human
being implicitly is "free" in this respect. What is involved here,
however, is not the freedom of the will to desire or intend, except
subjectively. Objectively (measurably) the active agent is the ability of the mind to learn causal relationships. This is underlined by
Rousseau in the statement that "the mind depraves the senses."
The power over nature acquired by man's increasing knowledge
increases his desires, and "it is in this manner that dissolute men
run into excesses." In other words, with his ability to learn how to
control nature, there goes no natural sense of proportion, no
freedom of the will to resist the demands of the "depraved
senses," heightened passions. Thus, "when nature ceases to speak,
the will still continues to dictate." Or more clearly, when our
original natural impulse to sustain life by eating is satisfied, our
appetite for food, aroused by our new power to acquire, continues to dictate that we eat and eat.

82. *Discourse on the Origin and Foundation of Inequality*, 186–87.

Now this account of free agency is really an account of the imperfect working of our faculty of perfectibility or improvement. It is remarkably similar to the frank description of perfectibility that begins two paragraphs later, and it contradicts Rousseau's second statement about free agency given in the intervening paragraph. There he writes in more conventional terms:

> Nature speaks to all animals, and beasts obey her voice. Man feels the same impulse, but he at the same time perceives that he is free to resist or to acquiesce; and it is in the consciousness of this liberty, that the spirituality of his soul chiefly appears; for natural philosophy explains, in some measure, the mechanism of the senses and the formation of ideas; but in the power of willing, or rather of choosing, and in the consciousness of this power, nothing can be discovered but acts that are purely spiritual, and cannot be accounted for by the laws of mechanics.[83]

This paragraph hangs in the air. It is at odds with the earlier account of human freedom already analyzed (which is convertible into Rousseau's view of perfectibility) and also has no sequel. It can refer only to the subjective sentiment of freedom and cannot be a cognitive concept. The sequel material—indeed, much of the rest of the book—is about the results of our perfectibility—our ability to learn. In thus rejecting freedom in favor of perfectibility as the characteristic human faculty, Rousseau has accepted the mechanistic necessitarian model of man of his supposed opponents—the materialists. As in the paragraph just analyzed, this ability is described as the source not only of our human good but also of human ill.

> It would be a melancholy necessity for us to be obliged to allow that this distinctive and almost unlimited faculty is the source of all man's misfortunes; that it is this faculty, which, though by slow degrees, draws him out of his original condition, in which his days would slide away insensibly in peace and innocence; that it is this faculty, which, in a succession of ages, produces his discoveries and mistakes, his virtues and his vices, and, in the long run, renders him both his own and nature's tyrant.[84]

83. Ibid., 187.
84. Ibid., 188.

If, then, Rousseau rejects free will in favor of perfectibility as the characteristic human quality, in what sense is his natural man free? And how does natural freedom relate to Rousseau's political theory? It must be a freedom that has an empirical reference, one that is measurable. And we know that this will be something different from free will, which has been reduced to a private sentiment. For political theory must be built on public concepts. Let us search for an answer to these questions in Rousseau's description of the state of nature.

In Rousseau's reconstruction of the primeval human condition, man's life is characterized by the operation of two sentiments, both of an unthinking, animal sort. On the one hand, there is the sentiment of self-love, which leads one to do what is necessary for self-preservation. On the other is the sentiment of pity, "a disposition suitable to creatures weak as we are, and liable to so many evils; a virtue so much the more universal, and withal useful to man as it takes place in him before all manner of reflection; and so natural, that the beasts themselves sometimes give evident signs of it."[85] Our first sentiments, therefore, embrace feelings for the other as well as for the self. Prior to all actual society, to the birth of reason and to the invention of language, there is ground laid for social order in our primitive sentiments of compassion for our fellow man. For Hobbes it was fear, triggering the activity of reason; and for Locke, self-interest enlightened by the experience of insecurity in a state of nature that produced regulations in the general interest. But for Rousseau it is the "natural sentiment" of pity that in every individual moderates "the activity of self-love" and "contributes to the mutual preservation of the whole species."[86]

We must be careful, however, not to make Rousseau's observations into a conception of natural sociality, for he himself explicitly denies such a final cause for the human person. He writes that it is from "the concurrence and the combination our mind is capable of forming between these two principles, without there being the least necessity for adding to them that of sociability, that . . . flow all the rules of natural right."[87]

85. Ibid., 201–02.
86. Ibid., 204.
87. Ibid., 171.

In Rousseau's state of nature, man's character is marked by a thoroughgoing independence; this is the sense in which natural man is genuinely free. Each man's free agency is fully operative; each is his own master and fully supplies his own needs. Each man relies on himself alone, and on no other. Here is at least a quasi-empirical or experiential basis for the private sentiment of free will.

For Rousseau, history is the story of the gradual collapse of this condition of freedom and equality, and the emergence of the unhappy inequalities of civilized social and political order as the result of a series of historical accidents. Rousseau's analysis of the political problem takes the form of a pseudohistory—the history of a Cartesian machine that has from its first operation run out of control.[88] The nature of man to Rousseau was not something given once and for all but a changing reality, infinitely malleable, formed by shaping circumstance and by our faculty of improvement or perfectibility. If unhappy and unguided circumstances—the uncontrolled world machine—produced inequality and unhappiness, we can well imagine that improvement of the human situation might be found in the construction of new circumstances, for example, in the remolding of the social environment. The machine might be rebuilt and put into controllable working order by a skilled social engineer.

But first we must recount the story of the haphazard construction and the destructive career of the uncontrolled machine. An exquisite irony of Rousseau's analysis is that the remarkable independence of primitive man was associated with "the life of an animal confined . . . to pure sensations."[89] But gradually the faculty of causal reason began to awake, as changing circumstance

88. Ibid., 177. Rousseau grants that his alleged facts "are not to be taken for historical truths, but merely as hypothetical and conditional reasonings." He compares them with the speculations of cosmologists on the origin of the world. Despite his disagreement with the materialists, Rousseau sometimes used a machine metaphor when talking about society. Thus in *A Discourse on Political Economy* he says "the citizens are the body and the members, which make the machine live, move, and work; and no part of this machine can be damaged without the painful impression being at once conveyed to the brain, if the animal is in a state of health." Here we have an interesting mixture of mechanical and biological metaphors. In Dodge, *Jean-Jacques Rousseau: Authoritarian-Libertarian?*, 1.

89. *Discourse on the Origin and Foundation of Inequality*, 212.

compelled men to become resourceful and inventive in order to subsist. Rousseau envisages, for example, developing pressure on resources resulting from historical accident—an unexplained increase in the number of people and adverse weather. The use of fire was introduced, and humans learned to make tools. Congruence and competition of interest gave rise to the idea of association in the pursuit of common goals of well-being. And this necessitated language, which in turn increased inventiveness. Families soon appeared and the beginnings of private property in family dwellings. From the new habit of living together developed "conjugal and paternal love."[90]

The organization of primitive society soon gave rise to new wants and desires and new conveniences to satisfy them—"the first source of evils."[91] Also, as people came to rely more and more on social living, jealousy and hatred grew up as companions to the feelings of love. Conceptions of distinction soon appeared, and from them "there arose on one side vanity and contempt, on the other envy and shame."[92] (Thus, unlike Hobbes, Rousseau discovered pride in the public world of cause and effect, which presumably renders it amenable to public control.) A sense of morality developed along with the need for laws to embody principles of civil comity and to prevent vengeance and other strong emotions from destroying social order.

Rousseau idealizes this late phase of the state of nature as "a period of the development of the human faculties, holding a just mean between the indolence of the primitive state and the petulant activity of egoism."[93] But then came more historical accidents that were radically to determine the future of the unguided social enterprise. With the introduction of metallurgy, the division of labor was required; and with improvements in agricultural methods, the division of property for the sake of efficiency. The happy state of nature was then at an end. For their original independence—the solid ground of their natural freedom of choice—men and women substituted a condition of dependence

90. Ibid., 216.
91. Ibid., 217.
92. Ibid., 218.
93. Ibid., 200.

and to that added, through the institution of private property, the dangerous condition of inequality.

From here on, mankind's political history was all downhill. "The usurpations of the rich, the pillagings of the poor, and the unbridled passions of all, by stifling the cries of natural compassion, and the still feeble voice of justice, rendered men avaricious, wicked, and ambitious."[94] The result of all these things was violent conflict and the emergence of the need for coercive government. Its construction Rousseau attributed to the wily rich, who convinced the poor that all stood in equal need of protection from oppression and of a means for securing their possessions. Thinking they were recovering liberty, they ran, instead, headlong into slavery. Soon religion was brought in to sanctify the governmental institutions thus established. "How necessary it was for the public tranquillity, that the will of the Almighty should interpose to give to sovereign authority a sacred and inviolable character."[95]

Forms of government varied with degrees of inequality. "Different states of the rich and the poor were authorized by the first epoch; those of the powerful and the weak by the second; and by the third those of master and slave, which formed the last degree of inequality, and the term in which all the rest at last end."[96] Thus we arrive at the unequal and despotic France of Rousseau's own experience. And the irony of human history has been laid before us—the price of the development of reason and creativity (perfectibility), of the human capacity for love and strong passion, of our sociability, and of our sense of morality has been the loss of our original independence. We have become subject to arbitrary force and have lost our freedom of choice.

Can the great value of the state of nature—individual freedom, defined as independence—be recaptured in society without sacrificing all the values that social life has created? In *Emile* and in the *Social Contract* Rousseau attempted an answer to this difficult question. In *Emile* the answer is given from the point of view of the individual considered as such. In the *Social Contract* it is given from the viewpoint of the citizen. Rousseau's starting point was

94. Ibid., 225.
95. Ibid., 237.
96. Ibid., 238.

such that he was not able to give a single answer to the question, valid for the human condition as such.

In Rousseau's Cartesian theory of value, freedom and perfectibility replace virtue or rather redefine it. In the tradition, to be virtuous meant to realize the model of excellence that God has fashioned as our natural end. By our reason we could know the divine plan, and by our good will we could fulfill it. But now God and his pattern of virtue have retreated into the world of myth. Masters notes that "in the footnotes of the 'Profession of Faith,' Rousseau clearly adopts the Savoyard Vicar's metaphysical 'first principle', whereas he does not similarly endorse the 'dogma' of the existence of God."[97] We are free of Divine mandates.

In a state of nature, we are free in the sense that we are independent of others in determining and fulfilling our needs and purposes. The sentiment that each of us has of the freedom of his will—which cannot, however, be theoretically demonstrated—implies that in the absence of Divine purpose, we are free to intend what we will—to create our own world of purpose and meaning. In society, mind as understanding or reason "leads me to judge about causes according to my natural reason [lumières naturelles]."[98] It yields knowledge of mechanical process, not of purposive movement. Purposes we supply for ourselves. Theoretical science, as a science of purpose and essence, no longer exists. Knowledge of the whole is not available.[99]

But how can every man create his own world of meaning? The result would be chaos, an ontological war of all against all—ideological warfare of an uncompromising kind as private purposes are acted out. For purpose there must be, yet in the absence of a natural pattern there are only the assertions of discordant wills. But there is no public, theoretical definition of free will available, only a subjective sentiment of it, so that free will is not a permanent and unalterable human characteristic. Two solutions to the problem are possible. On the one hand, we may attempt something like a literal return to the original state of nature, when individual independence was a reality. We may

97. Masters, *Political Philosophy of Rousseau*, 67, note 50.
98. *Emile*, 348 [my translation].
99. See Masters, *Political Philosophy of Rousseau*, 72.

reduce society to an aggregation of *promeneurs solitaires*, individual bohemian dreamers, each of whom, by keeping to himself alone, can freely live in the world he has willed for himself. But in so doing, we surrender society and all its potentialities for human growth and happiness. We surrender perfectibility—the unfolding of all human talents, the potentiality of moral growth, and the acquisition of vast power over nature. Our solution is antisocial or asocial. And as a practical matter, how many of us would choose to go in this direction? This is a life-style possible only for a few Rousseauistic philosophers. But perhaps an approximation to it can be found in a conception of private life, the life of the family man in the restricted sphere of his own *foyer*, to whose life-style he gives the distinctive stamp of his own will. This is the solution of *Emile*, who finds private freedom in a state that is less than ideal.

The second alternative is to redefine individual freedom, especially freedom of the will. We will have to fashion a social will and make the individual a citizen. We will have to surrender our natural will to a general will and redefine freedom in terms of equal sharing in the decisions of this new moral being. By making each man dependent only on the general will, in whose creation he shares, we allow him to live by a will that is truly his own. And we avoid the personal dependence of unequal historical society. For the independence of the state of nature we substitute mutual dependence on the law, while retaining our subjective (though now objectively false) sense of free will.

Rousseau's prescription for freedom defined in terms of citizenship is found in the *Social Contract*, whose focal concept is the general will. Establishing the mutual dependence of all citizens upon an impersonal system of law obviates, in Rousseau's view, the dependence of anyone on the will of another, which was the great impediment to individual freedom. "Finally, as each gives himself to all, he gives himself to no one and since there is no associate over whom one does not acquire the same right one grants him over oneself, one gains the equivalent of everything one loses, and more force to preserve what one has."[100]

---

100. *On the Social Contract*, book 1, chap. 6, 53.

Rousseau sought to demonstrate the liberal character of his model society by proving the identity of the will of the free individual with the general will. By virtue of our capacity for pity, we are outgoing, sharing persons, not closed monads like the men of Hobbes's and Locke's state of nature. Each of us has a *moi commun*, a self that is capable of living in community with other selves. This community-self can emerge and dominate the particular self (*moi propre*) when it acts in concert with other persons who are in all relevant respects its equals. There must be equality of material possessions of the same sort of property (for example, land, capital) to make identity of interests possible. There must also be a broad value consensus—shared opinions about the good and desirable. And there must be equality of participation in the formulation and application of the general will. It is a genuine community of interest that makes the general will possible. "It is what these different interests have in common that forms the social bond, if there were not some point at which all the interests are in agreement, no society could exist. Now it is uniquely on the basis of this common interest that society ought to be governed."[101]

When the requisite degree of community is present for the existence of a general will, decisions can be taken by a simple majority. Each citizen will ask himself, when voting, not what he can get out of the decision but rather what it is that the general will requires. If he finds himself in a minority, he will simply conclude that he was mistaken as to the general will and abide by the decision of the majority of his compatriots, for under such circumstances all of the characteristics of the general will are to be found as much in a majority as in the whole.[102] It is well, however, that the more weighty the matter under consideration, the closer the majority should approach unanimity.[103] When community is lost, however, and "private interests start to make themselves felt, . . . the general will is no longer the will of all . . . [and] when the social bond is broken in all hearts, when the basest interest

101. Ibid., book 2, chap. 1, 59.
102. Ibid., book 4, chap. 3, 111.
103. Ibid.

brazenly adopts the sacred name of the public good, then the general will becomes mute."[104]

Why is the general will not a perfect solution to the problem of freedom? We will recall that even Rousseau himself, in the first chapter of the *Social Contract*, referred to the solution he was about to present as one of "legitimate chains," not as a model of freedom. And it is clear from *Emile* and the *Reveries* that he thought the individual freer in private society in a poor political order, and as *promeneur solitaire* (the lone bohemian), than in the community of the general will, the best political society.

We can understand the problem best if we analyze the psychic and moral events that occur as we bring our citizens out of the state of nature into the society of the general will. Each to begin with is literally his own master, absolutely independent of all others for his security and his physical sustenance. He is radically free in action and also in thought, for he is free to act on the promptings of his will in fashioning his meanings and purposes. But each potential citizen will be prompted to leave the state of nature out of self-interest at the moment he feels himself dangerously threatened. "I assume that men have reached the point where obstacles to their self-preservation in the state of nature prevail by their resistance over the forces each individual can use to maintain himself in that state. Then that primitive state can no longer subsist and the human race would perish if it did not change its way of life."[105]

Each person, in joining civil society, seeks his self-preservation. But in pursuing this end through community, he must merge his very personality with those of others. "Instantly, in place of the private person of each contracting party, this act of association produces a moral and collective body."[106] How is this achieved? For the existence of a moral body implies a shared ethos, a common conception of good and evil. Yet in the state of nature, this does not exist. Each person is possessed of a sentiment of his own freedom, and a sentiment of pity for others. But conscience

---

104. Ibid., book 4, chap. 2, 108–09.
105. Ibid., book 1, chap. 6, 52.
106. Ibid., 53.

is not developed and consequently no one has a sense of right and wrong. These are the product of a teleological reason, which is entirely conventional and grows only within society. As Rousseau phrases it in *Emile*: "Reason alone teaches us to know good and evil. The conscience, which makes us love one and hate the other, although independent of reason, is therefore not able to develop without it."[107] But how are reason and conscience brought into play?

Having left nature for society, it remains the case that the ends of action arise from within us, from our sensed freedom of will, which creates a world of value and meaning. But this is not a public world, it is radically private. We are incapable of creating public societal meanings for a good and just (equal) society.[108] Our natural tendency will be, as Rousseau showed in the *Second Discourse*, to impose our private values on society, if we are the stronger, or to be imposed upon, if we are the weaker. A common system of moral meaning will have to be introduced from the outside to avert this result. Rousseau tells us that "[the blind multitude] must be made to see objects as they are, or sometimes as they should appear; to be shown the good path that it seeks; safeguarded against the seduction of private wills. . . . Individuals see the good they reject; the public wants the good it does not see. All are equally in need of guides. . . . From this arises the necessity for a legislator."[109]

Though no moral plan is given by nature or by God, people are used to thinking of morality as God-given, not as something imposed on the weak by the strong. Therefore the lawgiver must appear as a god. "The discovery of the best rules of society suited to all nations would require a superior intelligence, who saw all of men's passions yet experienced none of them; who had no relationship at all to our nature yet knew it thoroughly; . . . Gods would be needed to give laws to men."[110]

It is the Legislator, through his work of ideological teaching and institution building, who forms each of us into a new, social man by giving us common values and meanings.

---

107. *Emile*, book 1, 48 [my translation].
108. *On the Social Contract*, book 2, chap. 6, 67.
109. Ibid.
110. Ibid., book 2, chap. 7, 67–68.

One who dares undertake the founding of a people should feel that he is capable of changing human nature, so to speak; of transforming each individual, who, by himself, is a perfect and solitary whole, into a part of a larger whole from which this individual receives in a sense his life and his being; of altering man's constitution in order to strengthen it; of substituting a partial and moral existence for the physical and independent existence we have all received from nature.[111]

In effect, Rousseau is saying here that the Legislator must modify our subjective free will, if we are to participate in the general will. It is not simply a matter of cultivating our natural compassion for others or of arranging for equality of property and for equal political institutions. Crucial is the creation of a common value system, a common way of looking at the world, a common ideology of vision and aspiration. And this can only be done by remaking the natural man. We must be forced to be free by redefining our freedom in terms of the general will and by compelling our recalcitrant "particular selves," traces of individuality left over from the state of nature, to conform to the dictates of the general will. The general will cannot arise spontaneously within Rousseau's metaphysics as a natural will. For in that metaphysics, will, as such, is radically individual. It is known "by its action, not by its nature." For it has no nature—no naturally intelligible meaning and purpose—and therefore no theoretical status. Meaning and purpose that can be commonly willed must be artificially created. In socializing us, the Legislator establishes criteria of understanding to which individual wills are required to conform. The new will, as a carrier of meaning and purpose, is a carrier of inculcated myth—the myth of social and moral freedom. In this fashion the unplanned society of historical accident is replaced by the planned order of Rousseau's master engineer— the Legislator. But as an order, it has eliminated freedom. The two are incompatible. In this way Cartesian "spirit" (mind and will) is reduced to body in Rousseau's "people," and in the appetitive motives of the Legislator.

It is no wonder that in both the *Social Contract* and *Discourse on Political Economy* Rousseau lays great emphasis on the develop-

111. Ibid., 68.

ment by public authority of shared patriotic emotions and other common sentiments. He is especially concerned that religion, which treats of the highest realities and most profound values, be identified with the interests of the state. He praises Hobbes, who "dared to propose the reunification of the two heads of the eagle and the complete return to political unity, without which no State or government will ever be well constituted."[112] And he especially warned against expecting to create a well-ordered state with a population of Christians. For Christianity divides the allegiance of its adherents and in its most institutionalized forms sets up an independent ecclesiastical authority in the face of the authority of the state. In the *Discourse on Political Economy* he remarks that "it is not enough to say to the citizens, be good; they must be taught to be so; and even example . . . is not the sole means to be employed; patriotism is the most efficacious."[113] And patriotism was to be inculcated: "Create citizens, and you have everything you need . . . it is necessary to educate them when they are children."[114]

In this fashion, Rousseau, like Descartes in the Fourth Meditation, subjects "willing" to "knowing" by the artificial creation of a social mind. Liberty of indifference remains, indeed, for the particular will. But anyone who exercises it is guilty of error and sin.[115] In Rousseau's society of "legitimate chains" he may be compelled to conform to the cognitive "truth" of the norms mandated by the public Legislator.

Rousseau speaks honestly and prominently of his good society as "legitimate chains" at the outset of his book, even though he dissembles, as we have seen, in the course of the later argument. The legitimacy of Rousseau's chains derives from the fact that they are not perceived. Rousseau has arranged it so that his egalitarian system of the general will provides each man with the subjective experience of freedom in his equal participation in the formation of that will and in his equal subjection to self-made laws. That it is not the citizen, but rather a Divine Legislator who

112. Ibid., book 2, chap. 8, 127.
113. In Dodge, *Jean-Jacques Rousseau: Authoritarian-Libertarian?*, 7.
114. Ibid., 9–10.
115. *Meditations*, in Lafleur, ed., *Discourse and Meditations*, 114.

has fashioned the citizen's values and the character of his thought processes, does not come into view. His chains therefore do not appear as bonds. They appear as freedom. More importantly, they allow the establishment of a public order in which all the possibilities of human perfectibility—the ability to learn new behavior—may be worked out.

Rousseau's construction of the society of the general will is thus precisely as necessitarian as his analysis of the historical evolution of inequality. Given the "certain and invariable principles" of original human behavior, the problem Rousseau set himself was to manipulate these principles in such fashion as to produce out of the independent wills of natural man a community of equal and shared will. The Legislator is the sovereign engineer who brings Rousseau's system into being. Built according to the laws of social mechanism, its movements would be necessary, not free. The freedom of its members had to be redefined as equal participation in making and in subordination to the general will.

It is interesting to note that after the Legislator has established the political system, shaped the character of its members, and "enlightened" its will, he departs the scene. And with his departure leadership in effect ceases to be an aspect of Rousseau's politics. The government of Rousseau's best polity does not consist of leaders but of mere administrators of the general will, who are radically subordinate to the mandates of the popular assembly, which is sovereign. The government, or "prince," does not convoke the sovereign assembly; its regular meetings are set by law. During these meetings "all jurisdiction of the government ceases, the executive power is suspended, and the power of the humblest citizen is as sacred and inviolable as that of the first magistrate." "The people can establish and depose" the members of the government "when it pleases." And at the opening of every meeting of the assembly, two questions must be answered: "Does it please the sovereign to preserve the present form of government?" and "Does it please the people to leave the administration in the hands of those who are currently responsible for it?" The Rousseauistic coin that has "charismatic legislator" written on one side has "participatory democracy" inscribed on the other.[116]

Freedom in the *Social Contract*, I have argued, is a Rousseauistic myth. In his last work, *The Reveries of the Solitary Walker*, Rousseau in part lifts the veil from his work and shows us why this must be so. He is at last ready to grant that there is no way in nature of reconciling force with freedom. This can be done only by a conventional sleight of hand. He presents the key to his method.

The theme of the *Reveries* is Rousseau's separation from society and his break with the demands that society makes on him. As we follow Rousseau on the ten "walks" that constitute the book, we learn that much of his writing involved self-conscious dissembling, even lying, for the good of people unlike him—most people—who must live in society and seek their happiness there. On the Third Walk he tells us he has lied about founding his hope for future compensation on a belief in the ultimate justice of God.[117] He has also lied more generally in his elaborate defenses of God and religion.

> That he had frequently used specious or rhetorical arguments did not trouble him, for such arguments permitted him to silence his opponents. Even though Rousseau did not consider society to be man's natural end, he recognized that for the sake of self-preservation man was now forced to live in society. And . . . his concern with religion arose from this recognition of man's need for society and from his conclusion that good political life, that is, popular sovereignty, was not possible without a religious doctrine which would help each citizen fulfill his civic duties.[118]

On the Fourth Walk Rousseau deals more generally with the theme of lying and especially with the conditions that justify it. He also wants to explain how, despite "the pious lies he told to combat his contemporaries and defend the simple faith of citizens . . . he can nevertheless claim to be thoroughly dedicated to the truth."[119] As the walk begins, Rousseau defines lying as con-

---

116. *On the Social Contract*, book 3, chap. 1, 78–79; chap. 13, 100; chap. 14, 101; chap. 18, 106, 107.

117. In my discussion of the third and fourth walks, I follow Charles Butterworth's interpretive essay in his recent edition of Jean-Jacques Rousseau, *The Reveries of the Solitary Walker* (New York: New York Univ. Press, 1979). Quotations are from that edition.

118. *Reveries*, Interpretive Essay, 178.

119. Ibid., 181.

cealing a truth that ought to have been stated. And he concludes that to remain silent, or even to speak falsely to someone to whom we owe no debt, is not lying. This leads to the assertion that what we owe to others is "what is important or useful to them."[120] He follows this with an intricate piece of reasoning which concludes that, while self-serving lies are never excusable, those told in the interest of justice are.[121] Employing this standard justifies his behavior in *Emile* where "he contends that it was morally permissible to take a useful lesson from a false historical fact."[122] It excuses as well "the kind of lie he applauded in the *Social Contract* when he praised founding fathers for 'resorting to the intervention of heaven' . . . to make the citizens more willing to accept their civic duties."[123] But all these examples fail to touch the question of "whether Rousseau would consider a lie relating to the substance of his teaching as justified."[124] He gives us no direct answer to the question. Toward the end of the walk he excuses a lie about religion told in the interest of justice. But this matter he had already covered thoroughly on the Third Walk. Charles Butterworth concludes that "to raise the question directly, Rousseau would have to speak about problems that he [had] held in guarded silence for a number of years, and it is by no means clear that such candor would serve the cause of justice."[125]

> Even though the *Reveries* seems to be intended for no reader other than Rousseau, it is appropriate for him to be as guarded about the extent of his lying in this work as he was in his other writings. After all, his purpose here is to understand what justifies lying, not to confess to all the lies he may have told.[126]

The Fifth and Sixth Walks are the heart of Rousseau's book. In the one Rousseau describes his conception of the highest human

120. Ibid., 183.
121. Ibid., 188.
122. Ibid., 184.
123. Ibid., 188.
124. Ibid.
125. Ibid.
126. Ibid., 236.

happiness—the enjoyment, in the quiet of the passions, of the sentiment of one's own existence. In the other he spells out the implications for political society of his description of the highest happiness as solitude. In learning from them what Rousseau understood as true freedom, we indirectly learn also why all forms of political society, even the best, must exclude freedom and be understood as "legitimate chains."

On his Fifth Walk Rousseau reflects nostalgically on the happy time he had spent years before on St. Peter's Island in the middle of Lake Bienne, a small body of water in Switzerland. He describes it as a place "no traveler mentions" and as "very pleasant and singularly placed for the happiness of a man who likes to cut himself off." He asks what the happiness was that he had found there and replies that a "precious *far niente* was the first and the principal enjoyment I wanted to savor in all its sweetness, and all I did during my sojourn was in effect only the delicious and necessary pursuit of a man who has devoted himself to idleness." He contrasts this quiet life of reverie with the moments of "sweetest enjoyment and most intense pleasures" that he had known and finds far preferable to these fleeting moments "a simple and permanent state which has nothing intense in itself but whose duration increases its charm to the point that [he] finally find[s] supreme felicity in it."[127] The continual flux of things, bearing with it constantly changing affections, which one experiences so intensely in the affairs of social life, can be escaped in such moments of reverie as he experienced on St. Peter's Island. In reverie one escapes entirely from the passage of time into a present that "lasts forever . . . without any other sentiment of deprivation or of enjoyment, pleasure or pain, desire or fear, except that of our existence."[128] In such a state we enjoy "nothing external to ourselves, nothing if not our own existence. As long as this state lasts, we are sufficient unto ourselves, like God."[129]

Here we have a description of perfect Rousseauistic freedom: a retirement into subjectivity, absolutely cut off from the restless motions of Cartesian body, withdrawn into the quiet recesses of

127. *Reveries*, 62, 64, 67–68.
128. Ibid., 69.
129. Ibid.

solipsistic mind—the second resolution of the boundary problem of Cartesian dualism. If activity in society reduces reality to the feverish mechanical motions of body, reverie allows the mind to encompass body by erasing it. Cartesian will calls an imagined world into being; in reverie we recreate the world in serenity. "Movement which does not come from outside then occurs inside us. One rests less, it is true, but also more pleasurably, when light and sweet ideas only skim the surface of the soul, so to speak, without disturbing its depths."[130] Brought to perfection, the process of reverie, according to Rousseau, not only erases the world of body, it may actually absorb and transform it. Emerging from a reverie on his beloved island and perceiving the green world filled with flowers and birds around him, he "assimilated all these lovely objects to [his] fictions; and finally finding [himself] brought back by degrees to [himself] and to what surrounded [him], [he] could not mark out the point separating the fictions from the realities."[131] In reverie, Cartesian mind swallows up body and transforms it, conforms it entirely to the will of the subjective self. This is what Rousseau means by freedom; all else is chains.

On his Sixth Walk Rousseau describes the way in which society inevitably forges chains. He opens the walk with the statement that "there is hardly any of our automatic impulses whose cause we could not find in our heart, if we only know how to look for it."[132] As we read along we discover that he is concerned to explicate the action of one impulse—the desire to do good for others—and that his intention in the first sentence of the paragraph was to say that the desire and the act that follows upon it arise spontaneously from the self, from the complex of mind and will and not from some cause in the outer world. The spontaneous impulses of nature are acts of freedom. Rousseau illustrates the idea with an anecdote about the enjoyment he took in giving alms to a lame boy who customarily took up his post at the corner of a boulevard that Rousseau passed by daily. "At first I was charmed to see him; I gave to him very good heartedly and for

130. Ibid., 70.
131. Ibid.
132. Ibid., 74.

some time continued to do so with the same pleasure."[133] A little further on he writes of similar satisfying benevolences. "There were happier times when, following the impulses of my heart, I would sometimes make another heart content; and I owe myself the honorable testimony that, whenever I was able to savor this pleasure, I found it sweeter than any other."[134] "I liked, even passionately liked, being humane, beneficent, and helpful, as long as only my heart was involved."[135] Here is Rousseau, as natural man, spontaneously following one of the first impulses of the human heart, the impulse of compassion toward others.

But after a while, Rousseau tells us, the naturalness and spontaneity of such acts were lost, and his motive was altered by the fact that people came to expect good deeds from him as a matter of right and to impose a duty upon him to act well. With reference to the lame boy he writes that his pleasure in acting well, "having gradually become a habit, was inexplicably transformed into a kind of duty I soon felt to be annoying."[136] From that time on Rousseau avoided the boulevard crossing where the lame boy stood, for he found it painful to have a duty laid upon him, and he no longer took delight in the good act. Later he goes on to generalize: "I often felt the burden of my own good deeds by the chain of duties they later entailed. Then the pleasure disappeared, and the continuation of the very attentiveness which had charmed me at first no longer struck me as anything but an almost unbearable annoyance."[137] In the language of Cartesian dualism, his spontaneous act of freedom, proceeding only from himself, had been transformed by interaction with society—the world of body—into compulsion and thereby into something painful to him. "From these first good deeds, which my heart poured out effusively, were forged chains of subsequent liabilites I had not foreseen and whose yoke I could no longer shake off."[138] The obligations thus laid upon him against his will—he calls them

133. Ibid.
134. Ibid., 175.
135. Ibid., 77.
136. Ibid., 75.
137. Ibid.
138. Ibid., 76.

"these chains"—did not seem burdensome until he became a public figure. They then became intolerable.[139] "I saw that to do good with pleasure, it was necessary for me to act freely, without constraint, and that to take all the pleasure of a good act away from me, it was sufficient for it to become a duty for me."[140] The result, Rousseau explains, was that he ceased to follow the spontaneous promptings to goodness he felt and learned to abstain from good actions, fearful of the subjection to which he might subsequently have to submit.[141] And so, in his own eyes, he became worthless to society—"ineffectual. Unable to do good either for myself or for others, I abstain from acting . . . I avoid occasions to act even where I see only good to do."[142]

The conclusion Rousseau drew from these reflections was that he had "never been truly suited for civil society where everything is annoyance, obligation, and duty, and that [his] independent natural temperament always made [him] incapable of the subjection necessary to anyone who wants to live among men."[143] "As long as I act freely," he writes, "I am good and do only good. But as soon as I feel the yoke either of necessity or of men, I become rebellious, or rather recalcitrant; then I am ineffectual."[144] And he ends with a generalization about human nature:

> I have never believed that man's freedom consisted in doing what he wants, but rather in never doing what he does not want to do; and that is the freedom I have always laid claim to, often preserved, and most scandalized my contemporaries about.[145]

It is easy to see that such a view of freedom, as perfect spontaneity, allows no degrees or variations. Take it away, and one is subject to force, to chains. Writing about himself, he is also writing about natural man who, once brought into society, which by definition requires mutual obligations, must ipso facto submit to chains. There is no alternative in the Cartesian dichotomy within

139. Ibid.
140. Ibid., 76, 77.
141. Ibid., 78.
142. Ibid., 80.
143. Ibid., 83.
144. Ibid.
145. Ibid., 83–84.

which Rousseau's mind (and feelings) moved. Freedom must yield to force. Under these circumstances civil freedom could be nothing but a salutary illusion, an illusion that one is obeying one's own will in obeying the general will. Freedom in political society is a legitimating myth—morally meaningless but politically useful to the sagacious Legislator of egalitarian perfection.[146]

A Theoretical Summary

In the political theories of Hobbes, Locke, and Rousseau, the tensions between force and freedom develop within a hesitant and imperfect metaphysical effort to reduce Descartes's troubling dualism to the material pole, to body. The freedom that each sought to engineer had therefore to be consistent with necessity. For it signifies the orderly movement of bodies in a harmonious pattern. But, so ordered, would it be freedom any longer?

If we interpret Hobbes's work either as a failed or successful reductionism, the consistency of liberty and necessity are never established as freedom under law. Both vainglorious and rational man require Leviathan's harsh coercion to avert anarchy. Yet each, by the inner workings of his own nature, also stands ready to overthrow that power. Locke succeeds in stabilizing a similar system of possessive individualism only by socializing the citizenry to acceptance of a bourgeois myth. For them his system represents freedom under law. But for all others—anarchists, communists and others outside the myth—the power of the social

146. It is interesting to observe that Rousseau never acknowledged changing his view over the years, despite "the apparent substantive differences of [his] writings, the diverse circumstances and dates of their composition." By contrast, he "insists repeatedly that his view remained constant from the time he prepared the *First Discourse*." Terrence Marshall writes that "if Rousseau is taken at his word . . . a proper interpretation must discern how their paradoxes can be explained in harmony with his premises." ["Rousseau Translations: Review Essay," *Political Theory* 10 (February 1982):106.] I submit that my interpretation accomplishes this. Marshall also remarks that "the philosophical significance of the *Reveries* is that it contains Rousseau's 'first philosophy.' Appearing as a memoir to himself, in which the idea of God no longer mediates the base and the good, it reveals the ground of Rousseau's view of politics, nature, and men," (118). I have used the *Reveries* in this chapter consonantly with such a view of its function.

majority can be only arbitrary force. Rousseau's reductionism in the *Social Contract* achieves a similar reconciliation by socializing natural man to the conformism of the Jacobin nationalist. The Legislator stands beyond the political order as its founder. And for the solitary walker, civic obligations are burdensome chains of arbitrary power; he seeks freedom in solipsistic reverie. His willing and dreaming remain unreduced—but also asocial.

Theory as Practice: Foreword to a Complex Enterprise

This is primarily a book about tensional patterns in significant modern political theories. It is not a history of political culture and its multifaceted paradoxes. Nevertheless I believe that it is important to show that what happens at the fifth level of philosophical abstraction can also be observed in the thought that surrounds everyday politics. Human culture is a whole of related though diverse parts. In what follows in this chapter and in the last section of each of the next two chapters, I shall present some examples of how the paradox and ambivalence found in formal political theory are mirrored in the symbolic practices of political life. They are not representative of the whole but are intended to highlight problematic aspects of it.

The study of influence and causality in the history of philosophical ideas and the study of their diffusion through the various levels of social order is not an exact science nor will it probably ever be one. The data are exceedingly multiform and frequently elusive, and causes and influences are plural and difficult to sort out. One must rely on scholarly carefulness, good sense, and on insight in selecting and interpreting the phenomena involved, for there is no scientific canon at hand to provide a guide. The sociology of knowledge has made little progress in methodology since the seminal work of Karl Mannheim. And surely his *Ideology and Utopia* is not a work of science but a bold artistic interpretation of an important political reality.[147] To apply statistical methods in assessing library holdings and in estimating the size and character of the readership of particular books may be helpful, but it is an

147. New York: Harcourt, Brace and World, 1936.

incomplete method and may be a misleading one in measuring the diffusion of ideas. J. L. Talmon has commented eloquently on the problems involved in trying to assess in this way the influence of philosophers on the French Revolution:

> Statistics have been adduced to show that the works of the philosophers were neither widely distributed nor widely read in the years before the Revolution, and the influence of eighteenth-century ideas upon the Revolution has been seriously questioned. On becoming acquainted with the Revolutionary literature one is almost tempted to answer that statistics is no science. The prevalence of philosophical canon books in libraries or the number of their actual readers is in reality no index to their influence. How many people in our own days have actually read the *Capital* of Marx or the works of Freud? Few however would deny that the ideas propagated in these books have entered contemporary thinking and experience to a degree that defies measurement. There is such a thing as a climate of ideas, of ideas in the air.[148]

We need to stress that scholars have no certainty about the direction of causality in the relationship between highly sophisticated philosophy and what goes on in the minds of political leaders or of simple citizens or subjects as they act politically. Does the great philosopher cause and influence popular thought (either directly or indirectly), or does he rather represent a sophisticated statement of ideas that are operative in a society, independently of any causal action on his part? Is his work to be understood as the elegant statement of already operative ideas, as the work of a prophet, or as that of an evangelist? The roles of the philosopher are many and will vary with particular writers. We have no general theory that covers the matter in hand and no final answers to the sticky questions of intepretation we face.

The following discussion, therefore, is limited to reporting evidence about the reception of the work of the philosophers I have analyzed. I note significant parallels between paradoxes of force and freedom in the formal theories and important aspects of modern political culture that appear to display similar kinds of

---

148. J. L. Talmon, *The Origins of Totalitarian Democracy* (New York: Praeger, 1960), 69–70.

Cartesian ambivalence and tension. My aim is to point up important similarities, not to make definitive assessments about causality and influence, but nevertheless to take note of clear lines of influence where they can be shown to exist. The popular patterns of thought with which I shall deal are in some part historical but largely contemporary.

Hobbesian, Lockean, and Rousseauistic Ideas in Modern Political Culture

Hobbism

Even though Hobbes was a monarchist, he "received his worst political criticism from the Cavaliers" during the interregnum of 1649 to 1660, while he was in exile in France, "once the logic of his position [was] grasped" (He completed *Leviathan* in 1651 in France but had it published in London);[149] for he had written in plain language that in the state of nature nothing can be unjust.[150] And he saw no difference between the legitimacy of a commonwealth by institution and one by acquisition. Both have a de facto basis in fear, and from the de facto situation derives the de jure one.[151] Reading Hobbes's book in London, the parliamentarians in control took another view from the one they had earlier held of the author. "The powers that he had accorded to the Sovereign had shifted through historical caprice from Charles to Cromwell, and the fact that Hobbes could return to England safely was at least tacit recognition that the parliamentarians . . . had found them compatible with the new order."[152]

When the political tables turned once more with the Restoration, Charles II found no threat in the writings of the aging Hobbes and even gave him a pension and a place at court. But it is noteworthy that Hobbes's theoretical position "went against the entire trend of English constitutionalism as it was to develop in the Restoration."[153]

149. Reik, *Golden Lands*, 98.
150. *Leviathan*, 188.
151. Ibid., 252.
152. Reik, *Golden Lands*, 101–02.
153. Ibid., 102; see John Bowle, *Hobbes and his Critics* (London: J. Cape, 1951).

Most important for understanding Hobbes's ultimate political significance was the free-will controversy between Hobbes and the traditional intelligentsia of his time, which centered on the implications for human freedom and for human meaning in Hobbes's thoroughgoing mechanist outlook. Ralph Cudworth, "the most tough-minded and lucid" of Hobbes's opponents, saw that Hobbes's metaphysics took purpose out of the world. The world of Cudworth and Henry More "has creativity, novelty, vitality; Hobbes's is an automaton governed by the strict laws of motion. Their world is possessed of universal truth, absolute value, and qualitative distinctions. . . . Hobbes's world is a collocation of singulars, differing only in . . . spatial location, and velocity."[154] Samuel Johnson's reply to Hobbes's determinism, which stresses the subjective experience of free will, is peremptory— "Sir we know our will is free, and there is an end of it."[155] But it fits well with the more sophisticated replies given by later humanists (such as R. M. Hare in our own time) to later versions of Hobbesian positivism.[156]

The Hobbesian position on free will has been notably espoused in America by the Harvard behavioral psychologist, B. F. Skinner. And Skinnerian psychology has importantly affected public policy in the United States in opposite ways. Skinnerianism in practice has been Janus-faced—sometimes producing new and oppressive technical restraints on human behavior, at others, a greater freedom for the individual. But only the restraints are truly Hobbesian in spirit; the new freedoms might have surprised the philosopher.

Surveying our present condition, Skinner finds America to be a society that has worked through a good part of the Hobbesian prescription for a rational world in which freedom is reduced to the security of persons and property. But the persistence of a humanistic conception of freedom—what Skinner calls "autonomous man"—prevents complete rationalization. Indeed, at the penultimate moment of technological perfection, "autonomous man" threatens not only to destroy the fruits of rationalization

154. Mintz, *Hunting of Leviathan*, 102.
155. Quoted in ibid., 112.
156. See *Freedom and Reason* (London: Oxford Univ. Press, 1965), 61ff.

but the very existence of the world. Hobbesian security, almost attained, becomes fundamentally problematical. In Skinner's view, the humanistic values of freedom and dignity have become a "possessing demon," for they prevent the culmination of technological perfection. Like the vain man of Hobbes's state of nature, the free man of today refuses to come to terms with mechanical reality and refuses to submit to its rational laws. "It is not difficult," Skinner writes, "to demonstrate a connection between the unlimited right of the individual to pursue happiness and the catastrophes threatened by unchecked breeding, the unrestrained affluence which exhausts resources and pollutes the environment, and the imminence of nuclear war."[157] Our only salvation is to give up our freedom, to yield to the demands of rationality—the rationality of preservation. With Hobbes, we are compelled to give primacy to a single freedom—freedom from fear of violent death. The only way to secure it is through rational force in the form of a technology of human behavior.

> We could solve our problems quickly enough if we could adjust the growth of the world's population as precisely as we adjust the course of a spaceship, or improve agriculture and industry with some of the confidence with which we accelerate high-energy particles, or move toward a peaceful world with something like the steady progress with which physics has approached absolute zero. . . . But a behavioral technology comparable in power and precision to physical and biological technology is lacking, and those who do not find the very possibility ridiculous are more likely to be frightened by it than reassured. That is how far we are from "understanding human issues" in the sense in which physics and biology understand their fields, and how far we are from preventing the catastrophe toward which the world seems to be inexorably moving.[158]

In Skinner's view, human behavior does not depend on direction by some homunculus that inhabits the body but on the structure of the environment. Scientific analysis reveals "unsuspected controlling relations between behavior and environment."[159]

157. B. F. Skinner, *Beyond Freedom and Dignity* (New York: Alfred A. Knopf, 1971), 2–3, 200.
158. Ibid., 5.
159. Ibid., 19–20.

> In the traditional picture a person perceives the world around him, selects features to be perceived, discriminates among them, judges them good or bad, changes them to make them better . . . and may be held responsible for his action and justly rewarded or punished for its consequences. In the scientific picture a person is a member of a species shaped by evolutionary contingencies of survival, displaying behavioral processes which bring him under the control of a social environment which he and millions of others like him have constructed and maintained during the evolution of a culture. The direction of the controlling relation is reversed: a person does not act upon the world, the world acts upon him.[160]

The upshot of this analysis is the conclusion that we do not need better men but better environments.[161]

Skinner, à la Hobbes, thinks that an explanation of human behavior reveals that good and bad are simply labels for things that we find attractive (pleasurable) and things we find repulsive (painful). He expresses these in the language of reinforcement and within a framework of survival values. "Things are good (positively reinforcing)," he writes, "or bad (negatively reinforcing) presumably because of the contingencies of survival under which the species evolved."[162] "The only good things are positive reinforcers, and the only bad things are negative reinforcers."[163] Skinner does not expound this pleasure–pain psychology in detail and only mentions in passing that social survival, historically, has taken precedence over the deviant values of individuals. He expresses this as follows:

> Happiness may be taken to represent the personal reinforcers which can be attributed to survival value and esteem some of the conditioned reinforcers used to induce a person to behavior for the good of others; but all conditioned reinforcers derive their power from personal reinforcers (in traditional terms, public interest is always based on private interest) and hence from the evolutionary history of the species.[164]

160. Ibid., 211.
161. Ibid., 82.
162. Ibid., 104.
163. Ibid., 107.
164. Ibid., 110.

But it would appear that in the age of "autonomous man," history has let us down. Our false ideology of individual freedom has led us from a safe course of social survival to the irrational anarchy of individual choice. On the one hand, we have relaxed social control in the interests of individual freedom. And through the application of rational methods to technological development we have produced a culture of leisure, directed to the gratification of individual desires. Both have become dysfunctional in a time in which uncontrolled technological development in the service of individual whim has brought us to the verge of catastrophe. "Life, liberty, and the pursuit of happiness are basic rights. But they are the rights of the individual and were listed as such at a time when the literature of freedom and dignity were concerned with the aggrandizement of the individual. They have only a minor bearing on the survival of a culture."[165]

What must be done? Skinner's book is a plea for the abandonment of the illusions of freedom and a frank recognition of the vast perils these illusions produce. Our only alternative is to create a technology of human behavior and submit to being formed by it in the interest of general survival. Like Hobbes's Leviathan, this technology is the only warrant of rationality whose authority we will be induced to accept through fear of violent death. Skinner's role it to produce in us, with his writing, the rational reflex of terror—an artificial experience of the state of nature.

The gospel of Skinnerianism has received a wide hearing and the beginnings of a broad application during the decade of the 1970s. Researching the bibliography of the movement in the library of the university at which I teach, I found twenty-three book titles on the subject, not one of which predated 1972.

Techniques available for behavior modification are numerous. They include simple reward and punishment systems, subliminal suggestion, the administration of drugs, hypnotism, brainwashing, electronic controls, and psychosurgery. Targets for their application are also numerous: from keeping order in the public school classroom through business advertising; also improve-

165. Ibid., 180.

ment of marital sex relations, treatment of deviant sexual behavior, relief of the mentally ill to control criminal behavior, and even breeding of a particular kind of human being.

Controlling school behavior has received a lot of attention by applied behavioral psychologists, and behavior modification schemes in that area have received a substantial amount of criticism. A study reported in the *Journal of Applied Behavior Analysis* for 1972 asserted that programs of this sort produce a markedly passive child—one "who stays glued to his seat and desk all day, continually looks at his teacher or his text/workbook, does not talk to or in fact look at other children, does not talk unless asked to by the teacher, hopefully does not laugh or sing (at the wrong time), and assuredly passes silent in the halls."[166] A rebuttal argued that the classrooms studied were not representative and that efforts had also been made to employ behavior modification techniques to improve academic behavior as well as to control unruliness. The rebutter agreed though that programs aimed solely at docility were undesirable.[167]

Law enforcement officials have been eager to make use of a variety of behavior modification techniques to control the unruly populations of prisons. A conference of wardens heard from an M.I.T. psychologist about a variety of brainwashing techniques used by Asian communists on American prisoners that could be adapted for prison use. The techniques included systematic isolation and the production of mutual mistrust. According to Jessica Mitford, the technique has been put to work in at least one prison—the federal penitentiary at Marion, Illinois.[168] Drugs, electronics, and psychosurgery have also been employed in prison behavior modification programs. And large sums of federal money have been appropriated for research in the uses of these methods. Stolz reports that, in the past, informed consent of prisoners to

166. R. A. Winett and R. C. Winkler, "Current Behavior Modification in the Classroom: Be Still, Be Quiet, Be Docile," *Journal of Applied Behavior Analysis* 5 (1972): 499 ff., cited in S. B. Stolz, et al., *Ethical Issues in Behavior Modification* (San Francisco: Jossey-Bass, 1978), 49–50.

167. Ibid.

168. Cited in Vance Packard, *The People Shapers* (Boston: Little, Brown, & Co., 1977), 79.

total treatment programs has been lacking. And it is clear that at present it is the prison authorities and, through them, society, rather than the prisoners, who function as the client of professional psychologists in existing modification programs.[169]

The possibility of wholesale personality shaping through a variety of techniques is being canvassed by psychologists. They have experimented with imprinting behavior patterns in very young animals, and efforts are now being made to extrapolate these methods to human infants. Some psychologists interested in the possibilities of imprinting are motivated by disenchantment with what they consider the "haphazard educational procedures" employed by many families. But at least one such expert who is enthralled by the possibilities of psychogenesis is puzzled by the problem of adequate models. "To imprint for what?" he asks. "What kind of humans do we want to construct?"[170]

Technical capabilities for expanding the targets of behavioral control from special publics to the population at large exist in abundance. Computer technology has made feasible the pooling in one center of all the information held by twenty federal agencies on individual American citizens. And the establishment of a FEDNET is being pushed by agencies such as the General Services Administration. Television cameras that can control sections of cities as large as two miles square are already being employed to deter street crime and also to keep political protest gatherings under surveillance. Vehicular monitoring equipment that can tap into conversations in homes and also identify what television stations are being watched exist and are being used in many cities.[171]

It would be wrong to leave an impression with the reader that the technologies and behavior modification programs I have surveyed are wholly bad things or that their employment has had only negative results for a free society. Countless social and individual benefits can also be documented, especially in

169. Stolz, et al., *Ethical Issues*, 78, 82.

170. Cited in Packard, *People Shapers*, 64. See also the large and growing literature on genetic control, for example, Robert H. Blank, *The Political Implications of Human Genetic Technology* (Boulder, Colo.: Westview Press, 1981).

171. Packard, *People Shapers*, 114.

teaching skills to physically and psychologically handicapped children. Some of them cannot be helped by techniques other than Skinnerian, such as teaching machines. There is also no question that brain surgery has brought relief to many from painful and threatening psychic maladies. These techniques have manifestly contributed to the enhancement of human well-being and to individual freedom. The new techniques are truly ambivalent and paradoxical in their meaning for modern society.[172]

Lockean America

Though John Locke wrote with greater subtlety than Hobbes, his "new way of ideas," like that of Hobbes, generated considerable antagonism in the years following its appearance—the period of the accession of William and Mary. (I am referring to the *Essay Concerning Human Understanding*, not to the *Two Treatises of Government*.) Many critics "attempted to show the evil consequences to morality, religion, and exact thought which must follow from the acceptance of Locke's speculations."[173] Eventually, however, Locke's philosophy began to gain a sympathetic hearing and exert a large influence on the English intelligentsia. The uncertainty of Locke's dualism is represented by the fact that this influence led, on the one hand, to Berkeley's idealism and, on the other, to Humean empiricism and skepticism in the eighteenth century. Fowler observes that to "the ordinary common-sense Englishman . . . the systems both of Hume and Berkeley appeared to be given to the fatal objection of paradox."[174]

While Locke's writings on toleration and on the structure of constitutional government "may be said to have almost formed the recognized code of liberal opinion" in Great Britain in the nineteenth century, Locke's truest mirror has been on the other

172. For alleged direct Hobbesian influences on the constitutional foundations of American polity see Frank M. Coleman, *Hobbes and America: Exploring the Constitutional Foundations* (Toronto: Univ. of Toronto Press, 1977) and George Mace, *Locke, Hobbes and the Federalist Papers: An Essay on the Genesis of the American Political Heritage* (Carbondale and Edwardsville: Southern Illinois Univ. Press, 1979).

173. Thomas Fowler, *Locke* (London: Macmillan, 1909) 195.

174. Ibid., 196.

side of the Atlantic.[175] The ambivalence of Lockean politics is reflected clearly in the tensions and contradictions of American political culture. On the one hand, Locke's emphasis on effective processes of representative and constitutional government as necessary to the security of individual liberties against arbitrary private and public action moves in the direction of enlarged individual freedom, as does his concept of a popular political culture that enshrines natural rights. In a synthesis of empirical studies of leading American political ideals published in 1972, Donald Devine argues that "the values of Locke [along with those of other leading liberals of the seventeenth and eighteenth centuries] represent essentially the same values which comprise the American political culture at the present," despite "substantial environmental pressure."[176] Devine discovered that in a variety of studies carried out during the middle decades of the present century, the value of liberty, defined as freedom of press and speech and as representative government, was accorded the highest rank of seven values surveyed. [177] In the studies examined by Devine, belief in God was reported as virtually unanimous.

But there are also illiberal aspects to the American value consensus, just as there are illiberal elements in the political philosophy

175. Ibid., 194. I disagree with Gary Wills's thesis about Locke and the Declaration of Independence and follow instead the more traditional view as set forth by Carl Becker. See Gary Wills, *Inventing America* (New York: Vintage Books, 1979), esp. 169–74, 181–85, 193–96; Carl Becker, *The Declaration of Independence* (New York: Vintage Books, 1958). I do believe however that Wills makes a very good case that Jefferson's philosophy of life and of human nature was perhaps more influenced by the philosophers of the Scottish Enlightenment than by Locke. But in no part of his book does Wills establish that the ideas and language of the Declaration have that origin. Jefferson himself as he lay dying gave Locke as one of his sources for that document. Alasdair MacIntyre, in the first Rush Rhees Lecture, University of Rochester, 1983. See also Paschal Larkin, *Property in the Eighteenth Century, with special reference to England and Locke* (New York: Howard Fertig, 1969), 147, a cogent passage that supports this view.

176. Donald Devine, *The Political Culture of the United States* (Boston: Little, Brown & Co., 1972), 65. See also Neal Riemer, "Two Conceptions of the Genius of American Politics," *The Journal of Politics* 20 (November 1958):695–717.

177. Devine, *Political Culture of the United States*, 179–230. Devine's findings are detailed in my *Ideologies and Attitudes: Modern Political Culture* (Englewood Cliffs, N.J.: Prentice-Hall, 1974), 88–91, along with supporting studies.

of Locke. After commenting at length on the "natural liberalism" of American society, which unlike the liberal regimes of Europe was "born equal" and did not have to achieve liberal institutions through revolution, Louis Hartz speaks of the illiberal aspects of our culture. He writes that

> ironically, "liberalism" is a stranger in the land of its greatest realization and fulfillment. . . . Here is a doctrine which everywhere in the West has been a glorious symbol of individual liberty, yet in America its compulsive power has been so great that it has posed a threat to liberty itself. Actually Locke has a hidden conformitarian germ to begin with, since natural law tells equal people equal things, but when this germ is fed by the explosive power of nationalism, it mushrooms into something pretty remarkable. . . .
>
> I believe that this is the basic ethical problem of a liberal society: not the danger of the majority which has been its conscious fear, but the danger of unanimity . . . the "tyranny of opinion" that Tocqueville saw unfolding as even the pathetic social distinctions of the Federalist era collapsed before his eyes.[178]

In conformist America, public opinion may seek to "force" the deviant to be "free." Hartz writes that "when a liberal community faces military and ideological pressure from without it transforms eccentricity into sin, and the irritating figure of the bourgeois gossip flowers into the frightening figure of an A. Mitchell Palmer or a Senator McCarthy."[179] Hartz sees as the decisive American domestic issue our ability to muster liberal resources against the "unwritten tyrannical compulsion" our society contains.[180]

Hartz's literary analysis of the Lockean dualism of American political culture is borne out by empirical work on the subject. Robert Lane's fifteen "Eastporters" did not understand democracy in terms of majority rule and minority rights but rather in a Lockean majoritarian fashion.[181] Democracy for Lane's subjects consists of the "freedom of the nondeviant individual to do what the majority thinks is right."[182] And a study by Herbert McClosky, which compared leader and follower value attitudes, found that

---

178. *The Liberal Tradition in America* (New York: Harcourt, Brace, 1955), 11.
179. Ibid., 12.
180. Ibid.
181. See Kendall, *John Locke and the Doctrine of Majority Rule.*
182. Robert Lane, *Political Ideology* (New York: Free Press of Glencoe, 1962), 83.

political elites are much more sensitive to the constitutionalist and liberty-centered elements of the political culture than are the followership.[183] McClosky concluded that his study would "furnish little comfort for those who wish to believe that a passion for freedom, tolerance, justice and other democratic values spring spontaneously from the lower depths of society."[184]

All the empirical studies I have mentioned give clear evidence that, while many of the average men of Locke's "social majority" in America may have little regard for the rights of minorities who disagree with them, they all have very high respect for Lockean propertarian values—including those respondents with little in the way of property themselves. Lane's subjects accepted economic inequality along with the freedom to acquire property very strongly. And Lane noted that while America announces that "all men are created equal," it urges its members, in good Lockean fashion, to become unequal. The rich have a right to their wealth, and Lane's working men felt secure in contemplating the existence of a propertied elite overseeing the direction of the social order.[185] Americans seem to fit rather well Macpherson's definition of the "possessive individualist."[186]

Thus, American political culture appears to embrace contradictory values in which individual liberty and majoritarian force stand in tension with one another, as they do in the political theories of John Locke. Several writers have suggested that in our political practice we deal with this tension through the device of compromise, which has taken a variety of forms over the years—compromise between freedom and authority, between individualist freedom and egalitarian freedom, between property and conscience, and between laissez-faire liberalism and the liberalism of the welfare state.[187] One writer tells us that "in

183. Herbert McClosky, "Consensus and Ideology in American Politics," *American Political Science Review* 58 (June 1964):365. See also H. McClosky and A. Brill, *Dimensions of Tolerance* (New York: Russell Sage, 1983).

184. Ibid., 375. These and supporting studies are reviewed in detail in my *Ideologies and Attitudes*, 83–88, 91–103.

185. Lane, *Political Ideology*, 85–86.

186. See Larkin, *Property in the Eighteenth Century*, chap. 5, for an analysis of Locke's influence on the theory of property in America.

187. See citation of Staughton Lynd in Michael Kammen, *People of Paradox* (New York: Knopf, 1972), 237, and the examples of compromise in Kammen's text, 211–20, 270.

philosophy, Americans accepted the ambiguities and contradictions of the Lockean tradition . . . with even less difficulty than
Europeans. The primacy of sensation and the centrality of the
moral sense could flourish at once, as long as each of these
theories . . . did not push too far."[188] In this fashion, by compromise of antithetical principles, Americans have moderated
the tensions of force and freedom that lie at the heart of Lockean
doctrine. But what happens when the ability to compromise gives
out?

Rousseau and Modern Political Culture

Traditionally Rousseau has been thought of as a leading intellectual progenitor of the French Revolution. His name was popu-
larly associated with the symbolic victory of liberty and equality in
the celebration of the fall of the Bastille. A bust of Rousseau was
placed in the National Assembly in 1790 with copies of *Emile* and
the *Social Contract* arranged at its base. In 1791 the Assembly
accepted the presentation of Rousseau's complete works, and
busts of the philosopher were erected in meeting rooms of popular revolutionary societies. We know also that in 1791 a section of
Paris was named *Contrat Social* and a street named after Rousseau
as well. Festivals were held in his honor, and hymns and poems
dedicated to him in revolutionary and literary journals. Pilgrim-
ages to his original grave at Ermenonville were frequent. And as
an ultimate honor, the State decreed the translation of his remains to the Pantheon in 1794.[189]

188. Henry May in Kammen, *People of Paradox*, 218.

189. Joan McDonald, *Rousseau and the French Revolution, 1762–1791* (London:
Athlone Press, 1965), 156–58. McDonald argues that the revolutionary cult of
Rousseau built upon a preexisting literary cult that had developed in the decade
before the Revolution and was based largely on Rousseau's moralist and educational writings (161). Fundamental to this cult was the idea of radical moral
renewal, and it was this ideal that became a leading theme of Rousseau's revolutionary cult. McDonald denies, however, that the revolutionary cult could have
been based on the ideas of Rousseau's *Social Contract*, which was not widely
distributed in France between its first publication in 1762 and 1790. From this and
a variety of statistical evidence she concluded that the political ideas of the *Social
Contract* not only had little *direct* effect upon the Revolution but that they had no
effect at all, and that only a myth, not corresponding to the reality of Rousseau's

It is interesting to note that the enthusiasm of Jacobins such as Robespierre and St. Just for the moral regeneration of society by public authority during the Terror corresponds remarkably with Rousseau's description of the role of the legislator of the *Social Contract*, book 2, chapter 7, the political generator of the moral man. The political moralizing of the Jacobins also fits with Rousseau's statement that there are times, though they may be exceptional, when the moral fiber of societies can be restored through the blood and violence of revolutionary action. There are times when the "state, inflamed by civil wars, springs forth so to speak from its ashes, and regains the vigour of youth."[190] According to J. L. Talmon, the Rousseauistic paradox of employing force to create freedom extends in its influence far beyond the Terror of the French Revolution into the present, where it has begotten a political offspring peculiar to our time—the phenomenon of totalitarian democracy, the democracy of fanatic nationalism. Talmon writes:

> Rousseau's sovereign is the externalized general will, and stands for essentially the same as the natural harmonious order. In marrying this concept with the principle of popular sovereignty, and popular self-expression, Rousseau gave rise to totalitarian democracy. The mere introduction of this latter element, coupled with the fire of Rousseau's style, lifted the eighteenth-century postulate from the plane of intellectual speculation into that of a great collective experience. It marked the birth of the modern secular religion, not merely of a system of ideas, but as a passionate faith. Rousseau's synthesis is in itself the formulation of the paradox of freedom in totalitarian democracy in terms which reveal the dilemma in the most striking form, namely, those of will. There is such a thing as an

---

thought, had an effect (164). This extreme argument is called in question by an earlier statement that the general political ideas associated with the cult of Rousseau: liberty, equality, and the sovereignty of the people, were shared by all those who supported the Revolution and "cannot be regarded as peculiar to his political thought" (160). It is further modified by McDonald's references to a contributor to the *Revolutions de Paris* during 1789 and 1790, a person who insisted that the democratization of France required a thoroughgoing and general reform of morals and who, she says, was one of the few pamphleteers who understood Rousseau's political thought correctly (81–83).

190. *On the Social Contract*, 47.

objective general will, whether willed or not willed by anybody. To become a reality it must willed by the people. If the people do not will it, it must be made to will it, for the general will is latent in the people's will.[191]

Talmon has given here a succinct characterization of the attitude central to every modern totalitarian regime, from Hitler's Germany and Stalin's Soviet Union to the Ayatollah Khomeini's Iran. But I disagree with his formulation of it in one respect. I have tried to show that Rousseau did not regard the general will as "essentially the same as the natural harmonious order" but rather as something that had to be artificially created as a purposive and rational will by a person of great creative imagination, the Legislator figure, who draws around himself a mystical cloak of divine reason, a reason in which a Cartesian such as Rousseau did not believe. The general will, in its full development as an operative political will, is not natural but an ingenious human artifact. And we know that some who have played the Legislator role in our time saw it precisely in such terms. Adolph Hitler, for example, employed in all his public speeches throughout the life of the Third Reich a fanatic ideology of German nationalism. But to Hermann Rauschning he confided that nationalism and the idea of the superiority of the Aryan race were simply myths that he used as instruments of power.[192] As Rousseau wrote, "[The general will] must be made to see things as they are, sometimes as they ought to appear."[193]

In some cases the Legislator figure of a totalitarian regime is apparently a true believer in the ideals by which he artistically shapes his people. This is the case with conservative revolutions like that led by the Ayatollah Khomeini in Iran. His charismatic

191. Talmon, *Origins of Totalitarian Democracy*, 43. For a more sympathetic view of Rousseau's political philosophy as an archetype of liberal democratic thought, but one that also harbors within it the dangers of totalitarian nationalism on which Talmon focuses, see Alfred Cobban, *Rousseau and the Modern State* (London: George Allen and Unwin, 1934), especially chap. 8. For a criticism of Talmon's view see John Chapman, *Rousseau—Totalitarian or Liberal?* (New York: AMS Press, 1968), 78–80. Chapman sees Rousseau as a father of liberalism.

192. Hermann Rauschning, *The Voice of Destruction* (New York: G. P. Putnam's Sons, 1940), 232, 252.

193. *On the Social Contract*, 41.

gift is apparently as much a reality for him as it is for his people.[194] But his methodology remains genuinely Rousseauistic. This is strikingly revealed, for example, in the responses of Khomeini to questions about the Iranian revolution and his role in it that were posed to him by the Italian journalist Oriana Fallaci during an interview on September 12, 1979. Replying to Fallaci's comment that many Iranians say that there is no freedom in Iran and that the country is entirely in his hands, Khomeini responded: "Iran is not in my hands. Iran is in the hands of the people, because it was the people who handed the country over to the person who is their servant, and who wants only what is good for them."[195] And then in reply to a question whether Khomeini had not cultivated an authoritarian, fascist spirit of fanaticism the Imam said: "No, it is neither fascism nor fanaticism. . . . They yell like this because they love me, and they love me because they feel that I care for them, that I act for their good. That is, to apply the Commandments of Islam. Islam is justice. Dictatorship is the greatest sin in the religion of Islam."[196]

Khomeini also affirmed that his revolution was a distinctly democratic one: "The people fought for Islam. And Islam means everything, also those things that, in your world, are called freedom, democracy. Yes, Islam contains everything. Islam includes everything. Islam is everything." A little later in the interview, as an example of democracy, he told an anecdote about the behavior in a law class of Ali, the founder of the Shi'ite Moslem sect, that illustrated the ideal of equal treatment before the law. When Fallaci objected that democracy means much more than that and that the direction of Iranian political development was not clear, Khomeini replied that if dissident Iranians and foreigners did not understand the direction of his revolution, it was "too bad" for them and "none of [their] business." "You have nothing to do with our choices. If some Iranians don't understand it, too bad for them. It means that they have not understood Islam."[197] What

194. For Rousseau's influence on conservatives in his own time see McDonald, *Rousseau and the French Revolution*, 66–70, 123–25.

195. *New York Times Magazine*, October 7, 1979, 29.

196. Ibid.

197. Ibid., 30.

could be a better example of the Rousseauistic Legislator at work
forming and giving direction to the general will of his people—a
time when that general will does not get expressed in democratic
voting but is rather in process of "enlightenment"?[198]

I have presented examples of the historical work of the disciplinary Rousseau, making citizens of a people by supplying
"justice for instinct" and "the voice of duty" for impulse and
appetite.[199] In the act of political founding, when a legislator
gives "institutions to a nation," his discipline must take the form
of "changing human nature; of transforming every individual . . .
into a part of a greater whole," a condition of the citizen's "moral
freedom." In doing this "the Legislator puts into the mouths of
the immortals that sublime reason which soars beyond the reach
of common men, in order that he may win over by divine authority those whom human prudence could not move."[200] But there
are also historical examples of other more actively democratic
aspects of Rousseau's prophetic thought in action, which have
recently been dubbed with the name "participatory democracy."

Apparently, however, the participatory democracy of the *Social
Contract* had little appeal to Americans during the time of the
founders of the republic. Paul Spurlin has shown that while there
were sufficient library copies of the *Social Contract* in English for
the book to be fairly well known by the literate public during the
last quarter of the eighteenth century, and that many private
persons owned Rousseau's complete works, Rousseau's political
ideas were not well received by large numbers of people.[201]
Noah Webster, though much influenced by Rousseau in the
composition of the first edition of *Sketches of American Policy*
(1785), later repudiated him and penned in a margin of his
own book the sentence: "Many of these notions, taken from
Rousseau's *Social Contract*, are found to be chimerical."[202] Pronounced conservatives such as John Adams of course denounced

198. *On the Social Contract*, 41.
199. Ibid., 22–23.
200. Ibid., 23, 43, 45.
201. See Paul M. Spurlin, *Rousseau in America, 1760–1809* (University, Ala.:
Univ. of Alabama Press, 1969), especially chaps. 5, 6, 10.
202. Ibid., 61.

Rousseau roundly.[203] In 1764 the fiery James Otis did indeed refer positively to the philosopher as "the celebrated Rousseau." But no mention of his name or of the *Social Contract* is found in Farrand's record of the Constitutional Convention or in *The Federalist*.[204]

What is surprising is that we have no judgment on Rousseau by Thomas Jefferson, a leading exponent of the egalitarian and populist strand of American political culture in the period of our republican founding. There is no evidence that the thought of Rousseau had any influence on the composition of the Declaration of Independence, though we know that there was a copy of the *Social Contract* in Jefferson's second library. (The first was burned in 1770.) From Jefferson himself we have a stony silence about Rousseau. Spurlin found no reference to the *Social Contract* in any of Jefferson's writings, though he found it impossible to believe that the learned Jefferson had not read the book. He thinks that Jefferson concluded that the Frenchman's political thought simply had no value for him.[205] Overall, Spurlin concludes that "the *Social Contract* made no tangible contribution to eighteenth-century American political theory."[206] However, the book did become better known as the century closed and "evoked more comment in the decade of the French Revolution than in any other."[207] John Quincy Adams invoked Rousseau's name as authority in 1795.

Whatever possible influence, either direct or indirect, that the *Social Contract* may have had thereafter on American populist thought from 1800 on, striking resemblances to many of its central ideas are found in the ideological symbolism and political practice of the American New Left of the 1960s. In terms of explicit ideological commitment, we know that the New Left (or the counterculture) was a very mixed collection of Marxists, anarcho-syndicalists, and others. But the participatory ideal of Rousseau was shared by all, though very likely recognized by few

203. Ibid., 44.
204. Ibid., 63, 105.
205. Ibid., 65–66.
206. Ibid., 66.
207. Ibid., 104.

as having been given elegant statement by that philosopher. Robert Dahl writes in *After the Revolution?*:

> In his view of primary democracy as the only legitimate kind of state . . . Rousseau presents one of the most beguiling utopias since Plato's republic. That neither is achievable does not seem to distract and may even enhance, their attractiveness.
>
> The most recent visitation of the vision was during the 1960s when it revealed itself to some elements of the New Left who, not realizing how much they were merely restating an ancient tradition, insisted that people who are affected by decisions have the right to participate directly in making those decisions. Their demand for "participatory democracy" was simply a renewed assertion of Rousseau's insistence that the only legitimate source of authority is primary democracy.[208]

Like the men of the eighteenth century for whom Rousseau constructed his democratic society of the general will (in which he thought most could find happiness if not true liberty), the members of the New Left felt oppressed by what they saw as an unequal and atomistic society. In place of the arts and sciences they blamed technocracy (a problematic offspring of the blessings of scientific development) for their woes. They hungered for equality and community and turned their backs on rationality, which they identified with technocratic impersonality. Thus we find Louis Kampf writing:

> The pursuit of knowledge, we have assumed, is a good in itself and an agent of progress: it has led to the hydrogen bomb; the concept of rationality is at the foundation not only of scholarship, but of activities relating to work and political and social institutions: it has been used to justify the bureaucratic rationalization typical of industrial states. Intellectuals—the producers of such knowledge and instruments of rationalization—are under serious attack. They have manufactured the ideologies of the Cold War while hiding under the skirts of Western Civilization.[209]

The New Left attacked the atomism of the modern city and dreamed of decentralizing it into warm loving neighborhoods.

208. New Haven: Yale Univ. Press, 1970, 80–81.
209. Louis Kampf, "Notes Toward a Radical Culture," in Priscilla Long, ed., *The New Left: A Collection of Essays* (Boston: Porter Sergeant, 1969), 421–22.

Like Rousseau, they found a human spirit only in small face-to-face groups. Thus Rick Margolies writes:

> The city is built for commerce and travel. The roads are laid out for auto and truck traffic, not for people. The neighborhoods are segregated as either business or residential by bureaucratic zoning boards that are little influenced by the people who live in the area. The idea of reconstructing the city into humanly-scaled communal neighborhoods . . . is a threat to the propertied class which controls the zoning and redevelopment boards. People become nuisances.[210]

Rock and roll concerts and "Human Be-ins" were other New Left efforts to find community and a general will. In their political decision-making they enshrined the participatory ideal. The founders of Students for a Democratic Society (SDS) gave it prominent and succinct expression in their Port Huron Statement:

> As a *social system* we seek the establishment of a democracy of individual participation, governed by two central aims: that the individual share in those social decisions determining the quality and direction of his life; that society be organized to encourage independence in men and provide media for their common participation.
>
> In a participatory democracy, the political life would be based in several root principles:
>
> that decision-making of basic social consequence be carried on by public groupings;
>
> that politics be seen positively, as the art of collectively creating an acceptable pattern of social relations;
>
> that politics has the function of bringing people out of isolation and into community, thus being a necessary, though not sufficient, means of finding meaning in personal life.[211]

But as Robert Dahl pointed out, the New Left dream of a society of the general will proved an unrealizable utopia. They had an instinct for equal citizenship, but they never worked out an effective system of leadership. They made decisions after the

---

210. Rick Margolies, "On Community Building," in Long, ed., *The New Left*, 357.
211. "SDS: Port Huron Statement," in Massimo Teodoro, ed., *The New Left: A Documentary History* (Indianapolis & New York: Bobbs-Merrill, 1969), 167.

democratic fashion of *Social Contract*, book 3. But unlike the members of Rousseau's participatory polity, they were not first formed, molded, and "enlightened" by a charismatic totalitarian such as the founder figure with whom Rousseau presents us. They neither sought nor found a Legislator. Nor were they prepared to be "forced to be free." Most of them prized their individuality too much for that. But they had no formula or capacity for establishing responsible leadership.

It is interesting that the New Left movement of the 1960s was in part brought to birth intellectually by solitary walkers like Rousseau—the members of the Beat Generation of the 1950s, who were also called hippies. These men and women—for example, Jack Kerouac and Allen Ginsburg—found freedom and inspiration by retiring within their own consciousness, often with the help of drugs.[212] Many simple dropouts from our society, another kind of solitary walker, found their way into the movement as it got underway in the early sixties. And when it collapsed in the early seventies, they simply dropped out of society again. Others who came from the mainstream of society were not able to reintegrate themselves when the participatory dream ended and drifted about as part-time workers who earned enough to keep body and soul together and then went off to loaf. Some former prominent New Lefters have come to terms with the old society. Jerry Rubin, after acknowledging the death of the movement, reported from his San Francisco home in February 1973 that it was "time to begin life anew." "I am totally into self-development now, almost completely working on my body, on my mind. I do yoga, go to massage school, run every day, am into bio-energetics." He had become a very private person. "I want to lead a quiet life," he said.[213] Thus he moved from the freedom of an unworkable participatory vision to the freedom of the "solitary walker."

212. Thomas Clark, "Interview with Allen Ginsberg: The Art of Poetry," in Leo Hamalian and F. R. Karl, eds., *The Radical Vision: Essays for the Seventies* (New York: Crowell, 1970), 158.

213. *Rochester Democrat and Chronicle*, February 25, 1973, 29A.

4

The Failure of Dialectical Synthesis: Kant, Hegel, Marx, and Mill

Kant's Dualism of the Noumenal and Phenomenal Worlds: Their Nonsynthesis

It took more than a hundred years from the composition of Hobbes's *Leviathan* for a first-class philosophical mind to recognize the human emptiness caused by the various efforts to reduce Descartes's unhappy dualism to body in the understanding of political and social order. Why should the price of philosophical consistency and scientific accuracy have to be the freedom of the human soul? Immanuel Kant (1724–1804) was the first to confront this terrible dilemma and to attempt a solution that, in reestablishing moral freedom, would leave intact all the utilitarian gains of mathematized science.

Kant's starting point is orthodox Cartesianism—an ontology of consciousness in which the ability of the "I" to reflect on itself depends on the assumption of an external world of sense. In his *Critique of Pure Reason*, Kant wrote that "the consciousness of my existence is at the same time an immediate consciousness of other things outside me."[1] This brief sentence expresses clearly the epistemological and ontological relationship between spirit and body that Descartes had spelled out deviously and at length in the *Meditations*. (Kant thought he was correcting Descartes.) As in

1. Immanuel Kant, *The Critique of Pure Reason*, N. K. Smith, trans. and ed. (New York: St. Martin's Press, 1965), 244.

133

the secret argument of Descartes, the certainty of self and other is also quite independent of the concept of God. Kant rejected out of hand Descartes's superficial proof and stated explicitly in the first *Critique* that no ontological proof of the existence of God is possible.[2]

Now all this is strongly reminiscent of the similarities in the starting points of Hobbes, Locke, and Rousseau, especially the latter. Why, then, did Kant not tend, in his political theory, toward material reductionism like these three? The answer seems to lie in his way of conceiving the ontological status of matter or body. Descartes had identified body as an independent reality and had given sensation the initiative in creating, through imagination, our ideas. (Though, paradoxically, he had also made those ideas depend on the judgmental acts of intellect.) Hobbes, Locke, and Rousseau had followed him in asserting the autonomy and causal power of sensation. But Kant, working through the implications of Cartesian 'judgment,' came to the conclusion that our sensations of the outer world are mere appearances, which even as appearances cannot be known by us apart from certain categories furnished a priori by mind—such transcendental forms of intuition as 'space' and 'time' and the concept of 'causality'. These are the preconditions of all knowledge of the empirical world, though themselves quite independent of empirical experience. He writes: "There can be no question that I am conscious of my representations; these representations and I myself, who have the representations, exist. External objects (bodies), however, are mere appearances, and are therefore nothing but a species of my representations, the objects of which are something only through representations."[3]

These appearances are given meaningful form by the pure reason, which provides "the totality of the synthesis of the conditions, for a given conditioned."[4] Kant's thought is clearly and succinctly summarized in the following:

Experience . . . rests on the synthetic unity of appearances, that is, on a synthesis according to concepts of an object of appearances in

2. Ibid., 506–07.
3. Ibid., 346.
4. Ibid., 361–62.

general. Apart from such synthesis it would not be knowledge, but a rhapsody of perceptions that would not fit into any context according to rules of a completely interconnected (possible) consciousness, and so would not conform to the transcendental and necessary unity of apperception. Experience depends, therefore, upon *a priori* principles of its form, that is, upon universal rules of unity in the synthesis of appearances. Their objective reality, as necessary conditions of experience, and indeed of its very possibility, can always be shown in experience.[5]

But even in stressing the primacy of mind in knowing, Kant wants to stress the independent existence of body. For he makes it clear that apart from their significance in relation to the empirical world, "synthetic *a priori* principles are completely impossible. For they have then no third something, that is, no object, in which the synthetic unity can exhibit the objective reality of its concepts."[6]

In this fashion Kant radically subordinates body to mind, while saving the autonomy of the empirical world. This averts the possibility of reducing the basic concepts whereby we understand the world to a psychological artifact produced in us by the so-called educational work of some Legislator. It prevents the reduction of mind to body. It also gives a universal or public character to mind and eliminates the possibility of solipsism and cultural reductionism. The universality of Kantian transcendentals has also, ultimately, a democratic implication.

On this epistemological foundation Kant built a public order of moral freedom and, at the same time, a public order of right. For if moral choice was to be made compatible with mechanical order, it would first have to be shown to be an order. But how could Kant prevent freedom from being swallowed up by moral rules? He would have to draw the very idea of moral order out of the conception of human freedom. For to erect it independently, by reference to the purposes of a perfect being or any other way, would be reaction to an outworn idea of objective right. The new ontology and ethics had to be constructed entirely within the parameters of human consciousness. Kant in effect had elimi-

5. Ibid., 193.
6. Ibid., 194.

nated ontology in any traditional sense from the purview of his philosophy.

Kant's moral agent, like Hobbes's vainglorious dreamer and Rousseau's *promeneur solitaire*, is free in his moral choice of all constraints from the order of nature. Neither the passions and appetites of his own body or of another body impinging on his consciousness constrict or restrain his choices. He makes up his mind to act in entire freedom of the empirical world and its causal power, the world of 'phenomena', things as they appear to us to be. The maxims of his will are entirely his own creation, subject to one limitation only, which has no necessary connection with the world of sense—that they be consistent with the idea of law.

On what grounds could Kant assert such a restriction on choice? There were several. For one thing, the very idea of right action implies moral law defined as a public and universal order. More importantly, we must acknowledge that our own freedom implies that other persons whose existence we experience in the world are also free. I am required to respect that freedom if I expect to be treated as a free man by others. Therefore, the maxims of my will must be universalizable in order to be right. I must imagine them made operative as universal laws of nature. If their logical result, when so extended, would be the general frustration of their intended values, they cannot be right. But beyond this single procedural limitation of universalizability, I am free to create my own principles and rules of moral action. Kant called his discovery the 'noumenal' world.

The central concept of Kant's anthropology and ethics is personality. By virtue of his freedom from determination by the mechanical laws of nature—his ability to give law to himself—each man is an autonomous person and an end in himself. His value is absolute. Kant expresses the idea in these terms:

> Persons are . . . *objective ends*—that is, things whose existence is in itself an end . . . , for unless this is so, nothing at all of *absolute* value would be found anywhere.

> The law-making which determines all value must for this reason have a dignity—that is, an unconditioned and incomparable worth—for the appreciation of which, as necessarily given by a rational being, the word '*reverence*' is the only becoming expression. *Auton-*

omy is therefore the ground of the dignity of human nature and of every rational nature.[7]

The bourgeois role of Hobbesian and Lockean man and the citizen role of Rousseau's man fall away as the person emerges for the first time in modern philosophy, endowed with *Wille*, the ability to legislate for himself according to the pure idea of law embodied in the Categorical Imperative. As a person, one is irreducible to an effect of some empirical cause. For the person is a member of the noumenal world; the person transcends the empirical world, whose effects are produced by external and impersonal laws of motion. The person cannot be swallowed up by a concept of social and political need that reduces him or her to a mere means. Only policies defined in terms of the autonomous selfhood of persons are legitimate. Kant's ethics thus reinforces his ontological commitment to mind as free will and reason and raises thereby another barrier to material reductionism.

Kant's politics is devoted to the institutionalization of freedom and right. It had to be shown not only that the empirical individual *can* act rightly in respecting the freedom of others but also that one would in *fact* act rightly. These hard problems Kant treated in three brief works—*Idea for a Universal History, Conjectural Beginning of Human History*, and *Perpetual Peace*.[8]

A basic assumption of Kant's analysis is that behavior according to law implies purpose. In the *Idea for a Universal History* he writes:

> *All natural capacities of a creature are destined to evolve completely to their natural end.* Observation . . . of all animals confirms this for them. An organ that is of no use, an arrangement that does not achieve its

7. Immanuel Kant, *Groundwork of the Metaphysics of Morals*, H. J. Paton, trans. (New York: Harper and Row, 1964), 96, 103. For a detailed study of Kant's doctrine of personality see Hardy E. Jones, *Kant's Principles of Personality* (Madison: Univ. of Wisconsin Press, 1971), especially chapter 7. A good collection of Kant's political writings with a useful introduction is Hans Reiss, ed., *Kant's Political Writings*, H. B. Nisbet, trans. (Cambridge: Cambridge Univ. Press, 1970). See also Frederick P. van de Pitte, *Kant as Philosophical Anthropologist* (The Hague: Martinus Nijhoff, 1971) and Yiramiahu Yovel, *Kant and the Philosophy of History* (Princeton, N.J.: Princeton Univ. Press, 1980).

8. See L. W. Beck, ed. and trans., *Kant on History*, (Indianapolis: Bobbs-Merrill, 1963).

purpose, are contradictions in the teleological theory of nature. If we give up this fundamental principle, we no longer have a lawful but an aimless course of nature, and blind choice takes the place of the guiding thread of reason.[9]

This appears to hark back to the Scholastic tradition, and one wonders whether ideas of this sort can be combined with the Cartesian assumptions that form the basis of Kant's metaphysics. Within this framework they can be justified only as transcendentals—ideas that originate in the mind and that are necessary for us to make sense out of our experience. 'Causality' is such a concept that is necessary to make sense of the phenomenal world, as is the idea of 'fundamental right' in order to make our moral experience intelligible. Kant treats natural teleology in the same way. Thus, he writes, in finding purposes in nature, "we do not observe or infer this providence." Rather, "we can and must supply it from our own minds in order to conceive of its possibility by analogy to actions of human art." The concept is "transcendent from a theoretical point of view." But "from a practical standpoint, with respect, for example, to the ideal of perpetual peace, the concept is dogmatic."[10] If functions as an article of faith.

Kant finds man's natural purpose not expressed in the individual life but in that of the species, which also distinguishes his teleology from the premodern tradition. In defining human purpose, Kant tells us that the freedom of the will in its appearances (that is, in human actions) is determined by universal laws, just like every other natural event. These are not universal moral laws, which express only the abstract concept of law as principle or standard (the Categorical Imperative, for example), but rather laws of nature. They signify invariant mechanical action, not moral behavior. Yet Kant believes that observing their play over a long period of time reveals a pattern of moral development of the will—"a steady and progressive though slow evolution of its original endowment."[11]

That the movement of the species over time might be more lawful than the movement of an individual will, Kant derived

9. Ibid., 12–13.
10. *Perpetual Peace*, in *Kant on History*, 106–08.
11. *Universal History*, in ibid., 11.

from the idea of statistical regularity in large numbers of natural events. The free will (as spontaneous choice) of individuals affects decisions about marriages and births. Yet statistical tables show predictable behavior in these things "according to laws stable as [those of] the unstable weather."[12] Analogously, while individuals follow their own purposes, the race together might, in its movements, reveal an overall pattern of change, Kant thought.[13] In the realm of moral evolution we have here a concept something like Adam Smith's "unseen hand" of the market. In the latter, each individual pursues only his own well-being and profit. But the action of self-centered individuals en masse produces the well-being of all, the common good.

Now what purpose does human life reveal? Again following the Scholastic tradition, Kant frames his answer in terms of the perfection of natural functions—"the development of all the capacities which can be achieved by mankind."[14] And this requires the creation of "the society with the greatest freedom." Thus the establishment of the "perfectly just civic constitution, is the highest problem Nature assigns to the human race." It will be a society in which "freedom under external law is associated in the highest degree with irresistible power."[15]

Since the specifically human capacity is free moral choice, defined as self-determination under universal rules of procedural right, the fulfillment of human nature requires the development of moral sensitivity. And this means the sensitivity of everyone, in his actions, to the "rights of man"—the treatment of all individuals as ends in themselves. Ironically, however, we do not observe this sensitivity increasing in the present. Just the opposite; history reveals the prevalence of selfishness and violence. Yet like the selfishness of individual behavior in Adam Smith's theory of the unseen hand, this is working toward the final goal of perpetual peace and freedom. The Fourth Thesis of the *Idea for a Universal History* is that "The means employed by Nature to bring about the development of all the capacities of

12. Ibid.
13. Ibid., 11–12.
14. Ibid., 16, 21.
15. Ibid.

men is their antagonism in society, so far as this is, in the end, the cause of a lawful order among men."[16] In the sequel Kant calls this antagonism an "unsocial sociability." It is the opposition of combative egos "propelled by vainglory, lust for power, and avarice" that, in the condition of society, enlarges human powers and talents.[17] Kant has here transmuted Hobbes's "war of all against all" from a problem to be overcome by reason into a vehicle for the expression of reason. But reason is now no longer solely a capacity of self-conscious individuals but a power of nature working unconsciously through the race. The idea of 'history' as rational teleological process has been born.

In *Perpetual Peace* Kant spells out the steps in the historical process that lead to the realization of freedom as the condition of human fulfillment. He describes there the movement of "that great artist, nature, who in her mechanical course" aims at producing "a harmony among men, against their will, and indeed through their discord."[18] Through war and conflict she fills up the globe and makes all parts of the world inhabitable through the ingenuity that selfishness engenders. The drive for security, awakened by conflict and the threat of conquest and exploitation, leads people to band together to form states for self-protection. In modern times it eventuates in the development of the liberal republican order as the best guarantee of the security of all. No individual may will the protection of the rights of all. But out of self-interest all will be driven to enter into a political contract to establish the rule of law and a system of checked and balanced powers. History reveals a dialectic of interest through which selfishness produces its opposite—the public good.

> The problem of organizing a state, however hard it may seem, can be solved even for a race of devils, if only they are intelligent. The problem is: "Given a multitude of rational beings requiring universal laws for their preservation, but each of whom is secretly inclined to exempt himself from them, to establish a constitution in such a way that, although their private intentions conflict, they check each

16. Ibid., 15.
17. Ibid.
18. In *Kant on History*, 106.

other, with the result that their public conduct is the same as if they had no such intentions."[19]

The natural attachment of every people to its own language and mores together with their mutual rivalries prevents the emergence of a monolithic world society that would stifle freedom and individuality. But world law comes to be established through the principle of free association embodied in the federal idea. "With advancing civilization reason grows pragmatically in its capacity to realize ideas of law."[20] In this fashion, through institutional constraints, every person is guaranteed that he or she will be treated by others as an end, not only as a means. And the Categorical Imperative becomes the general rule of public behavior. Equality of political right and freedom of every individual from unjust coercion are established.

All this analysis, however, is within the terms of the phenomenal world, the world of nature. We have not observed the working of human freedom but rather a determinate dialectical process whereby people come to treat one another as the free have a right to be treated. But is there true moral development that takes place pari passu with the institutional evolution of political and social freedom? The working out of the perfect constitution is compatible with the continuance of selfishness as enlightened self-interest. And within Kant's system we have no way of measuring moral change. For the noumenal world—the world of internal freedom and moral right—is not open to public scrutiny. Kant can only make an act of faith that in a regime of freedom intentional morality (a true "kingdom of ends") will flourish. He writes that "providence is justified in the history of the world, for the moral principle in man is never extinguished." If we assume "that humanity never will or can be improved, the only thing which a theodicy seems unable to justify is creation itself, the fact that a race of such corrupt beings ever was on earth."[21] But there is no way in which we can achieve a point of view from which it is possible to verify a judgment we make on the question.

19. Ibid., 112.
20. Ibid., 128.
21. Ibid.

Kant has endeavored to overcome Cartesian dualism in such a way as to avoid materialist reduction by weaving noumenal freedom and right together with phenomenal motion in a dialectic of history. In this way the free creativity of the moral self is retained for every individual and for mankind as a whole and enshrined as a principle of growth in the determinate motions of the material world. But has he succeeded? An acid test of success might be a finding that freedom and right have, in a specific instance of human behavior, been a causal force.

Kant has managed to avoid Rousseau's reductionist pitfall by generalizing good will at the outset. No Legislator is required to renovate nature to make it good by substituting the general for the particular will. All men in their natural condition have the general will by knowing the Categorical Imperative. And they are also capable of living by it. But since they are free, *will* they in fact do so? The evidence at present is that they will not—at least now *do* not in large numbers. Thus nature in her mechanical course is taking the steps described to compel us, by ingenious structures working through self-interest, to treat one another as we ought. As Hans Saner paraphrases Kant's thought, "Antagonism in general expands the natural creative process and advances the human one. The idea of political struggle is thus subject to the same determination by laws as the idea of cosmological struggle." "Unity comes about by lawful struggle."[22] For our freedom to act rightly gives us rights. But when nature's work is done, will compulsion still be needed? Will noumenal will take over?

Since the noumenal self, which is capable of moral action, transcends the phenomenal self—is radically other than the phenomenal self—how can I or anyone else know when the choices I make are actually free? For in the world of appearances, every action must have a measurable cause to be explained. And freedom—the noumenal self—cannot be measured. Since knowing and being are both radically dual, how can I ever know that my action is unaffected by desire? There is no common measure of freedom and necessity. Will not the choices of phenomenal man always be reducible to phenomenal causes? And does the noumenal man as such not *always* act well—in idea?

22. Saner, *Kant's Political Thought*, 15, 311.

Kant himself seems to give up on the question when he writes, "How pure reason can be practical—All human reason is totally incapable of explaining this, and all the effort and labor to seek such an explanation is wasted."[23] Edward Ballard has pointed up in more detail the problem that Kant's reworking of Descartes's dualism has engendered.

Man as phenomenal can be known to be causally determined; nevertheless as rational (noumenal) man may be believed to act freely and to initiate sequences of events for which he is responsible (*Pure Reason*, A66, B679). But it also follows that we cannot *know* ourselves to be both moral and empirical. We cannot in principle know that our will is completely undetermined by empirical inclinations and desires. Moreover, we cannot discover a schematic structure of the will which shows that moral law (the law of rational being) necessarily applies to any sort of value objects, for example, to our experienced motives. Strictly speaking, therefore, we cannot know that our motives are moral even if they are.[24]

Kant seems to have saved man's interior moral freedom by detaching it from the world of action altogether. He has solved the problem of the tension between mechanical force and human freedom only by removing noumenal man from the world. For Kant the phenomenal world is essentially a field of force in which moral ends may be achieved but not by knowably moral acts. We shall never be able to *observe* freedom working in it, because freedom and necessity are incompatible. We can put noumenal freedom into this world only by an act of faith. In the cognitive order, noumenal freedom and morality are mysteries.[25]

Hegel: Dialectical Synthesis of Subject and Object— the Necessary Freedom of Absolute Spirit

Though Kant had failed, his successors did not abandon the dialectical approach to resolving the problem of the duality of

23. *Groundwork of the Metaphysics of Morals*, 129.

24. Edward G. Ballard, *Philosophy at the Crossroads* (Baton Rouge: Louisiana State Univ. Press, 1971), 158.

25. For a parallel statement see Yovel, *Kant and the Philosophy of History*, 297–300.

mind and body. On the contrary, they embraced it with fervor and have richly developed the crude outline sketched out by Kant. In particular, they have made bold efforts to overcome the radical disjunction between noumenal and phenomenal existence that frustrated Kant's efforts at synthesis. For Hegel and Marx, the dialectic was a sesame to the mystery of freedom and the key to understanding and predicting the course of human history. To their numerous epigones, the concept is still pregnant with the future.

Georg Friedrich Hegel (1770–1831) was both a good Cartesian and a good Kantian, to a point. Like Descartes, he believed that meaningful philosophizing had to take place within the boundaries of consciousness, within sense experience. And with Kant he agreed that consciousness itself could have meaning only through an 'Absolute Idea'. His use of the raw materials of sense was to be rather different from Descartes's in explaining and developing the structure of knowledge, however. And in his peculiar way of marrying the Idea to sense experience, he was to move far from the personalism that is characteristic of the work of Kant.

Though Descartes used the expression "the mind" as an abstract universal, his philosophical analysis never took him beyond the reality of particular minds. And, as we saw in chapter 2, this results in puzzles that can be resolved within Cartesian terms of reference only by a materialist reduction or by asserting the pure privacy of solipsistic free will. Kant saw the difficulty and sought to deal with it through his doctrine of transcendental forms and concepts—some of them logical and ontological, others ethical and teleological. But he never went beyond describing these concepts as properties of individual minds. As we have seen, in the noumenal world of freedom, it is the thinking and willing individual person, not mind and will in general, that has absolute value. But this made it impossible for him to give an account of the whole that unites our minds or to bridge existentially the noumenal and phenomenal worlds. Subject and object remained disjoined for him, discrete realities. But for Hegel such an analysis was inadequate precisely because it failed to capture and express the nature of the whole. It therefore failed to constitute true knowledge.

Another problem that Descartes and Kant had skirted in their ontologies was the problem of change, in the most general sense. It seemed odd to Hegel to affirm that an obviously transient being 'is', and it also appeared to him that every being in our ken is fundamentally ephemeral. The world of our experience is one of constant change, of 'becoming' rather than of 'being'. And our philosophy to be adequate must reflect this basic reality of our consciousness. Hegel's solution to the problem of the whole (the unity of body and spirit and of particulars and universals) and to the problem of change was to discover Universal Mind and Will at work in the particulars of sense as principles of development, as the Absolute in the process of coming to be.

The starting point of Hegel's dialectic is the Cartesian recognition of the absolute interdependence of mind and body or of the self and that which is other than the self. Hegel's unique conclusion from this insight was the proposition that somehow the self must come to its fulfillment, its complete consciousness, through interaction with the other. The process involves first alienation in otherness but finally a restoration to selfhood in which the original dualism is transcended. The puzzling and stressing opposition and antagonism is done away with in a new integration of self and other, a harmonious unity of opposites. Charles Taylor has succinctly capsulized the thought in writing that for Hegel "a subject is necessarily a being who incorporates his other (his embodiment) and 'returns to himself' through this other, that is, comes to self-consciousness in his other."[26]

In the epistemological analysis of *The Phenomenology of Mind* Hegel first distinguishes mind from body in the order of immediate apprehension. It is in sensually apprehending the world that we become aware of the difference between self and other. "In sense experience pure being breaks up into . . . two 'thises,' . . . one this as I, and one as object."[27] A little reflection then leads us to an awareness that our apprehension of particular "thises" is not direct but rather is mediated by universal concepts. But the universal also becomes lively for us only as *it* is mediated by particu-

---

26. Taylor, *Hegel*, 150.

27. G.W.F. Hegel, *The Phenomenology of Mind*, J. B. Baillie, trans. (New York: Harper and Row, 1967), 150. Parenthetical page references are to this edition.

lars, which negate and cancel one another in a time series, the order of change.

> I, *this* I, see the tree, and assert the tree to be the Here; *another* I, however, sees the house and maintains the Here is not a tree but a house. Both truths have the same authenticity—the immediacy of seeing and the certainty and assurance both have as to their specific way of knowing; but the one certainty disappears in the other. (154)

Thus mind and body, universal and particular, are shown to be necessary to one another in the order of cognition and to function to provide knowledge by dialectical interaction. But at this level "the I *qua* universal" eludes final definition and understanding, as do all universal concepts. We must mount higher on the dialectical ladder.

Hegel follows this introduction with a further analysis of perception in which he stresses the need to comprehend one aspect of reality by denying or excluding all else. Perception is necessarily selective and therefore incomplete. We must seek a way to unite our partial perceptions in a higher unity—that of 'understanding'. Here reason reduces particulars to a unity, the unity of a field of forces, held together as a 'kingdom of laws', the laws of physical motion. Hegel does not follow Kant, however, in radically distinguishing the abstract noumenal world from the phenomenal. Whether observing particulars or understanding the underlying forces that move them, we are still dealing with phenomenality. The real opposition is between phenomenality and the conscious self. "Consciousness does not as yet find itself in it [the unified abstract world of law]. It is empty, for it is merely the nothingness of appearance, and positively the naked universal" (191). "The play of forces is what understanding has directly to do with; but the real truth for it is the inner world bare and simple. The movement of force is consequently the truth only by being in like manner something simple" (193–94). The 'kingdom of laws' is, thus, meaningless.

The problem of meaning is not, as for Kant, that reason is too limited to see the real nature of things in themselves behind the veils of their phenomenality. It is a result "simply of the nature of the case, because in the void there is nothing known, . . . because its very characteristic lies in being *beyond* consciousness" (192). What Hegel seems to be saying here is that beyond the world of phenomena understood as a 'kingdom of laws', there *are* no 'things in themselves'. There is simply consciousness. Value and meaning are not inherent properties either of the sensible or the intelligible world but of consciousness. "It is manifest that behind the so-called curtain, which is to hide the inner world, there is nothing to be seen unless we ourselves go behind there, as much in order that we may thereby see, as that there may be something behind there which can be seen" (212–13). Hegel is a better Cartesian than Kantian. His conclusion also points to the need for a further analysis if our effort to know is to succeed. We must study self-consciousness.

In the exploration of self-consciousness, Hegel moves from contemplation to action. Knowing enters the order of power. I am conscious of myself as I become aware that my perceptions represent objects different from me. And I seek unity by absorbing them into myself. My action "consumes the inorganic nature, and I express myself thereby as a living being" (223). I become involved in the ebb and flow of life. In this way, "self-consciousness is . . . assured of itself through sublating the other, which is presented to self-consciousness as an independent life, self-consciousness is *Desire*" (225).

The next step toward knowing is taken when self-consciousness has before it another self-consciousness. It is now that a recognition occurs of what self-consciousness is—the reality of mind. "Only so and only then *is* it self-consciousness in actual fact; for there first of all it comes to have the unity of itself in its otherness. Ego which is the object of its notion, is in point of fact not '*object.*' . . . With this we . . . have before us the notion of *Mind* or *Spirit*" (227).

At this point, Hobbes's "war of all against all" begins. For the self "must cancel this its other . . . in order . . . to become certain of itself as true being." In doing this,

> it . . . proceeds to sublate its own self, for this other is itself. . . . Through sublation, it gets back itself, because it becomes one with itself again through cancelling of *its* otherness; but secondly, it

> likewise gives otherness back again to the other self-consciousness,
> for it was aware of being in the other, it cancels thus its own being in
> the other and then lets the other again go free. (229–30)

Thus we move ultimately to the unity of Kant's "kingdom of
ends," the republic of self-conscious freedom. But this is only
the abstract process, capsulized. The kingdom of freedom does
not arrive so easily. As for Kant, it comes into being for Hegel only
through struggle.

> The relation of both self-consciousnesses is in this way so consti-
> tuted that they prove themselves and each other through a life-and-
> death struggle. They must enter into this struggle, for they must
> bring their certainty of themselves, the certainty of being for them-
> selves, to the level of objective truth. . . . It is solely by risking life
> that freedom is obtained. (232–33)

The struggle for freedom—the full realization of what it means
to be a conscious self—proceeds through a number of historical
phases. In *The Phenomenology of Mind* Hegel catalogs its purely
intellectual (or ideological) phases.[28] Ancient Stoicism established
that "consciousness is essentially that which thinks, is a thinking
reality" (244). Later, this notion was fulfilled in Scepticism, "the
actual experience of what freedom of thought is" (246). "Thought
becomes thinking which wholly annihilates the being of the world
with its manifold determinateness, and the negativity of free
self-consciousness becomes aware of attaining, in these manifold
forms which life assumes, real negativity" (246). Scepticism in
turn develops into "the unhappy consciousness" of the otherworldly Christian. This consciousness stands "midway, at the
point where abstract thought comes in contact with the particularity of consciousness *qua* particularity. . . . It is the union of
individuality and individuality" (257). It manifests itself especially
in a yearning for the unity of the beyond and yields its freedom of
decision to the beyond in the person of the mediating agent, the
priest. The mediator announces the right and the just on behalf

---

28. A detailed political application of his developmental epistemology is
found in Hegel's *Philosophy of History*, J. Sibree, trans. (New York: Dover Publications, 1956), and in his *Philosophy of Right*, T. M. Knox, trans. (London: Oxford
Univ. Press, 1952).

of 'Absolute Being', which guides the acts of consciousness. Consciousness disclaims as well the fruit of its labor and its enjoyment. The ego is stripped away and converted "into a 'thing' into an objective external existence" (266).

The Renaissance brings self-consciousness still further along toward knowledge. The process of reason as empiricism or experimental method is not, as earlier, a passive one. "It itself settles the observations to be made and the experience to be had" (281). Having rejected the "Beyond," Reason now actively seeks itself in the world. "It seeks its 'other,' while knowing that it thus possesses nothing else but itself: it seeks merely its own infinitude" (281). But empiricism does not avail to find it. The inadequacy of observational method, including the formulation of laws describing observed regularities, is revealed in the analysis of thought itself—in psychology. The method cannot give an account of mind without interpreting the context that conditions it. And here no clear causality can be established. Ideologies may flow from a culture. But they can also revolutionize one. As Taylor puts it, "Observing reason cannot really cope with the meshing of the given and the self-made in man."[29]

When consciousness seeks itself in moral practice it does better. Now it discovers itself as a "thing" that informs the life of society as universal custom. For custom "is nothing else than the absolute spiritual unity of the essential substance *(Wesen)* of individuals in their independent reality; it is an inherently universal self-consciousness" (375). This is an important juncture in the development of Hegel's epistemology. For it is here that the individual loses the moral independence he had for Kant. He comes to see himself as "only a 'this,' a given existent unit" that bears and exemplifies the universal consciousness (376). In this way, the "realization of self-conscious reason . . . finds its complete reality and fulfillment in the life of a nation" (376). When seekers after knowledge have reached this point of awareness,

> they are conscious within themselves of being these individual independent beings through the fact that they surrender and sacrifice their particular individuality, and that this universal substance is

29. Taylor, *Hegel*, 162.

their soul and essence—as this universal again is the action of themselves as individuals, and is the work and product of their own activity. (376)

Dialectical method, of course, does not present this as loss for the individual but as a way to fulfillment. Hegel writes: "As the individual in his own particular work *ipso facto* accomplishes unconsciously a universal work, so again he also performs the universal task as his *conscious* object. The whole becomes *in its entirety* his work, for which he sacrifices himself, and precisely by that means receives back his own self from it" (377). The individual finds himself most fulfilled in the life of the "free nation" in which "reason is in truth realized." For here he himself is the "essential being, and has also attained his destiny" (378). The thought is very much like Rousseau's concept of the general will. When I can identify with a will that I form, I exist only for myself. I see only myself in the other and in the whole, which is a perfect unity.

After tracing the path that leads to knowledge up to its culmination in the self-conscious moral life of a free nation, Hegel moves in an opposite direction. He describes a variety of individualist phenomena—hedonism, subjectivist moral sentimentalism (the Romantic movement), reformist idealism that strives to perfect mankind through individual action, and the cult of self-expression. At the end of this section he also criticizes the formalist ethics of Kant in which individuals test their maxims by universal and abstract procedural criteria. We seem to be moving away from the goal. But then we realize that we have simply been thinking dialectically, proceeding from the universal to the particular pole. We emerge at last with the final synthesis. The heightening of individuality at several levels has prepared us for the community of free men. We have left the beginnings of ethicality in unthinking custom—our first grasp of the universal— and passed through self-conscious individualism to free community.

The living ethical world is spirit in its truth. As it first comes to an abstract *knowledge* of its essential nature, ethical life (*Sittlichkeit*) is destroyed in the formal universality of right or legality (*Recht*). Spirit, being now sundered within itself, traces one of its worlds in the element of its objectivity as in a crass solid actuality; this is the

realm of Culture and Civilization; while over against this in the
element of thought is traced the world of Belief or Faith, the realm
of the Inner Life and Truth (*Wesen*). Both worlds, however, when in
the grip of the notion . . . are thrown in confusion and revolutionized through individual Insight (*Einsicht*), and the general diffusion of this attitude, known as "Enlightenment" (*Aufklaerung*).
And the realm which had thus been divided and expanded into the
"present" and the "remote beyond," into the "here" and the "yon-
der," turns back into self-consciousness. This self-consciousness,
again, taking now the form of Morality (the inner moral life) ap-
prehends itself as the essential truth, the real essence as its actual
self: no longer puts its world and its ground and basis away outside
itself, but lets everything fade into itself, and in the form of Conscience (*Gewissen*) is spirit sure and certain (*gewiss*) of itself. (461)

I have been examining Hegel's way of bringing body and mind
together in a harmonious unity of necessity and freedom in *The
Phenomenology of Mind*. Though this work embraces a discussion
of social and cultural change, as we have seen, its focus is on
individual consciousness—its levels and the dynamic of its development. In *The Philosophy of History* and *The Philosophy of Right*
Hegel shifts his emphasis to society and politics. In the first of
these works he traces the institutional history of freedom from
oriental despotism ("One is free") through Greek and Roman
democracy ("Some are free") to the beginnings of what he saw as
a modern liberal state ("All are free") in the Prussia of his time.
The Philosophy of Right presents a cross-sectional analysis of the
emerging liberal order. I shall note the way Hegel's epistemological position receives expression in the two works.

Section 3 of part 4 of *The Philosophy of History* opens with a
statement that the present period of history is "the period of
Spirit conscious that it is free, inasmuch as it wills the True, the
Eternal—that which is in and for itself Universal."[30] Later we are
told that from the "painful struggles of History" has emerged a
"recognition of the Secular as capable of being an embodiment of
Truth."[31] The modern state turns out to be the special vehicle in
which the truth is expressed. We have come to recognize that

30. G.W.F. Hegel, *The Philosophy of History*, J. Sibree, trans. (New York: Dover
Publications, 1956), 412.

31. Ibid., 422.

"there is nothing higher or more sacred" than "Morality and Justice in the State."[32]

The triumph of morality and justice in the state involves also the triumph of embodied will.

> Secular life is the positive and definite embodiment of the Spiritual Kingdom—the Kingdom of the *Will* manifesting itself in outward existence. . . . The Freedom of the Will *per se*, is the principle and substantial basis of all Right—is itself absolute, inherently eternal Right, and the Supreme Right . . . , it is even that by which Man becomes Man, and is therefore the fundamental principle of Spirit.[33]

Hegel closes the *History* with a note that such a general formulation as this tells us little, and he indicates that he will elsewhere present a consideration of the "metaphysical process by which the abstract Will develops itself, so as to attain a definite form of Freedom, and how Rights and Duties are evolved therefrom."[34] This task he carries out in *The Philosophy of Right*.

It will be useful at this point to review the leading aspects of Hegel's dialectical method as I have traced it so far. Hegel's point of departure was the Cartesian dichotomy of body and spirit, and the dilemma he set out to resolve was the puzzle about the precise interrelationship of these two principles of reality. He found himself in agreement with Kant that the illumination of the meaning of human experience and the judgment of right and wrong must be the province of autonomous mind defined as will and reason (or as reasonable will). These are, in a sense, the primary reality. He also agreed that one could not give will the status of subjective individual intention, as Descartes had done. But Kant's assignment of the principles of right and meaning to a transcendental status, which individual minds could know but might not act upon, was to Hegel a flawed resolution of the Cartesian dilemma, for it failed to supply the missing connection between body and spirit. Recent history might contain hints that the unintelligible motions of the phenomenal world were contributing to the realization of the purposes of noumenal intelli-

32. Ibid.
33. Ibid., 443.
34. Ibid.

gence. But to believe so remained fundamentally an act of faith, not established knowledge. Also, spirit itself was infinitely fragmented in the Kantian system. Hegel proceeded, therefore, to argue that spirit, as reasonable will, must be understood as a force that actually shapes, forms, and moves, as well as comprehends empirical reality (body). He avoided a monistic reduction of the dual Cartesian system to spirit by asserting that spirit could only become conscious of itself—and therefore truly 'be'—by embodying itself in the particulars that constitute sense experience (body). To account for the confusion, conflict, and frequent "mindlessness" of empirical experience and to give full recognition to the sharp contrast between spirit and body, Hegel wrote of the process of embodiment as one of alienation. Spirit by becoming its polar other at first becomes lost in the other. Its empirical manifestations are partial, distorted, one-sided. Eventually, however, spirit returns to itself as human consciousness, immeasurably enriched by the experience of embodiment. But only at the end of a long historical process is the development to full self-consciousness of embodied spirit accomplished.[35]

Hegel's solution to the Cartesian dilemma was ingenious and, surely at one level, a success. It specified, plausibly, a precise causal relationship between spirit and body and in such a way as to account for all aspects both of individual and social (institutional) experience, over time, without monistically reducing either to the spirit or body pole. It did not, however, eliminate the tension between individual freedom and political force. The dialectic, rather, incorporated the tension.

Hegel's dialectical system reifies *Geist*, "Absolute Spirit." Spirit becomes a being—in a sense, the only being—and one that expresses itself in the particulars that men as individuals are. Existence and essence (intelligibility) are joined in the affirmation that only the Universal truly 'is,' and is known by itself to 'be'. Even though concrete embodiment is necessary to the fulfillment of spirit, the particulars that constitute the vehicle of that embodiment are in themselves, as particulars, necessarily unintelligible and unreal or, rather, a second-class kind of reality, which is

35. See *Philosophy of Right*, 216.

always in flux, in process of becoming—accidental. Hegel has eliminated not only Cartesian subjective individuality but also the moral individuality of Kant's noumenal man. The individual is free and fulfilled only as he participates in the life of *Geist*.

The process by which individual persons are brought to freedom within the concrete Universal of fulfilled Absolute Spirit is a necessary one. For Hegel had translated the teleological and ethical concepts of the natural law tradition into laws of historical necessity modeled on the laws of logic and of physics. This is clear from his remarks on the Renaissance, when men came to realize, Hegel tells us, that "thought is not only a higher reality than external things, but that rational thought *determines* the course of things."[36] Individuals are shaped by the lawful processes of *Geist* in the same way that Rousseau's men of the general will are shaped and formed by the work of the Legislator. The two systems differ in that the freedom for Hegel's *Geist* to manipulate individuals is the freedom of an Absolute Being who indwells them. At the end of an unconscious process, the individuals subjected to the process themselves become free as they become conscious of their identity with the Absolute. The free machinations of Rousseau's Legislator are arbitrary and (literally) unjustified. In each case, however, men are forced to be free.[37]

The politics implicit in Hegel's dialectic is spelled out in *The Philosophy of History* and *The Philosophy of Right*. In both volumes the individual, to win his freedom, must pass through a process of moral rehabilitation presided over by society. The idea is not

36. Taylor, *Hegel*, 161.

37. Patrick Riley comments on Hegel's insistence that the claims of subjective will must give way to those of objectively rational will "whether it be recognized or not by individuals" (P. R. 157) as an assertion "reminiscent of Rousseau in its intimation that people may have a real will that they fail to recognize." But Riley goes on to say that the passage is *not* reminiscent "of [Rousseau's] claim that they may be 'forced to be free'" (191). Patrick Riley, *Will and Political Legitimacy: A Critical Exposition of Social Contract Theory in Hobbes, Locke, Rousseau, Kant, and Hegel* (Cambridge, Mass.: Harvard Univ. Press, 1982). I fail to see why this is not a case of being "forced to be free," despite the fact that the "forcing" is being done not by an arbitrary Legislator but by an "objectively rational" Absolute Spirit. The latter, after all, is supposed to be embodied in the state and therefore acts through its agencies. As Riley also notes, "the recognition of conscience in the *Phenomenology* becomes the recognition of the state in the *Philosophy of Right*" (193).

presented as a moral wish but as a natural necessity. Taylor has succinctly (though perhaps unwittingly) revealed this aspect of Hegel's thought in writing that

> man must be lifted to universality so that his aspirations correspond to the universal good; but this requires a long formation and discipline, it requires a hard-won transformation. It is foolish to think that our unreconstructed spontaneous feeling will be one with the universal. . . .
>
> The highest ethic is also one which is fulfilled. It is not just an 'ought,' something that should be. . . . Spirit living in a people shows us laws which are at the same time *Sein*, real existence.[38]

Since reason and will indwell individuals not as such but in the institutions that collectivities of individuals share, Hegel, not surprisingly, reifies Absolute Spirit in the institution of the state. Thus in *The Philosophy of Right* he tells us that "the national state is mind in its substantive rationality and immediate actuality and is therefore the absolute power on earth."[39] In another place he writes that "the concrete Ideas, the minds of the nations, have their truth and their destiny in the concrete Idea which is absolute universality, i.e., in the world mind."[40] This obviously makes the norms of a national culture authoritative, in an ultimate sense, for all the individuals who are members of the culture. The individual's freedom is therefore to be found in subscribing to established ideals and ethics.[41]

Within Hegel's rational state, the task of cultural development and diffusion is given to an official class of civil servants who constitute one of the "Estates" (*Staende*) represented in Hegel's corporatively organized legislature. A democratic aspect is given to this estate of experts in their recruitment from the whole society by competitive examination. One of their functions is to participate with the unofficial agricultural and business estates in

38. Taylor, *Hegel*, 165, 169–70.
39. *Philosophy of Right*, 212.
40. Ibid., 219.
41. Riley also remarks, in interpreting Hegel, that "since the only worthwhile will is the rational will, and since rationality cannot be found in mere Kantian moral universality, it must be looked for in the concrete rationality of the customs and institutions around us." *Will and Political Legitimacy*, 192–93.

framing general legislation through which standards are established for the society as a whole.[42] Another is to implement this
legislation through administration by applying universal principles to specific cases—the executive function.[43]

George Kelly tells us that this universal class is

> an elite which, principally by means of its philosophical absorption
> in culture, creates structures which regulate society, encourage its
> orderly advance, and guarantee a reciprocity of rights and duties
> and a recognition of belongingness. . . . As *Staatsbeamten*, their func-
> tion in political matters is not dissimilar to that of philosophically
> oriented pedagogues in educational ones: they translate the will of
> a culture from the inchoate premises of its base into the most
> articulate and effective forms, while fending off the modern ten-
> dency of politics to degenerate into either the clash of particular
> interests or their invidious compromise. This depends on their
> prior training in a philosophical, cultural, and humanistic thrust.[44]

When change occurs, self-appointed, World Historical Individuals may lead the way to new formulations of the Idea, and the
role of all other individuals is to follow the leader. At any time,
one nation in particular "is entrusted with giving complete effect
to . . . the advance of the self-developing self-consciousness of
the world mind."[45] This nation has an "absolute right of being
the vehicle of this present stage in the world mind's development,
the minds of the other nations are without rights." This looks
like a justification for cultural imperialism.[46] Not only are indi-

42. For a description and discussion of the various institutions of Hegel's state
see my *Theories of the Political System*, 3rd ed. (Englewood Cliffs, N.J.: Prentice-
Hall, 1978), 392–95.

43. *Philosophy of Right*, 176.

44. George A. Kelly, *Hegel's Retreat from Eleusis* (Princeton, N.J.: Princeton
Univ. Press, 1978), 14–16.

45. *Philosophy of Right*, 217.

46. Ibid., 218. T. M. Knox, however, claims that Hegel did not mean this as a
justification of the status quo, since he does not read Hegel's description of the
rational state as one of an actually existing state. "Hegel and Prussianism," in
Walter Kaufmann, ed., *Hegel's Political Philosophy* (New York: Atherton Press,
1970), 18. Shlomo Avineri denies that the passage involved gives any particular
World Historical Nation a right to political hegemony but that this "*absolute* right
is . . . in the sphere of cultural leadership." "Hegel and Nationalism" in Kaufmann, *Hegel's Political Philosophy*, 130. It is not clear to me how leadership in this
sphere can readily be distinguished from cultural imperialism.

viduals forced to be free, according to the standards of their culture, but cultures too must be fashioned to freedom through surrendering their rights to the culture of the dominant nation. It is not surprising that for Hegel, in the relations of nation states vying for supremacy in a given moment, there is an "ethical moment in war."[47] "War is . . . the moment in which the ideality of the particular attains its right and is actualized. War has the higher significance that by its agency, . . . 'the ethical health of peoples is preserved in their indifference to the stabilization of finite institutions.'"[48]

In the event, the tension between force and freedom in Hegel's world is resolved by identifying individual freedom with a necessary end phase of the development of the Absolute Idea, or *Geist*. The individual is not free qua individual but only as a 'moment' of the idea. And the freedom of the Idea itself culminates in the contemplation of necessity. (See appendix B for a critique of some leading literature on the relationship of freedom to necessity in Hegel's politics.)

The Necessary Freedom of the Species-Being: Hegelian Dialectics Inverted

"Life is not determined by consciousness, but consciousness by life," wrote Karl Marx (1813–1883) in *The German Ideology*. "In the first method of approach the starting point is consciousness taken as the living individual; in the second method, which conforms to real life, it is the real living individuals themselves, and consciousness is considered solely as *their* consciousness."[49] This

47. *Philosophy of Right*, 209.

48. Ibid., 210. Errol E. Harris gives another reading to Hegel's views on war. He writes: "In external relations the state is sovereign or it is not a state, and its sovereign status has to be recognized. It follows that its relations with other states are . . . entered into by its own will and determined solely by its own interest, or, where agreement fails, enmity and war. It is here that ordnance becomes *ultima ratio regum* and Louis XIV is vindicated. To say this is not to glorify or romanticize war, it is simply to state what is inevitably true so long as states are sovereign," in Donald P. Verene, ed., *Hegel's Social and Political Thought* (Atlantic Highlands, N.J.: Humanities Press, 1980), 142. It seems to me that the passage I have quoted from Hegel in its normative emphasis is quite different from Harris's purely descriptive sentences.

49. Karl Marx and Friedrich Engels, *The German Ideology*, S. Ryazanskaya, trans., in Robert C. Tucker, ed., *The Marx–Engels Reader*, 2nd ed. (New York:

is not so much a statement of materialist ontology as a protest against the idealist mystification that Marx judged Hegel's *Weltgeist* to be. For Marx, the conception of a World Spirit evolving to self-conscious freedom, far from giving meaning to human life, detracted greatly from a clear appreciation of the sensuous reality that we experience in daily living. Despite Hegel's insistence that the Idea, to be realized, requires empirical embodiment and despite Hegel's effort to build his analysis entirely within experienced categories of individual consciousness, *Geist* remained for Marx a pale and vapid abstraction. In setting forth his own ontology, Marx stressed the ultimate reality of the individual as a sensuous being. It was to be expected that this would bring with it a corresponding emphasis on the material pole of the body–mind dichotomy. But we should be mistaken if we classified Marx as a materialist of any simplistic sort.

Like Descartes, Marx was impressed by the radical dependence of our mental experience on sensation. In *The German Ideology* he goes so far as to speak of ideas as "phantoms formed in the human brain" and to call them "sublimates of their material life-process, which is empirically verifiable and bound to material premises."[50] Descartes had described people as "thinking things," an expression that stresses "thingness" as much as "thinking." But also like Descartes, Marx recognized an active, vitalistic power in the individual, which could not be reduced to a mere epiphenomenon of bodily processes. For in the same essay, Marx wrote, "We set out from real, active men."[51] And in the *Theses on Feuerbach*, which he wrote in the spring of 1845 as he and Engels began their joint authorship of *The German Ideology*, he expressly repudiated a narrow version of materialism, saying that "the materialist doctrine that men are products of circumstances and upbringing and that, therefore, changed men are products of other circumstances and changed upbringing, forget that it is men who change circumstances and that it is essential to educate the educator him-

W. W. Norton & Co., 1978), 155. Quotations from the *Reader* are with permission of W. W. Norton & Company, Inc., copyright © by W. W. Norton Co., Inc., 1978.

   50. Ibid., 154.

   51. Ibid.

self."[52] Also, in criticizing Feuerbach's materialism in the Fifth Thesis, Marx wrote that Feuerbach did "not conceive sensuousness as practical, human-sensuous activity," an expression of a vitalistic rather than mechanistic character, which attributes a certain autonomy to the striving human person.

In another early essay we have an ontological statement of a similar dualistic intent. "For a Ruthless Criticism of Everything Existing" tells us that "the socialist principle represents, on the whole, only one side, affecting the *reality* of the true human essence. We have to concern ourselves just as much with the other side, the theoretical existence of man, in other words to make religion, science, etc., the objects of our criticism."[53] William L. McBride, in a recent study of Marx's ontology and method, points out that "Marx never leaned very heavily on the 'materialistic' label," and in his early writings in particular liked to characterize himself as a "naturalist" who was also a "humanist." "At all times he was anxious . . . to distinguish his philosophy from the crude, mechanistic materialism of . . . Helvétius and Holbach."[54] Unlike these writers, Marx felt free to employ such expressions as "the human spirit." For he knew that his readers would understand that "no metaphysical claim about the existence of a world of spirits or souls, radically distinct from the world of natural objects in which we ordinarily think of ourselves as living, is entailed thereby."[55] Descartes would certainly have understood and sympathized with his intention.

A Cartesian sort of dualism (mutually implicative mind and body) is as characteristic of Marx's late period as it is of his early period. In the afterword to the second German edition of *Capital*, composed in 1873, Marx contrasts his epistemology with Hegel's, asserting that

> to Hegel, the life process of the human brain, i.e., the process of thinking, which, under the name of 'the Idea,' he even transforms

52. Karl Marx, *Theses on Feuerbach*, in Tucker, *Marx—Engels Reader*, 144.
53. Ibid., 13.
54. William L. McBride, *The Philosophy of Marx* (London: Hutchison, 1977), 79–80.
55. Ibid., 83–84.

into an independent subject, is the demiurgos of the real world, and the real world is only the external, phenomenal form of 'the Idea.' With me, on the contrary, the ideal is nothing else than the material world reflected by the human mind, and translated into forms of thought.[56]

This statement does not reduce ideas to matter in motion any more than it affirms a radical independence for them. À la Descartes, it asserts instead a radical interdependence of mind and body. Still another formulation of a dualist position from Marx's middle period is found in a passage of *The Eighteenth Brumaire of Louis Bonaparte* (1852) in which Marx asserts that "Men make their own history, but they do not make it just as they please; . . . but under the circumstances directly framed, given and transmitted from the past."[57]

Nevertheless, Marx's attempt to avoid materialist reductionism and to affirm a certain duality in human motivation, like Descartes's effort, is fraught with ambiguity and ambivalence. For in *The German Ideology*, immediately after saying that the point of departure of his analysis is "real, active men," Marx writes that "on the basis of their real life-process we demonstrate the development of the ideological reflexes and echoes of this life-process."[58] If our mental experience becomes, in the second instance, a mere reflex and echo of the life process, what has become of the "real, active man," with whom we started, the man who shapes circumstance? He seems to have become a mere feedback mechanism. Like Descartes, Marx wished to have his necessity and his freedom as well. But how the two may be combined is far from clear. Let us see whether Marx's dialectical analysis of the historical development of human life clarifies and resolves the problem.

Central to Marx's view of man, and the most original element in it, is the concept of *homo faber*—man as worker, as producer. Basic is the simple fact that men, working with the raw materials of nature, produce for themselves the necessities of life. Marx writes that "life involves before everything else eating and drinking,

56. Tucker, *Marx–Engels Reader*, 301.
57. Ibid., 595.
58. Ibid., 154.

habitation, clothing and many other things."[59] But the concept is much richer than this. One ultimately discovers that beyond such obvious empirical generalizations, it contains an entire normative ethics.

In the *Manuscripts of 1844* Marx observes that under capitalist conditions of production, most men do not find their work satisfying. They do not receive back as their own the ever-expanding product of their efforts but are constrained to sell their labor for a subsistence wage. The relationship between wages and productivity is, in fact, increasingly negative. "The worker becomes all the poorer the more wealth he produces, the more his production increases in power and range."[60] Under capitalism, the worker is bought and sold as a commodity like the products of his labor. He is at the mercy of the market, and "his own activity is to him an unfree activity . . . performed in the service, under the dominion, the coercion and the yoke of another man" (78). The worker takes no joy in his work but labors simply to keep body and soul together. He is free only in "his animal functions—eating, drinking, procreating." His work is merely "a *means* to satisfy needs external to it," and very primitive ones at that (74).

Under these circumstances, the worker's product confronts him "as *something alien*, as *a power independent* of the producer" (71). His labor becomes "an external existence . . . that exists *outside him*, independently, as something alien to him" (72). Appropriation also appears as "*estrangement*, as *alienation*" (72). In fact, the whole of nature, the "sensuous external world," becomes "an alien world antagonistically opposed to him" (74). The worker also comes to realize that "in the very act of production he was estranging himself from himself" and himself from his fellow man. "Estranged labour estranges the *species* from man. It turns the *life of the species* into a means of individual life" (73, 75). The worker does not produce for society but for his employer and, minimally, for himself in order to keep alive.

Beneath the language of alienation, and in the interstices of its description, lies Marx's normative theory of man—a conception

59. Ibid., 156.

60. *Economic and Philosophic Manuscripts of 1844*, in Tucker, *Marx–Engels Reader*, 71. Parenthetical page references are to this edition.

of man as he *ought* to be and as he *might* be under altered economic circumstances. The *un*alienated man is at one with himself, with his fellow man, and with nature. He is not a narrow and isolated individual, but a species-being, a social animal, who is fulfilled in the work of social production. ("The proposition that man's species nature is estranged from him means that one man is estranged from the other, as each of them is from man's essential nature.") When alienation is overcome, man works for the sake of the work itself, in which he takes joy. For "he contemplates himself in a world that he has created" (76). Subject (the worker) and object (his product) are now harmoniously united. Nature (the external world), worked over by the social creativity of mankind, is no longer hostile and alien but an extension of humanity. We are given a picture of free, satisfying creativity in a cooperative commonwealth of outgoing persons who mutually sustain one another as subjects, instead of using one another as objects.

> Man is a species being, not only because in practice and in theory he adopts the species as his object . . . but because he treats himself as the actual, living species; because he treats himself as a *universal* and therefore a free being.

> The productive life is the life of the species. It is life-engendering life. The whole character of a species—its species character—is contained in the character of its life activity; and free, conscious activity is man's species character. Life itself appears only as a *means* to life. (75, 76)

Marx's normative theory of man as a species being is a logical extrapolation from a combination of Cartesian and Hegelian concepts. If in a Cartesian world, body and spirit, sensation and thought, are mutually interdependent in a radical way, then I am both an extension of nature (the physical world) and an active agent that frames the world through my consciousness. Neither external nature nor I as a thinking, willing being is a given. Rather, we form one another, in perfect interdependency, as a naturalistic, organic whole. This seems to be precisely the idea that Marx spells out in the texts reviewed here. It makes sense for him to write, on the one hand, that "the phantoms formed in the human brain are . . . necessarily, sublimates of their material life-process" and also to assert that "man makes his life-activity itself the object of his will and of his consciousness. He has conscious life-activity. It is not a determination with which he directly merges."[61]

Descartes did not conceive of any disruption of the harmonious interplay of spirit and body. Nor did he face up to the problems involved in specifying precisely how the interaction of mechanical reflex and free will occurs. He left us instead with a paradox. Hegel attempted its resolution, as we have seen, with an historical theory in which necessity and freedom are dialectically interwoven to a culminating point that lies somewhere on the edge of history. Central to Hegelian dialectics was a process of alienation whereby spirit, or The Idea, becomes its "other" through embodiment in the particularity (and therefore partiality, one-sidedness) of concrete existence. So embodied, the Idea suffers distortion, a distortion that is never fully corrected but which diminishes over time as *Geist* moves through ever more perfect concretizations.

Marxist alienation is different and closer in its metaphysical categories to those of Descartes than to those of Hegel. Nature (body) is not conceived as in itself an alienated form of creative individuality (spirit). Rather, nature under the special circumstances of capitalist production comes to be viewed by the individual worker as a distorted and antagonistic reality that impedes the self-expression of creative mind. Mind and body do not work together in their natural harmony but are at odds with one another. And mind itself (as a world only of individuals) is fragmented not by virtue of the existence of individuals as such but by the opposition of person to person in conflictual and exploitative relationships. Particularity therefore dominates over universality because no sense of unity exists between men, between man and nature, or between the worker and himself. But when the existing circumstances of production have been radically altered and universalized, man's natural universality will be made manifest. And universality involves the harmonious interaction of men with one another, with nature, and of each man with himself. Universality, unity, rationality, freedom—all are one. Marx writes,

61. *The German Ideology* and *The Manuscripts of 1844*, ibid., 154, 76.

The universality of man is in practice manifested precisely in the universality which makes all nature his *inorganic* body—both inasmuch as nature is (1) his direct means of life, and (2) the material, the object, and the instrument of his life-activity . . .

An animal produces one-sidedly, whilst man produces universally. It produces only under the dominion of immediate physical need, whilst man produces even when he is free from physical need and only truly produces in freedom therefrom. An animal produces only itself, whilst man reproduces the whole of nature. . . . Man knows how to produce in accordance with the standard of every species, and knows how to apply everywhere the inherent standard to the object. Man therefore also forms things in accordance with the laws of beauty. . . .

Through and because of this production, nature appears as *his* work and his reality . . . He contemplates himself in a world that he has created.[62]

In these formulas, Marx has avoided reifying mind and will. There is no World Spirit or Absolute Idea. There are only individual men who are both body (sensuous activity) and spirit (creative and rational will). But the harmonious interactions of body with spirit that characterize Marx's universal man, the species-being who happily "contemplates himself in a world that he has created," are a normative ideal not an existing actuality. They represent a way of life to be achieved.

Marx asserts that the satisfying life of the universal man, the freely creative species-being, will become a reality for all men when a universal (that is, communist) system of production has been created the world around. Communism is the key to overcoming the crippling alienation that prevents man from fulfilling himself. He celebrates the idea in a ringing passage from the *Manuscripts of 1844*:

Communism as the positive transcendence of *private property*, or *human self-estrangement*, and therefore as the real *appropriation* of the human essence by and for man; communism therefore as the complete return of man to himself as a *social* (i.e. human) being—a return become conscious, and accomplished within the entire wealth of previous development. This communism, as fully-

62. *Manuscripts of 1844*, ibid., 75–76.

developed naturalism equals humanism, and as fully-developed humanism equals naturalism; it is the *genuine* resolution of the conflict between man and nature and between man and man—the true resolution of the strife between existence and essence, between objectification and self-confirmation, between freedom and necessity, between the individual and the species. Communism is the riddle of history solved, and it knows itself to be this solution.[63]

Here is Marx's solution to the Cartesian body–mind problem. He has specified a precise connection between the two elements of reality and the social and economic conditions under which a perfectly harmonious interaction of the two elements will occur. But one part of the solution is still lacking. He must specify the process whereby communism, the system in which freedom and necessity will live in happy conjunction, will be created.

It is in the early *German Ideology* that we find Marx's most complete description of the historical teleology by which spirit and body will be brought into harmonious and fruitful interaction. Tucker tells us that "Marx never again set down a comprehensive statement of his theory of history at such length and in such detail."[64] The following analysis draws on part 1 of this work. Since its organization follows the outline of the "Theses on Feuerbach," Tucker infers that it was written by Marx alone, even though the work as a whole was a product of Marx's collaboration with Engels and was published over both their names. If Tucker is correct, the difference that some writers allege to exist between Marx's humanistic emphasis on *praxis* and Engels's naturalistic determinism is an extremely narrow one indeed. The philosophy of history implicit in the later *Foundations of the Critique of Political Economy* (1857–58) and of *Capital* itself (1867), Marx's masterpiece, is perfectly consonant with it.

Marx tells us in *The German Ideology* that men begin "to distinguish themselves from animals as soon as they begin to *produce* their means of subsistence" (150). Produce seems to have here the rich meaning of "fashion, shape, create." It conveys a sense of actively reworking the materials given by raw nature. (Animals,

63. Ibid., 84.
64. Ibid., 146. Parenthetical page references are from *The German Ideology*, in Tucker, *Marx–Engels Reader*.

presumably, live passively, taking their subsistence from nature as nature presents it to them, already fashioned by her for their use.) The manner in which production takes place Marx calls a "mode of production," a term that encompasses much more than "the reproduction of the physical existence of individuals." It is rather "a definite form of activity of these individuals, a definite form of expressing their life, a definite *mode of life* on their part" (150). Marx seems to be trying to describe what we today call a culture or a way of life. And he tells us that a given culture can be defined by its mode of production. "As individuals express their life, so they are. What they are, therefore, coincides with their production, both of *what* they produce and with *how* they produce. The nature of individuals thus depends on the material conditions determining their production" (150).

Modes of production are various and are distinguished from one another by the degree to which each has "developed its productive forces." And this is "shown most manifestly by the degree to which the division of labour has been carried" (150). The various forms of division of labor are, in turn, "just so many different forms of ownership." Or, in other words, a given division of labor "determines also the relations of individuals to one another with reference to the material, instrument, and product of labour" (150–51).

The various modes of production form a time series of increasing productivity that Marx calls "the various stages of development in the division of labour" (151). To understand history is to understand how these stages are organized and how they change. Marx writes: "It is quite obvious from the start that there exists a materialistic connection of men with one another which is determined by their needs and their mode of production, and which is as old as men themselves. This connection is ever taking on new forms, and thus presents a 'history' independently of the existence of any political or religious nonsense which would especially hold men together" (157).

The key concept in the group we have just presented is "division of labor," the social relationship that is both the basis of human productivity and of human conflict. As Marx's history unfolds we see that its hallmark is an enormous irony. The advance from communal ownership to private property, both in antiquity and in modern times, through increasing the division of labor, has on the one hand produced the material basis of the good life by overcoming scarcity. At the same time it has enormously magnified class antagonisms and heightened the ruthlessness of exploiting ruling classes. Marx's division of labor is the institution whereby the historical process is forcing us to be free.

Tribal ownership, the earliest form of property, "corresponds to the undeveloped stage of production" in which "the division of labor is . . . still very elementary," Marx tells us. Its social structure is that of the extended family, fundamentally a harmonious and nonexploitive system, despite the presence of slaves at the bottom of the social scale. Marx describes slavery as "latent" in this form of social order and tells us that it "only develops gradually with the increase of population, the growth of wants and with the extension of external relations, both of war and of barter" (151). In the second form of ancient ownership— the commune—private property is found at the beginning beside, though subordinate to, public property and rapidly acquires scope and prominence. Under this system "the division of labour is already more developed. We already find the antagonism of town and country; later the antagonism between those states which represent town interests and those which represent country interests, and inside the towns themselves the antagonism between industry and maritime commerce. The class relation between citizen and slaves is now completely developed" (151). In modern history a similar development can be traced, beginning not with the closed society of the tribe but with the communalism of the feudal manor and guilds. And in place of slaves we find serfs tied to the land and journeyman apprentices. Again, "there was little division of labor" (153). But then came an "extension of the division of labour" with the "separation of production and commerce, the formation of a special class of merchants" (178). Capitalism was born.

The division of labor represents for Marx not only a central principle of economic efficiency but also the idea of particularity— a particularity that embodies selfishness and alienation. "The division of labour," he writes, "implies the contradiction between the interest of the separate individual or the individual family and the communal interest of all individuals who have intercourse with one another" (160). As its complexity increases, so does individualism, which destroys primitive community while paradoxically creating the material basis of the ultimate communist society. It is an individualism that is utterly incompatible with human freedom. For in "natural" (as opposed to "voluntary") society "man's own deed becomes an alien power opposed to him, which enslaves him instead of being controlled by him. For as soon as the distribution of labor comes into being, each man has a particular, exclusive sphere of activity which is forced upon him and from which he cannot escape" (160). And so it goes throughout history, until the final communist revolution, when the last ruling class, the proletariat, seizes power. As the division of labor broadens into "world-historical activity," individuals "become more and more enslaved under a power alien to them . . . a power which has become more and more enormous and, in the last instance, turns out to be the *world market*." Only after the communist revolution will "this power . . . be dissolved" (163). Until then, impersonal historical process, not free human will, governs the evolution of society. It acts "as an alien force existing outside them, of the original end goal of which they are ignorant, which they thus cannot control, which on the contrary passes through a peculiar series of phases and stages independent of the will and the action of men, nay even being the prime governor of these" (161). Until the coming of world communism—whose advent must be an act of faith—freedom is sacrificed to the necessity of dialectical process. Praxis can be no more than compulsory role-playing in the here and now. Though humanists seek to distinguish them, it is not clear how Marx, in the necessitarian and impersonal history he inscribed in book 1 of *The German Ideology*, differs from Engels in the similarly necessitarian and impersonal history of his *Socialism: Utopian and Scientific*.

The passages of the *Foundations* and of *Capital*, volume 1, which refer to the historical process, fit perfectly into the theoretical framework I have just adumbrated. And both these books are indisputably the work of Marx alone. Thus, in the *Foundations*, Marx writes that it was only in the eighteenth century that social relations came to "confront the individual as a mere means to-ward his private purposes, as external necessity."[65] Speaking of the mode of production, Marx writes that "in all forms of society there is one specific kind of production which predominates over the rest." And he tells us that each mode of production "is a particular ethos which determines the specific gravity of every being which has materialized within it."[66] In contemporary times it is of course capital that "is the all-dominating economic power of bourgeois society."[67]

In a sketchy outline of eight "points to be mentioned here and not to be forgotten," which appears at the head of section 4 of the Introduction to the *Foundations*, Marx briefly mentions the problem of freedom. Following a brief discussion in point 6 of *"the uneven development of material production relative to e.g. artistic development,"* Marx writes, in point 7, that *"this conception appears as necessary development."* To this he adds: "But legitimation of chance. How. (Of freedom also, among other things.)" The ensuing text, however, contains no mention of freedom as a possibility for the historical here and now. One passage in "The Chapter on Capital" refers only to the historical development of freedom in the future. Marx writes of capital's

> ceaseless striving towards the general form of wealth [which] drives labour beyond the limits of its natural paltriness [*Naturbedürftigkeit*], and thus creates the material elements for the production of the rich individuality which is all-sided in its products as in its consumption, and whose labour also therefore appears no longer as labour, but as the full development of activity itself, in which natural necessity in its direct form has disappeared.[68]

Somewhat further along Marx addresses the idea of individuation, which was a leading theme of *The German Ideology*. The original human condition, he reminds us, was that of the *"species-being [Gattungswesen], clan being, herd animal*—although in no way whatever as a ξῷον πολιτικόν [political animal] in the political

65. Karl Marx, *Grundrisse. Foundations of the Critique of Political Economy*, trans. Martin Nicolaus (New York: Random House, 1973), 84.

66. Ibid., 106–07.

67. Ibid., 107.

68. Ibid., 109, 325.

sense."[69] This herd animal was, of course, not like the species-being that man is to become in the communist society of the future—the free participant who is also a fully social animal. (This is what the disclaimer about not being a ξῶον πολιτικόν is meant to convey.) Individuation, he tells us, is the product of exchange, which makes "the herd-like existence superfluous and dissolves it."[70] But the individual so produced "relates himself only to himself."[71] In a sense, the individual remains a member of a community but of an unequal and domineering sort. As "proprietor" he has "objective being," because that is what the community is all about—private property. But even in this role he lives under conditions that "chain him to the community, or rather form a link in his chain." The suffering worker in a bourgeois society "stands there purely without objectivity, subjectively." Marx notes here, with irony, that "the thing which *stands opposite* him has now become the *true community* [*Gemeinwesen*], which he tries to make a meal of, and which makes a meal of him."[72] This is hardly a picture of individuals engaged in free and meaningful praxis.

The end, as the beginning of capitalism, forms part of a necessary process in the categories of the *Foundations*. Marx writes that at a certain point in its development, capitalism becomes a barrier to the expansion of productive power. It is then "necessarily stripped off as a fetter."[73] The contradictions into which capitalism falls lead to "explosions, cataclysms, crises." The recurrence of these catastrophes at last leads to the system's "violent overthrow."[74] Force persists to the last moment, before the advent of freedom.

The tone of *Capital* is no different. In the preface to the first German edition (1867) Marx tells us that the standpoint from which he has viewed the economic evolution of society sees that evolution "as a process of natural history," that is, of impersonal

69. Ibid., 496.
70. Ibid.
71. Ibid.
72. Ibid.
73. Ibid., 749.
74. Ibid., 750.

forces. Such a standpoint, he writes, "can less than any other make the individual responsible for relations whose creature he socially remains, however much he may subjectively raise himself above them."[75] Prior to the communist revolution, the individual is simply a pawn in the hands of historical process. As he maintained in his earlier works, so also later in *Capital*, Marx tells us that

> the life-process of society, which is based on the process of material production, does not strip off its mystical veil until it is treated as production by freely associated men, and is consciously regulated by them in accordance with a settled plan. This, however, demands for society a certain material ground-work or set of conditions of existence which in their turn are the spontaneous product of a long and painful process of development.[76]

That process itself is not the work of freedom but of necessity. Dialectics may in the end accomplish the harmonious fusion of body and spirit that brings with it human freedom. But its method is force. Force is the only reality that Marx actually observed. Freedom was a reality for the future, and its coming remained for Marx, as for Kant, an act of faith. Marx was not able to *demonstrate* that it could become an actuality. The dialectical movement of history was the necessary movement of force, not freedom. The dialectical resolution of the duality of mind and body and of freedom and force in practice sacrifices freedom to force.

The Contradictions between *On Liberty* and Mill's Concept of an Authoritative Clerisy

It may seem strange to include John Stuart Mill (1806–1873) in a chapter on dialectical thought. He is not thought of as an Hegelian or Kantian, and certainly no one would classify this apostle of middle-class liberalism as a Marxist. We call him a utilitarian. But his utilitarianism is not that of Bentham. It contains ideas that are characteristic of the work of Kant, Hegel, and

---

75. *Capital*, in Tucker, *Marx–Engels Reader*, 297.
76. Ibid., 327.

Marx, especially their view that the processes of history will eventually renovate human nature and make of selfish individualists, whose interests today collide, a race of sociable beings who are also free men. With Kant, Hegel, and Marx, Mill envisaged the coming age as one of great intellectual and cultural development as well as one of moral growth. Like them he expected that the ' future of harmonious cooperation would come about only after a long period of antagonism and conflict, and, indeed, as its result. Though his concept of progressive conflict was far less violent than theirs—the conflict of ideas in a free marketplace rather than of nations and classes—it was nevertheless dialectical in character. For Mill viewed development as the result of combining opposites. The eclecticism of his thought reflects a dialectical approach to truth. Joseph Hamburger writes:

> Believing that opposites could be combined, Mill attempted such combinations. Indeed his intellectual life after the early 1830's . . . consisted of such attempts. The competitive principle and private property were balanced against a sympathetic understanding of the possibilities of socialism; his father's method of deduction would be reconciled (after a fashion) with Macaulay's crude empiricism; St. Simonian elitism and Coleridge's idea of a clerisy would be combined with the Benthamite argument for democracy . . . ; and so on, the eighteenth century would be reconciled to the nineteenth; as roads to improvement, moral regeneration would be combined with institutional change.[77]

How well did Mill's dialectical effort succeed?

A glance at the essay *On Liberty* seems to put Mill, unlike the paradoxical dialecticians whose work I have just reviewed, unequivocally on the side of freedom. In his introductory chapter Mill writes that the purpose of his essay is "to assert one very simple principle, as entitled to govern absolutely the dealings of society with the individual in the way of compulsion and control." The principle is that neither individual nor collectivity has a right to interfere with the liberty of action of any person except for

77. "Mill and the Traditions of Liberalism" (Paper delivered at the Annual Meeting of the American Political Science Association, San Francisco, September 1975).

self-protection. Mill means it to apply to the coercive force of public opinion as well as to the use of force as a sanction of law. He is especially concerned with freedom of thought and expression and with freedom of life-style. "The appropriate region of human liberty," Mill writes,

> comprises, first, the inward domain of consciousness; demanding liberty of conscience in the most comprehensive sense; liberty of thought and feeling; absolute freedom of opinion and sentiment on all subjects, practical or speculative, scientific, moral or theological. . . . Secondly, the principle requires liberty of tastes and pursuits; of framing the plan of our life to suit our own character . . . Thirdly, . . . freedom to unite, for any purpose not involving harm to others.[78]

Mill did not view individual liberty as an end in itself but as a utilitarian device. And he regarded utility as the "ultimate appeal on all ethical questions." Thus he defined it "in the largest sense, grounded on the permanent interests of man as a progressive being" (136). And freedom he believed to be a primary instrument of human progress. Free expression furnished a guarantee that fallible ideas would be subjected to a running criticism. "Complete liberty of contradicting and disproving our opinion," he wrote, "is the very condition which justifies us in assuming its truth for purposes of action; on no other terms can a being with human faculties have any rational assurance of being right" (145). The forum of debate he insisted be kept open to all, not only to elites (165). Provision should be made for the "fullest and freest comparison of opposite opinions" (185).

From the competition of such a broad and free market in ideas, Mill expected that settled truth would eventually proceed. "As mankind improves," he wrote, "the number of doctrines which are no longer disputed or doubted will be constantly on the increase: and the well-being of mankind may almost be measured by the number and gravity of the truths which have reached the point of being uncontested" (171). Not through the clashing

78. *On Liberty*, in Mary Warnock, ed., *Utilitarianism, On Liberty, Essay on Bentham* (Cleveland and New York: World Publishing Co., 1962), 137–38. Parenthetical page references are to this edition.

interests of hostile classes but through the clash of opposed ideas and ideals would the agreement of mankind ultimately emerge.

Freedom of life-style, the encouragement of "experiments in living," Mill thought important for sharpening critical judgment and independence of mind. The rule of custom leads, by contrast, to "ape-like . . . imitation" (187). In his own time especially, conformity was the rule; "they like in crowds," he wrote. "They exercise choice only among things commonly done: peculiarity of taste, eccentricity of conduct, are shunned equally with crimes: until by dint of not following their own nature they have no nature to follow" (190). European culture would stagnate without the leaven of persons willing to fashion their lives along novel lines, disdainful of approval by the mediocre majority, and willing to be original. Genius, creative originality, may indeed belong only to a few. But "genius can breathe freely only in an atmosphere of freedom" (194). Nor was Mill concerned only with new ways of life that ultimately might be converted into customs. The full development of each individual required freedom to be oneself. "The same things which are helps to one person toward the cultivation of his higher nature are hindrances to another" (197). Moral and cultural flowering in all its dimensions requires full, unhindered play for the dialectics of freedom. We approach the age of freedom and community not through force and conflict, as our other dialecticians would have it, but through the fullest liberty.

Such is the argument of *On Liberty*. But it is an argument that is not consistent with the doctrine of other major expressions of Mill's political and social thought, according to Gertrude Himmelfarb, an astute commentator on Mill's work.[79] An early statement of the ideas of this "other" Mill is found in a series of essays entitled "The Spirit of the Age," which he published anonymously in the *Examiner* in 1831—five years following the spiritual crises that led him away from the cold and impersonal utilitarianism of Bentham and his father toward the Romantic warmth of Coleridge's and Wordsworth's poetry. In the *Examiner* essays Mill's point of departure is the same as that of *On Liberty*—the

79. See Gertrude Himmelfarb, *On Liberty and Liberalism: The Case of John Stuart Mill* (New York: Alfred A. Knopf, 1974).

malevolent influence of public opinion in a democratic age. But his conclusion about the remedy for the evil was quite opposite to that of *On Liberty*.[80]

Mill derived the frame of reference in "The Spirit of the Age" from the work of St. Simon and Comte—that historical development alternates between "natural" and "transitional" periods.[81] In a transitional period, old ideas and institutions have been discredited and are in process of dissolution. It is a time of "intellectual anarchy" in which there is found great "increase of discussion" without a parallel "increase of wisdom."[82] Mill identified the England of his time as a society that was passing through just such a period of transition.

In the "Spirit of the Age," Mill tells us that, while widespread discussion may be effective in exposing errors, it is not a guarantee that new truth will emerge. Indeed, it creates an atmosphere hardly suited to the production of truth, a penchant to rely on "private judgment," and an unwillingness of the careless many to defer to the careful reasoning of the better educated.[83] He did not believe the majority would "ever have sufficient opportunities of study and experience, to become . . . conversant with all the inquiries which lead to the truths by which it is good that they should regulate their conduct."[84] Only an intellectual elite can be "expected to make the evidence of such truth a subject of profound meditation and to make themselves thorough masters of the philosophical grounds of those opinions of which it is desirable that all should be firmly *persuaded*, but which they alone can entirely and philosophically *know*."[85] Most men ought and, except in "transitional periods," "always do" form their opinion "on all extensive subjects" on the authority of the experts.[86] Here we have an elitist doctrine of truth that is worlds away from the democratic libertarianism of *On Liberty*.

80. Ibid., 37.
81. See ibid., especially fn. 28, in which Himmelfarb explains the difference between the terms used by St. Simon and Comte for these periods and the terms coined by Mill.
82. Ibid.
83. Ibid., 37–38.
84. Quoted in ibid., 39.
85. Ibid.
86. Ibid.

Mill also tells us that when an "ignorant or a half-instructed person" relies solely on his own judgment he is easily perplexed and readily led astray by the "artful sophist."[87] The man with the cleverest tongue, not the truth, will prevail under such conditions. This is hardly an expression of optimism in the free market in ideas. He continues by expressing the view that the transitional period of his own time would soon give way to a new "natural state . . . in which the opinions and feelings of the people are, with their voluntary acquiescence, formed *for* them, by the most cultivated minds."[88] By contrast, the generalized intellectual and moral self-reliance of *On Liberty* and the need for extensive "experiments in living" are depicted there as the desired shape of the intellectual world for a very long time to come.

One might attempt to explain these very opposite ways of thinking about individual liberty as a function of intellectual development; the older Mill, one would say, simply became more optimistic about generalized liberty of expression. But Himmelfarb points out that this is not the case at all. "On the contrary," she writes, "themes from this series reappear in almost all his later work, sometimes alluded to casually, at other times developed at some length."[89] In an essay on "Civilization" published in 1836 in the *London and Westminster Review*, Mill blames the vast quantity of books of his time and the enormous increase in the size of the reading public for the shallowness and confusion of the age, while *On Liberty* saw in the widespread diffusion of a variety of ideas the foundation of intellectual progress. The essay on Coleridge, published in the same *Review* in 1840, recommends the "endowed establishment" of an intellectual elite, a pluralistic "clerisy," representing all the groups that contributed to national culture. Its work was to be both the development and diffusion of that culture to all members of society. In the same essay Mill stresses the importance of a cohesive core of national ideas and values that remain settled and considered "above discussion"—a fixed and enduring political culture.[90]

87. Ibid.
88. Quoted in ibid., 41.
89. Ibid., 42.
90. Ibid., 45–46.

Much closer to the composition of *On Liberty* is a diary entry of 1854 in which Mill laments the "multitude of thoughts" of the time that unsettled conviction and produced uncertainty on all sides. "Those who should be the guides of the rest," he writes, "see too many sides to every question . . . they feel no assurance of the truth of anything."[91] Soon *after* the publication of *On Liberty* Mill once again expressed himself in ways entirely contrary to the spirit of that essay. In an exchange of letters with his friend Alexander Bain, Mill says expressly that in matters of religion, as they relate to the doctrine of *On Liberty*, he was interested in bringing over to his own skeptical standpoint only the moral and intellectual elite—"really superior intellects and characters." For the rest he would rather "try to improve their religion than to destroy it."[92] This reservation, which is entirely absent from *On Liberty*, Himmelfarb believes undermines the entire doctrine of that essay, assuming that Mill's motive for exempting religion from dissolving analysis was because he saw it useful as a support for public morality. She draws out the logic of the reservation by saying that it "implied that something less than the whole truth was more desirable than the whole truth, that a religion based upon intellectual error was preferable to an agnosticism which may have been intellectually sounder." If this was Mill's intention, it plainly contradicted the basic argument of *On Liberty*.[93]

Behind Mill the libertarian, have we discovered a hesitant advocate of opinion management by the man who "knows," for the sake of public order and cohesion? We do not seem to be far from Locke's theory of a social and intellectual elite that inculcates principles of enlightened interest in the guise of a divinely mandated natural law. Or perhaps we are in the presence of a mild-mannered Rousseauistic Legislator.[94]

It would hardly be fair to Mill to say that he ever directly advocated thought control or opinion management. Indeed, we

91. Quoted in ibid., 48.

92. Quoted in ibid., 52.

93. Ibid.

94. Cf. Graeme Duncan on Mill's conception of an intellectual elite and their politico-social role with Rousseau's legislator in *Marx and Mill: Two Views of Social Harmony* (Cambridge: Cambridge Univ. Press, 1973), 283.

know that he was critical of Auguste Comte's political science precisely because of its authoritarian and manipulative features. In *On Liberty* Comte plays the role of a whipping boy, and even in the more sympathetic estimate that Mill made of Comte's work later, in 1865, the tone in places is severe. Mill published his review of Comte's philosophical works originally as two articles in *The Westminster Review* for April and July of 1865.[95] In the first of these essays, which he devotes to a critique of Comte's major philosophical work, the *Cours de Philosophie Positive*, Mill writes that the "general idea" of Comte's scheme of cultural control by an intellectual elite is

> while regulating as little as possible by law, to make the pressure of opinion, directed by the Spiritual Power, so bearing on every individual, from the humblest to the most powerful, as to render legal obligation . . . needless. Liberty and spontaneity on the part of individuals form no part of the scheme. M. Comte looks on them with as great jealousy as any scholastic pedagogue, or ecclesiastical director of conscience. Every particular of conduct, public or private, is to be open to the public eye, and to be kept, by the power of opinion, on the course which the Spiritual Corporation shall judge to be the most right. (327)

Commenting on this authoritarian plan, Mill simply remarks that it "is not a sufficiently tempting picture to have much chance of making converts rapidly, and objections to the scheme are too obvious to need stating" (327).

In his second essay, Mill vigorously attacks the passion for unity and system that forms a central theme of Comte's later work, especially the *Système de Politique Positive*, his major political writing. "The *fons errorum* in M. Comte's later speculation," Mill writes, "is the inordinate demand for 'unity' and 'systematization'." Mill decries Comte's requirement that every person "regard as vicious any care at all for his personal interests, except as a means to the good of others," a radical self-abnegation without which one's existence "is not 'systematized', is not in 'complete unity'." And he marvels that Comte should suppose "that all perfection consists in unity" (336–37).

95. Citations here are from John Stuart Mill, *Essays on Ethics, Religion, and Society, Collected Works*, vol. 10, J. M. Robson, ed. (Toronto: Univ. of Toronto Press, 1969). Parenthetical page references are to this edition.

Why is it necessary that all human life should point but to one object, and be cultivated into a system of means to a single end? May it not be the fact that mankind, who after all are made up of single human beings, obtain a greater sense of happiness when each pursues his own, under the rules and conditions required by the good of the rest, than when each makes the good of the rest his only object, and allows himself no personal pleasures not indispensable to the pres- ervation of his faculties? . . . There is a standard of altruism to which all should be required to come up, and a degree beyond it which is not obligatory, but meritorious. . . . So long as they are in no way compelled to this conduct by any external pressure, there cannot be too much of it; but a necessary condition is its spon- taneity. . . . As a rule of conduct, to be enforced by moral sanctions, we think no more should be attempted than to prevent people from doing harm to others, or omitting to do such good as they have undertaken. (337–39)

In all these passages, from both essays on Comte, the liberal and individualist Mill speaks clearly. The passages are a plain indictment of Comte's political science. Nevertheless, though he found "capital errors" in the *Cours de Philosophie Positive*, Mill's overall view was that it contained "an essentially sound view of philosophy." And though he deemed the later works (especially the *Système de Politique Positive*) to be "in their general charac- ter . . . false and misleading," he found in them "a crowd of valuable thoughts, and suggestions of thoughts in detail" (265). "There are many remarks and precepts . . . which, as no less pertinent to our conception of morality than to his, we fully accept" (339–40). In striking contrast to the critical remarks just quoted at length and in the very same paragraph as the last of these quotations, we find Mill saying that it was as much a part of his own scheme as of Comte's

that the direct cultivation of altruism, and the subordination of egoism to it, so far beyond the point of absolute moral duty, should be one of the chief aims of education, both individual and collective. We even recognize the value, for this end, of ascetic discipline, in the original Greek sense of the word. . . . We do not doubt that children and young persons will one day be again systematically disciplined in self-mortification; that they will be taught, as in antiquity, to control their appetites, to brave dangers, and submit voluntarily to pain, a simple exercise in education. Something has been lost as well as gained by no longer giving to every citizen the training necessary for a soldier. (339)

It is difficult to see how such an idea logically falls under the general moral rule that society attempt no more than "to prevent people from doing harm to others." It is also difficult to reconcile with this moral rule Mill's approval of a Comte-like clerisy, a cultural directorate of society, and of Comte's notion of a public "Religion of Humanity," despite his liberal dilution of both concepts. The dialectical combination of opposites, as a method of philosophizing, requires more than the sequential assertion of opposed concepts. It requires that one demonstrate the existence of a fundamental metaphysical harmony beneath an apparent tension. But has Mill anywhere provided such a demonstration?

Mill's failure to resolve, in a coherent and cogent fashion, the dialectical tension of force and freedom is stressed by Himmelfarb in the commentary referred to earlier. Citing a passage from a revised version of his *Autobiography*, which Mill published in the late 1850s when he was at work on his essay *On Liberty*, Himmelfarb remarks that Mill

> was trying to straddle two positions that were further apart than he cared to admit, to have the best of two worlds that were, if not mutually exclusive, at least in important respects antithetical. There is something almost pathetic in his retrospective attempt to super-impose the principle of *On Liberty*—"unchecked liberty of thought, perfect freedom of individual action in things not hurtful to others" (The wording is almost identical with that of *On Liberty*)—upon the Comtean vision of an organic society so firmly based upon reason, morality, and a "general unanimity of sentiment" as to preclude any further change.[96]

96. *On Liberty and Liberalism*, 53. The passage cited by Himmelfarb reads: I looked forward, through the present age of loud disputes but generally weak convictions, to a future which will unite the best qualities of the critical with the best of the organic periods; unchecked liberty of thought, perfect freedom of individual action in things not hurtful to others; but along with this, firm convictions as to right and wrong, useful and pernicious, deeply engraven on the feelings by early education and general unanimity of sentiment, and so well grounded in reason and in the real exigencies of life, that they shall not, like all former and present creeds, religious, ethical and political, require to be periodically thrown off and replaced by others.

She calls the passage an "unconvincing synthesis of the critical and the organic."[97]

Several other students of Mill have also pointed to the ambivalence of Mill's thought. Maurice Cowling's judgment is severe. He accuses Mill of "moral totalitarianism" because of his hope for an ultimate moral consensus embodied in a highly integrated social order, a consensus that would bring an end to the free competition of ideas. Even the essay *On Liberty* Cowling interprets as a document that is much less liberal in import than the reading given us by Himmelfarb. Its end, according to Cowling, is "not of diversity of opinion pure and simple, but of diversity of opinion within the limits of a rationally homogeneous, agreed, social consensus about the method of judging and the right end to be approached." He argues that "there is beyond the libertarian character of the means an assumption of a fundamental homogeneity of all rational judgment."[98] Instead of the dialectical play of force eventuating in democratic freedom (as in Marx), a dialectic of freedom ultimately gives way to a static order of enforced agreement—an ideological orthodoxy presided over by Mill's established clerisy. Again we find a sharp tension between opposed conceptions of force and freedom.

Graeme Duncan, though he calls Cowling's critique of Mill a "peevish and one-sided assault," agrees with Cowling that Mill's ideal of an elite-managed moral orthodoxy was "a significant strand in Mill's thought."[99] And he thinks that "certain of Mill's comments and assumptions" support Cowling's interpretation.[100] Duncan points out that even in *On Liberty* Mill speaks of increased agreement resulting from the improvement of mankind, "a gradual narrowing of the bounds of diversity of opinion." And he notes that Mill thought liberty of discussion valuable only "until mankind are much more capable than at present of recognizing all sides of the truth," far distant though that day might be.[101] Yet he nevertheless believes that Mill's qualifications and

97. Ibid.

98. Maurice Cowling, *Mill and Liberalism* (Cambridge: Cambridge Univ. Press, 1963), 26, 44, cited in Duncan, *Marx and Mill*, 277, and fn. 58 in chapter 8.

99. Duncan, *Marx and Mill*, 278.

100. Ibid., 277.

101. Ibid., 278, citing *On Liberty* (London, 1960), 103, 114.

modifications of the Comtean doctrine on unity and consensus put Mill on the side of democratic freedom rather than of aristocratic force in his conception of the historical culmination of social order. He writes,

> Mill's image of the homogeneous community . . . was vague and not at all a matter of immediate concern for him. If it came into being at all it would be as a result of a lengthy and peaceful historical process, and not at the instigation of moral tyrants or philosopher kings. . . . he was optimistic about human improvement, and his concern with social cohesion and with rational agreement between free men, and his belief that good ends and enlightened men and groups would harmonize in the end, blur simple contrasts between his social vision and that of Marx.[102]

In Duncan's interpretation of the Millian utopia, the authority of the clerisy seems to have given way to broad rational agreement as the basis of social harmony.

While Cowling understood Mill's theory to proceed through liberty to restrictive (and therefore coercive) organicism, Duncan treats Mill's processual theory as a mixture of force and freedom eventuating in the free democratic association pictured in the last quotation. His analysis emphasizes the polarity of Mill's fear of the common man in the present and hope for his future development. "He did not regard the intellectual and moral condition of the masses as fixed," writes Duncan.

> They were not passive, inert stuff, to be manipulated forever by elites, no matter how moral. . . . But as their development presupposed both restraint, against their destructive desires and fantasies, and participation in managing their social destiny, a vital tension built up in Mill's thought. His own resolution of the problem was to insist that the threat which they posed to liberty, culture and government in the public interest was in "the present stage of things," and that substantial changes would and must occur.[103]

During the period of developmental change, power could not be vested solely, or even dominantly, in the many. Representative government, ad interim, could not mean full democracy, if the

102. Duncan, *Marx and Mill*, 278.
103. Ibid., 234.

necessary progress in moral and intellectual development were to occur. The common man had to be prepared for his eventual entry into complete political and cultural control of his destiny. And in Duncan's reading, the elite responsible for this preparation was to be the Victorian middle class. The result would inevitably be class rule based on class interests, however optimistic Mill might be about middle-class virtues. "The question to be faced . . . is the ambiguous and even hostile relationship between the political virtue defined and discussed by Mill, and the actual or likely class interests of those whom he wished to see in authority. That Mill himself was uneasily aware of the conflict does not remove it."[104]

Duncan finds a philosophical defect in Mill's doctrine of classless elites and in Mill's own awareness of the problem, graphically exemplified in his theory of plural voting. The theory required that additional votes be awarded to persons of intellectual superiority, "but because of the weakness of the prevailing educational system, another and temporary ground of differentiation was required."[105] The substitute test of intellectual merit Mill called "superior function"—"which meant that employers, manufacturers, merchants, bankers, and suchlike would have voting privileges."[106] Also, since higher education was available to the rich and not to the poor, "what from one angle seemed a protection of superior merit was from another a defence of property."[107] Mill himself recognized the difficulty inherent in his schema: the political privilege assigned to education, "right in itself, is further and strongly recommended by its preserving the educated from the class legislation of the uneducated, but it must stop short of enabling them to practice class legislation on their own account."[108] Duncan calls this statement "a fatal concession to Marx." One could also view it as a dim recognition by Mill that his political theory was ensnared in the force–freedom paradox.

We have focused on the tension, ambivalence, and ambiguities of Mill's theory of freedom. When analyzed by commentators

104. Ibid., 280.
105. Ibid., 281.
106. Ibid.
107. Ibid.
108. From *Representative Government*, cited in Duncan, *Marx and Mill*, 281.

from a variety of ideological standpoints, as we have seen, the complexities of Mill's thought are reduced to a variety of emphases. We discover that there is not only the "other" Mill but *many* "other" Mills. For Himmelfarb the problem becomes an unresolved contradiction between libertarianism and authoritarian organicism—an incomplete paradox that leaves Mill perched uncomfortably on both of Descartes's metaphysical poles. Cowling presents us with an inverted paradox—through freedom to the endless coercion of "moral totalitarianism." Duncan, by contrast, finds the paradox in its normal form but mitigated by Mill's liberal sensibilities and personal distress at the force (as class rule) implicit in the preeminent role he assigned to middle-class virtue.

A look at Mill's philosophy of social science may help us to understand the philosophical ground of the tension between force and freedom in Mill's work. This Mill set down systematically in part 6 of his *System of Logic*, which he entitled *On the Logic of the Moral Sciences*. The statement of his intention in the first chapter of the book leads one to suppose that Mill was a thoroughgoing mechanist. The physics of his time was mechanistic, and it was Mill's judgment that human reality was, in basis, no different from that of the physical world. Social inquiry, à la physics, is nomological, a search for laws—the "laws of our rational faculty," and "laws of mind." In his opening sentence Mill tells us that "the backward state of the Moral Sciences can only be remedied by applying to them the methods of Physical Science, duly extended and generalized."[109] The laws of mind are simply a complex case of the same order of phenomena that we designate as physical reality and are to be comprehended by a variation of the same scientific method we employ to understand physical laws. "In scientific investigation, as in all other works of human skill, the way of obtaining the end is seen as it were instinctively by superior minds in some comparatively simple case, and is then, by judicious generalization, adapted to the variety of complex cases" (833). Truth is of one piece.

109. In *Collected Works*, vol. 8, J. M. Robson, ed. (Toronto: Univ. of Toronto Press, 1974), 833. Parenthetical page references below are to this edition.

Substantive knowledge, whether of physics or of human reality, proceeds from empirical investigation. "The laws of our rational faculty, like those of every other natural agency, are only learnt by seeing the agent at work" (833). But the methods of inductive inquiry, to be adequate, must be adapted to the specific character of the phenomena at hand. Thus arises the important role of the philosopher of science or methodologist. And it is in this role, not in that of the substantive inquirer, that Mill casts himself in the *Logic*.

In chapter 2 Mill attempts to remove objections to the basic assumption of his endeavor—that "the actions of human beings, like all other natural events, [are] subject to invariable laws" (835). For if this is not accomplished, it "would be fatal to the attempt to treat human conduct as a subject of science" (835). The chapter is entitled "Of Liberty and Necessity." And at the outset Mill declares himself on the necessitarian side of the argument about free will "which, from at least as far back as the time of Pelagius, has divided both the philosophical and the religious world." "The affirmative opinion is commonly called the doctrine of necessity, as asserting human volitions and actions to be necessary and inevitable. The negative maintains that the will is not determined, like other phenomena, by antecedents, but determines itself. . . . I have already made it sufficiently apparent that the former of these opinions is that which I consider the true one"(836).

Mill appears in this passage to have opted, à la Hobbes, for a materialist and mechanist reduction of Descartes's dichotomy, of which one pole was the free and autonomous will. But in the next several paragraphs we find that he was not a reductionist at all but a Cartesian dualist, for he takes great care to distinguish his own version of the necessitarian doctrine from that of the fatalist.

A fatalist believes . . . not only that whatever is about to happen, will be the infallible result of the causes which produce it (which is the true necessitarian doctrine), but moreover that there is no use in struggling against it; that it will happen however we may strive to prevent it. . . . [He believes] that his nature is such, or that his education and circumstances have so moulded his character, that nothing can now prevent him from feeling and acting in a particular way, or at least that no effort of his own can hinder it. . . . His

character is formed *for* him, and not *by* him; therefore his wishing
that it had been formed differently is of no use; he has no power to
alter it. (840)

Mill terms this view "a grand error." He insists, as did Descartes,
that a person has "to a certain extent, a power to alter his character." Mill goes on to say, "His character is formed by his circumstances (including among these his particular organization);
but his own desire to mould it in a particular way, is one of
those circumstances, and by no means one of the least influential. . . . We are exactly as capable of making our own character, *if
we will* as others are of making it for us" (840).

Two paragraphs later Mill tells us that "we shall find that this
feeling, of our being able to modify our own character *if we wish*, is
itself the feeling of moral freedom which we are conscious of." "A
person feels morally free who feels that his habits or his tempta-
tions are not his masters, but he theirs: who even in yielding to
them knows that he could resist; that were he desirous of altogether throwing them off, there would not be required for that
purpose a stronger desire than he knows himself to be capable of
feeling" (841). Mill's thought here seems very close to that of
Descartes writing in the *Discourse on Method* that his freedom was
secure if he learned to "conquer [himself] rather than fortune,
and to alter [his] desires rather than change the order of the
world."[110]

But what motivates us to use our will to form our character one
way rather than another? Descartes, we recall, makes an accurate
judgment of intrinsic possibilities the criterion of a good or well-
ordered (and therefore, truly free) will. And it is clear that the
range of possibilities, that is, the order of value, is given for
Descartes by body, by the passions or appetites. Thus free will
when it judges accurately becomes the engineer who works out a
logical structure of realizable desire from the chaos *initially* given
by the passions. Free will does not extend to the fashioning of goal
values but only to our instrumental behavior. Thus a paradox
appears; in the exercise of our freedom of will, we fit ourselves
into a determinate mechanical order. In the end, Descartes can

---

110. *Discourse*, in Lafleur, ed., *Discourse and Meditations*, 20.

admonish us to treasure our thoughts as the only things that are truly ours. Unlike the lower animals, we are free to recognize the order of necessity. But if our rational thoughts simply mirror the necessity of the world, it is body and its determinate motions that are ultimately real. Only if our thoughts, by legislating for us the structure of reality, *create* the world are we free in a genuine— and, indeed radical—sense. For then body disappears altogether into sovereign will. As we know, Descartes himself was never able to judge which was the truth of the matter. What about Mill?

Mill does not move from the idea of free will as self-mastery to either of the possible Cartesian poles—freedom as the recognition of physical necessity or freedom as solipsistic creation of the world. In the *Logic of the Moral Sciences* he speaks rather of fulfillment of freedom in the development of virtue.

> It is of course necessary, to render our consciousness of freedom complete, that we have succeeded in making our character all we have hitherto attempted to make it; for if we have wished and not attained, we have, to that extent, not power over our own character, we are not free. Or at least, we must feel that our wish, if not strong enough to alter our character, is strong enough to conquer our character when the two are brought into conflict in any particular case of conduct. And hence it is said with truth, that none but a person of confirmed virtue is completely free. (841)

But what is Millian virtue? An avowed religious skeptic, Mill gave no cognitive value to the traditional Judeo–Christian moral code. Nor did he acknowledge the authority of a natural moral law. In an essay on "Nature," written between 1850 and 1858, he expressly repudiated this concept.[111]

> From the general use of the expression "natural justice," it must be presumed that justice is a virtue generally thought to be directly implanted by nature. I believe, however, that the sentiment of justice is entirely of artificial origin; the idea of natural justice not preceding but following that of conventional justice.
>
> . . . the duty of man is the same in respect of his own nature as in respect to the nature of all other things, namely not to follow but to amend it. (397)

111. This essay was published posthumously as one of three essays on religion in a volume so titled by Mill's stepdaughter, Helen Taylor, in 1874. Parenthetical references here are from that volume as it appears in Mill's *Collected Works*, vol. 10.

A few paragraphs further on Mill adds that "conformity to nature, has no connection with right and wrong" (400). Precisely and meaningfully used, "nature" signifies either "the entire system of things, with the aggregate of all their propensities, or . . . things as they would be, apart from human intervention" (401). Nature is properly only "a collective name for all facts, actual and possible" (374).

Mill closes his essay on "Nature" with the statement that the "duty of man is to cooperate with the beneficent powers, not by imitating but by perpetually striving to amend the course of nature—and bringing that part of it over which we can exercise control, more nearly into conformity with a high standard of justice and goodness" (402). In this essay, and in another one on "Theism" written between 1868 and 1870, Mill makes it clear that he is a skeptic but admits the *possibility* of the existence of a "Principle of Good" that

> *cannot* at once and altogether subdue the power of evil, either physical or moral; could not place mankind in a world free from the necessity of an incessant struggle with the maleficent powers, or make them always victorious in that struggle, but could and did make them capable of carrying on the fight with vigour and with progressively increasing success. Of all the religious explanations of the order of nature, this alone is neither contradictory to itself, nor to the facts for which it attempts to account. (389)

But if "a high standard of justice or goodness" is not revealed in the order of nature, *where is it revealed?* Just *how* does one go about specifying moral principles for the "amendment" of nature? Nowhere in his writings does Mill give us a clear answer to this question. We know that he rejected out of hand the Benthamite principle of pleasure maximization and Bentham's "felicific calculus" with its purely quantitative standard.[112] In his essay on Bentham, Mill writes that "man is never recognized [by Bentham] as a being capable of pursuing spiritual perfection as an end; of desiring, for its own sake, the conformity of his own character to his standard of excellence, without hope of good or fear of evil from other sources than his own inward consciousness. Even in

112. See the essay on Bentham, *Collected Works*, vol. 10, 77ff.

the more limited form of Conscience, the great fact in human nature escapes him."[113] But if for Mill "conscience" is a "great fact in human nature," he never explained what principles a conscientious man will follow. The Mill who loves freedom and who stresses the freedom of the will to conquer and amend nature presumably must leave the definition of a "conscientious act" up to each individual—as a part of the realm of his autonomy. Self-determination of the standard of goodness must be part of such a concept. But how, then, can the question of value be invested in a clerisy? If it *is* so invested, must it not be arbitrary myth? For Mill has surely given us no cognitive standard of moral truth. Mill tells us in the *Logic of the Moral Sciences*:

> The application of so improper a term as Necessity to the doctrine of cause and effect in the matter of human character, seems to me one of the most signal instances in philosophy of the abuse of terms, and its practical consequences one of the most striking examples of the power of language over our associations. . . . The free will doctrine, by keeping in view precisely that portion of the truth which the word Necessity puts out of sight, namely the power of the mind to co-operate in the formation of its own character, has given to its adherents a practical feeling much nearer to the truth than has generally (I believe) existed in the minds of necessitarians. The latter may have had a stronger sense of the importance of what human beings can do to shape the characters of one another; but the free-will doctrine has, I believe, fostered in its supporters a much stronger spirit of self-culture.[114]

This passage, and the ones on which I have just commented, are perfectly consonant with the self-development doctrines of *On Liberty*. But they surely contradict the opening paragraph of the chapter in which they occur—a paragraph in which, as I have noted, Mill ranges himself with the necessitarians *against* the voluntarists. By the end of his chapter, "Of Liberty and Necessity," Mill's definitional effort has produced, in the plainest terms, the central dilemma of Cartesian dualism. It is impossible, with logical consistency, to assert the validity of both concepts at once. Mill's strange dialectic is a vehicle by which his thought

113. Ibid., 95.
114. *Logic of the Moral Sciences*, in *Collected Works*, vol. 8, 841–42.

wanders back and forth between the poles of force and freedom, perpetually unable to assert any sort of coherent relationship between them. Mill does not ultimately resolve the puzzle of Cartesian dualism. He remains to the end enthralled by it.

Summary and Political Patterns

The moral freedom sought by the philosophers discussed in this chapter is a far cry from the *haut bourgeois* freedom-as-propertarianism of Hobbes and Locke. It is also very different from the *petit bourgeois* egalitarianism and fraternalism of Rousseau, though it is framed in the language of moral regeneration borrowed from him. Freedom in this chapter is the longed-for goal of conscientious, gradualist liberalism, stated in concepts of human fulfillment (Kant, Mill, and one version of Hegel). It is also ambivalently (and here reminiscently of Rousseau) the voice of revolutionary liberalism, perverted ultimately to fascism, waving bloody banners of nationalistic moral crusade (another version of Hegel). Finally, it is the voice of proletarian anger, outraged at the ineffectiveness of liberal conscience and at the hypocrisy of bourgeois revolution in its Janus form (Marx). In each case, freedom is a prophecy and an image of a historically evolved "New Man." It is a freedom that requires a special kind of moral regeneration—the creation by historical process of a noble free spirit to direct the harmonies of free body.

In none of these several forms is the goal of moral freedom achieved. In the work of some of its liberal articulators the ideal of freedom remains incoherent (Kant, Mill). In its fascist, nationalistic form and as orthodox Marxist communism, it sacrifices freedom to force (Hegel, Marx).

Kant and the United Nations

Immanuel Kant's vision of a world federation of republican states captured the imagination of young Germans such as Friedrich Schiller, who in his *Ode to Joy* contemplated the coming of a universal political brotherhood of man. Schiller in turn inspired the apocalyptic chords of Beethoven's choral movement in his last symphony.[115] Beginning at the turn of the next century with the World Peace movement and World Court and continuing with the construction of the League of Nations and the United Nations, liberal democratic statesmen sought to turn Kant's dream into a working moral and political system.

Hans Morgenthau has called the period of American foreign policy that begins with the administration of William McKinley and extends through that of Franklin D. Roosevelt "Utopian." By Utopian he means a period in which the president substituted abstract moral principles for strategic conceptions of national interest in the formulation of U.S. foreign policies. Morgenthau finds the spirit of utopianism epitomized especially in Woodrow Wilson's Fourteen Points and in his conception of the structure and working of the League of Nations as well as in Franklin Roosevelt's and Cordell Hull's hope for the United Nations. Writers like Walter Lippmann and the members of the so-called realist school of foreign policy—such as George Kennan, Kenneth W. Thompson, and Charles Burton Marshall—agree with him.[116]

Of Wilson, Morgenthau writes that his thought "not only disregards the national interest, but is explicitly opposed to it on moral grounds," and he cites Wilson's Mobile speech of October 27, 1913, as evidence: "It is a very perilous thing to determine the foreign policy of a nation in the terms of material interest. It not only is unfair to those with whom you are dealing, but it is degrading as regards your own actions. . . . We dare not turn

115. Carl J. Friedrich, *Inevitable Peace* (Cambridge, Mass.: Harvard Univ. Press, 1948).

116. Hans J. Morgenthau, *American Foreign Policy: A Critical Examination* (London: Methuen, 1951), 23ff; George Kennan, *American Diplomacy 1900–1950* (New York: Mentor Books, by arrangement with Univ. of Chicago Press, 1951); Hans J. Morgenthau, ed., *Peace, Security and the United Nations* (Chicago: Univ. of Chicago Press, 1946); William G. Carleton, *The Revolution in American Foreign Policy* (New York: Random House, 1957); Kenneth W. Thompson, *Morality and Foreign Policy* (Baton Rouge and London: Louisiana State Univ. Press, 1980); Kenneth W. Thompson, *Ethics, Functionalism, and Power in International Politics: The Crisis in Values* (Baton Rouge & London: Louisiana State Univ. Press, 1979). See also Charles W. Hendel, *The Philosophy of Kant and Our Modern World* (New York: Liberal Arts Press, 1957).

from the principle that morality and not expediency is the thing that must guide us, and that we will never condone iniquity because it is most convenient to do so."[117] One hears echoed in Wilson's words the contrast that Kant, in *Perpetual Peace*, draws between the "moral politician," who seeks peace "as an ethical problem" and the "political moralist," a strategist for whom the "first principle . . . pertaining to civil and international law . . . is merely a problem of technique." The political maxims of the "moral politician" are not derived "from the welfare or happiness which a single state expects from obedience to them . . . but rather from the pure concept of the duty of right, from the *ought* whose principle is given a priori by pure reason, regardless of what the physical consequences may be." The latter, the strategist, glosses over "principles of politics which are opposed to the right with the pretext that human nature is not capable of the good as reason prescribes it."[118] À la Kant, Wilson wants us to behave like noumenal people.

In the Fourteen Points that Wilson recommended to Congress as the basis for the peace settlement of 1919, the substance of two of the preliminary articles (2 and 3) that Kant laid down in his model treaty for perpetual peace appear prominently. The intention of its second definitive article and second appendix also appear. Point 4 calls for the "reduction of national armaments to the lowest point consistent with domestic safety." Points 6, 7, 9, 10, 11, 12, and 13 all demand national independence and political self-determination for a dozen liberated peoples; and point 1 requires "open covenants of peace openly arrived at, with no secret international agreements in the future." Culminating the list is point 14, which calls for the establishment of "a general association of nations, . . . for the purpose of affording mutual guarantees of political independence and territorial integrity to great and small states alike."

If the peace were written in this fashion, World War I, Wilson thought, might indeed have been a war to end wars and one to make the world truly safe for democracy, because democracy (Kant's republicanism) would make the world safe. Such a culmi-

117. Cited in Morgenthau, *American Foreign Policy*, 23–24.
118. *Perpetual Peace*, in *Kant on History*, 121, 124–25, 127.

nation would also have justified the spirit of total struggle with which the war was waged. Paraphrasing Wilson's reflection on the matter, George Kennan writes:

> Our cause is holy; . . . violence must know no limitations short of unconditional surrender . . . A democracy is peace loving. . . . [But] when it has once been provoked to the point where it must grasp the sword . . . it fights for the very reason that it was forced to go to war. . . . It fights to punish the power that was rash enough and hostile enough to provoke it . . . Such a war must be carried to the bitter end. . . . [Also there would this time] be "an organized peace," [secured by] a League of Nations which would mobilize the conscience and power of mankind against aggression. Autocratic government would be done away with. Peoples would themselves choose the sovereignty under which they wish to reside. . . . The peace would be just and secure.[119]

In Hans Saner's paraphrase of Kant's thought we have a parallel: "Unity comes about by lawful struggle. It presupposes a will to the right and a will to freedom, not a need for peace and quiet."[120] (Albeit Kant was ambivalent on this point. He had written in *Perpetual Peace* that "the solution of the problem of political wisdom . . . remembering discretion, . . . does not precipitately hasten to do so by force; rather, it continuously approaches it under the conditions offered by favorable circumstances.)[121]

Kennan and the realist school of foreign policy criticize Wilson for seeing the war, which he was so reluctant to enter, as a total, all-out holy war and for attempting, once and for all, to end power politics rather than to reestablish a working balance of power, according to traditional formulas. The breakup of the Austro-Hungarian Empire into self-determined and national states and the separation of Russia from France by ideological revolution destroyed the possibility of effective counterweights to German power. "There was nothing effective to take [the balance of power's] place." And Germany, the defeated power, "smarting from the sting of defeat and plunged into profound social unrest

119. Kennan, *American Diplomacy*, 66.
120. Saner, *Kant's Political Thought*, 311.
121. *Perpetual Peace*, in *Kant on History*, 125.

by the breakup of her traditional institutions, was left nevertheless as the only great united state in Central Europe."[122]

The European equilibrium never was reestablished during the interwar years. America retreated to its traditional isolationism, and the League of Nations failed to "mobilize the conscience and power of mankind against aggression." And so Nazi–Fascist aggression came on and with it the Second World War. With a more astute feeling than Wilson had for the magnitudes of international power, Franklin Roosevelt saw early on the need to shore up Britain with American strength and was able to establish the Lend–Lease policy. But when America finally entered the war, the spirit of an apocalyptic holy war once again took over, and once more it was supposed that a world federation—this time the United Nations—could solve the problem of mobilizing world opinion for peace. Both Roosevelt and his secretary of state, Cordell Hull, put great reliance on the United Nations to solve the problems of the peace. As Hans Morgenthau has put the matter: "For the United States the new world organization in the form of the United Nations was a substitute for power politics; it was supposed to do away with the balance of power, spheres of influence, alliances, the very policies seeking national advantage and aggrandizement. In one word, the United Nations was an end in itself, the ultimate end of American foreign policy."[123]

This time the utopian spirit, though modified in Allied policy by the shrewd political sense of Winston Churchill and by other factors, threatened for a while to allow the unlimited spread of influence and power by a dynamic Russian Communist regime. However, the first Russian veto in the Security Council produced widespread disillusionment, and a realistic policy of "containment" was shortly announced by the new president in the form of the Truman Doctrine in March 1947. The cold war replaced the age of utopian internationalism.

Kant saw the process of evolving a world federation of republics that might produce perpetual peace as a more gradual process than either Wilson or Roosevelt and Hull envisaged. But Wilson's attempted substitution of the dictates of noumenal con-

122. Kennan, *American Diplomacy*, 69.
123. Morgenthau, *American Foreign Policy*, 100.

science for strategic calculation was what Kant had hoped for in the motivation of statesmen. The substitution, however, did not lead "directly to the end" (that is, toward peace), as Kant had declared.[124] Rather, it appeared as naiveté and contributed instead to an unworkable peace in 1919 and, indirectly, to the renewal of general war in 1939.

Kant's belief that struggle, by enlightening interest, might through the "mechanism of nature" bring widespread authority to the republican (or liberal democratic) ideal and to the idea of a world republican federation also proved illusory. We may, indeed, be motivated like a "race of devils," as Kant put it, but the devils have not had the sense to establish justice, as Kant had predicted they would in *Perpetual Peace*. Instead, totalitarian governments have appeared, both fascist and communist, of a severity far greater than Frederick II's barracks monarchy along with a proliferation of other kinds of dictatorial regimes, especially in the Third World. American policy, instead of encouraging the growth of liberal democracies the world around, has given support to reactionary, traditional dictatorships and to military juntas in an effort to offset the spread of Russian and Chinese Communist power. From moralism our political leaders have frequently descended to open cynicism in the conduct of foreign policy. Henry Kissinger's approach was frankly one of realpolitik. And Jimmy Carter's blundering return to ineffective moralism has been followed by power-political strategies in Ronald Reagan's administration, which thunders against violations of human rights in the USSR while excusing them in the traditional dictatorships among our allies.

I cannot assert, despite all this, that Kantian internationalism has been entirely without good fruit. The United Nations provides a useful forum for international negotiation. And since the publication of the Universal Declaration of Human Rights, there is no question that world opinion has become sensitized to violations of human rights, even though frequently (if not always) no adequate remedy is at hand. Witness the small successes of Amnesty International, for example, which are achieved almost entirely through publicity of governmental wrongdoing. Never-

124. *Perpetual Peace*, in *Kant on History*, 125.

theless, the Kantian approach to freedom and peace has proven at best ambivalent in its working out and at worst absolutely utopian and counterproductive in its application. Kenneth W. Thompson sums the matter well when he writes: "The search for norms and values that can provide practical standards for evaluating American foreign policy, or any nation's foreign policy, is primarily a quest for viable and coherent guides to action. Those who seek moral answers must find their way through the twisted wreckage of a multitude of earlier endeavors that have failed from an excess of either cynicism or too lofty idealism."[125]

Hegelianism—Right and Center

Divergent tendencies within the Hegelian school of thought were already noticeable in the 1820s, and during the following decade they "became more obvious and more extreme."[126] H. Stuart Hughes claims that after the middle of the nineteenth century this counted for little in terms of philosophical development; however, from that point on Hegel "remained little but a memory. Only through his Marxist heirs did he survive as a living force."[127]

It may be true that the conservative Hegelianism of writers such as Bernard Bosanquet has never been a "living force," but surely, at least for a brief period, the Hegelianism of Giovanni Gentile had significance as a vehicle for expressing the official doctrine of Fascist Italy. And there are few who would question the importance of a very different political ideology—welfare liberalism—that roots in the thought of such Hegelian thinkers as Thomas Hill Green and in the much more attenuated Idealist concepts from which John Dewey's pragmatism developed.

Giovanni Gentile, a leader among the intelligentsia of pre-Fascist Italy and a neo-Hegelian, served as minister of education in Mussolini's government. Beside Mussolini himself, who borrowed eclectically in his ideological formulations from many sources, Gentile was the chief theoretician of Fascist Italy. Hegel's

---

125. *Morality and Foreign Policy*, 175.

126. John E. Toews, *Hegelianism: The Path toward Dialectical Humanism, 1805–1841* (Cambridge: Cambridge Univ. Press, 1980), 203.

127. H. Stuart Hughes, *Consciousness and Society: The Reconstruction of European Social Thought, 1890–1930* (New York: Vintage Books, 1958), 185.

insistence on identifying living philosophy with that which is actualized in historical life, by contrast with mere speculation, is mirrored in such expressions of Gentile as this: "Fascism is hostile to all Utopian systems which are destined never to face the test of reality. It is hostile to all science and all philosophy which remain matters of mere fancy or intelligence."[128] The statement that Fascism is "a living thought, a principle of universal character daily reflecting its inner fertility and significance" also has a Hegelian ring. So does the statement that "both Fascism and nationalism regard the State as the foundation of all rights and the source of all values in the individuals composing it." Gentile also mentions "the Corporations of Syndicates," which reminds us of Hegel's "Estates," and says that they "are a device through which the Fascist state goes looking for the individual in order to create itself through the individual's will. But the individual it seeks is not the abstract political individual whom the old Liberalism took for granted. He is . . . the individual who exists as a specialized productive force." Interesting for the thesis of this book is Gentile's statement that Mussolini "once chose to discuss the theme of 'Force or Consent?', and he concluded that the two terms are inseparable, that the one implies the other and cannot exist apart from the other."[129]

So there are certainly Hegelian-sounding phrases to be found in Gentile's Fascism, whether Hegel himself would have found the political order with which they were associated acceptable or not. Ernst Nolte, however, a careful student of Fascism, treats Gentile's philosophy as window dressing and argues that "in adopting the Hegelian terminology via Gentile . . . Mussolini succeeds in producing a remarkable mystification." The formulas of Gentile "testify little to the specific form of the fascist state, to its relationship to the peculiar reality of the party."[130] And Nolte concludes: "It was not in its theory that the Fascist party exerted

128. Giovanni Gentile, excerpt from *The Philosophical Basis of Fascism*, in Carl Cohen, ed., *Communism, Fascism and Democracy: The Theoretical Foundations*, 2nd ed. (New York: Random House, 1972), 340.

129. Ibid., 343.

130. Ernst Nolte, *Three Faces of Fascism*, Leila Vennewitz, trans. (New York: Holt, Rinehart, and Winston, 1965), 244.

its strongest impact on Mussolini, but in the basic structure of its practice." "The reality of fascist Italy was completely dependent on the will of the Duce and his trend of thought of the moment."[131] Nevertheless, it cannot be without significance that Mussolini found Hegelian language useful to his purposes.[132]

Welfare liberalism, insofar as it can be traced at all to a philosophical system, presents us with still another Hegelian face. Its English beginnings are found in the writings of Thomas Hill Green, a nineteenth-century English don, who "from Kant and Hegel . . . learned . . . a grand scheme which the spiritual heirs of Locke and Hume had failed to discern."[133] Green's philosophy constitutes an argument with the utilitarians, whose point of departure was the assumption that good can be reduced to pleasure and that society arises from the agreement of contracting individuals. Green's starting point was the Idealist assumption "that the various parts of the natural world are related to form a system," a spirit-penetrated system, and that men and women are self-determining moral beings capable of living in a community of shared good, in whose realization all fulfill their best possible selves.

Green was a believer in private property and in the free market economic system of competition and private profit as necessary to human perfection. The capitalist middle class was for him, in fact, Hegel's universal class, but in an ideal order its membership would be societywide. "Reform legislation would transform members of the labouring class into full-fledged capitalists."[134] A central aspect of this reform program involved bringing the educational system under social control. For this was needed "to prevent children from growing up in that kind of ignorance which practically excludes them from a free career in life."[135] To

131. Ibid., 249.

132. For Hegel as a father of totalitarian thinking see also Karl R. Popper, *The Open Society and Its Enemies* (Princeton: Princeton Univ. Press, 1950), part 2.

133. I. M. Greengarten, *Thomas Hill Green and the Development of Liberal-Democratic Thought* (Toronto: Univ. of Toronto Press, 1981). Green's works were reprinted in three volumes in 1973 by AMS Press from a 1911–18 edition published by Longmans, Green and Co., London. His *Prolegomena to Ethics* and *Lectures on the Principles of Political Obligation* form part of volume 2.

134. Greengarten, *Green*, 71, 88–89, 99.

135. Greengarten, *Green*, 95, citing "Liberal Legislation," *Works*, volume 3.

this Green added a stress on the democratization of parliament (with reference to the Reform Act of 1867) not only to defend worker interests but as a moral education as well—learning to take a share in community responsibilities and thereby to grow as a person.[136] In short, it was the state's responsibility through legislation to "maintain the conditions without which a free exercise of the human faculties is impossible." For the state, in Green's eyes, à la Hegel, is "a society of societies, in which all . . . claims . . . are mutually adjusted."[137] In this way, classical liberalism's "night-watchman state" would become the active state of welfare liberalism. The social legislation of the British Liberal governments of 1906 to 1916 was passed in this spirit.[138]

The American welfare state, created under the leadership of Franklin Roosevelt, developed piecemeal and in an experimental manner. It sprang in the first instance from urgent social necessities, apparently without benefit of philosophy. As Harry Girvetz has put it, "Contemporary liberalism . . . is not a fixed or systematically elaborated body of doctrine, nor is it a product of the practical and theoretical labors of one or two or even of several great men. There are no towering [philosophical] figures . . . associated with the standpoint of contemporary liberalism."[139] Nevertheless, the welfare liberal language of freedom as "self-realization" and "actualization," the language of "human development" and of the "realization of potentialities" is Idealist in character. And we know that American intellectuals have been acquainted with Hegelian thought from Emerson through Dewey to the present. It is certainly the case that Dewey's notion of the "truth" of society as something that people make and that grows historically rather than as a static and abstract given shows the

136. Greengarten, *Green*, 95–96.

137. Greengarten, *Green*, 51, 96, citing *Principles of Political Obligation* and "Liberal Legislation."

138. Greengarten, *Green*, 128. Following C. B. Macpherson, Greengarten casts doubt on the compatibility of Green's capitalist assumptions, which imply a self-seeking individualist model of man, and those deriving from Hegelian organicism, which imply a cooperative, socially minded nature. See especially 102–06. See also Shlomo Avineri, *Hegel's Theory of the Modern State* (Cambridge: Cambridge Univ. Press, 1972), 81–98, for a discussion of Hegel's critique of capitalism.

139. Harry Girvetz, *The Evolution of Liberalism* (New York: Collier Books, 1963), 153.

influence of his early reading of Hegel, as do his concepts of "the public" and "The Great Community." We also know that in his semipopular political essays as well as in *The Public and Its Problems* Dewey expressed a critique of the atomistic, individualist features of classical liberal American society in a typically welfare liberal vein.[140]

Much ink has been spilled in arguing the question whether Franklin Roosevelt's deficit spending to fund a variety of emergency welfare measures in the 1930s conquered the Great Depression. But there is no doubt that the vast social welfare programs he launched, from emergency relief and unemployment insurance to social security enacted during the 1930s and expanded in the 1970s, have raised millions of Americans above the poverty line into the competitive ranks of middle-class America. It has also been argued that the expansion of the welfare state since Kennedy's New Frontier has been disastrously costly and has been channeled to the wrong people. And there is strong argument that a large number of hard-core poor have not been helped and may not be reachable by existing welfare measures. Also, regulatory agencies designed to establish federal control in the general interest over the free forces of a competitive economy have been taken over and used for their own purposes by the groups they were supposed to regulate. And much evidence has been brought forward that central economic planning has failed.[141]

A high rate of inflation, an enormous national debt that requires vast sums for its funding, the defection of many leading intellectuals from the welfare liberal ideological camp, the election of Ronald Reagan and his attempt to dismantle many welfare programs, and debate about the future funding of the social security program are all testimony that welfare liberalism has not been an overall success. Indeed, Theodore Lowi has argued that over the years, by giving free rein to the ideology of "Interest Group Liberalism" (an indigenous ideology at least since Madison), the welfare state has seriously damaged the ability of the federal

140. See the essays of John Dewey, *Problems of Men* (New York: Philosophical Library, 1946) and *The Public and Its Problems* (New York: Holt, Rinehart and Winston, 1927).

141. See, for example, Theodore Lowi, *The End of Liberalism*, 2nd ed. (New York: W. W. Norton & Co., 1979).

government to function in an orderly, rational and just fashion.[142] Underlying Lowi's argument lies the assumption that instead of controlling and modifying individualist motivation, welfare liberalism in practice has exacerbated the fragmenting power of individualism and has expanded the ability of individuals to use the political system to achieve purely selfish purposes. In Lowi's view, the power of the national government to serve the public interest has been seriously eroded, if not destroyed.

Hegel would no doubt argue that all this has happened because Americans put the republic into the hands of "civil society," an expression he used to characterize the individualist spirit of commercial life. He would further argue that too much power over public policy has been given to public opinion, which in his view "becomes infected by ignorance . . . and perversity, by . . . mistakes and falsity of judgment," and is therefore to be "despised for its concrete expression."[143] Most important, he would lament the fact that America has neither developed a universal class, a philosophically oriented body of civil servants imbued with the spirit of the common good (the will of Absolute Spirit), nor handed prime authority to such a body. For only such a class of regenerated, unselfish souls, effectively in control of public decisions, can, in Hegel's view, help the average man to see his true interest and to follow it. Only such an elite group can save us from collapsing into subjectivist freedom (in other words, anarchy) and move us instead toward objective freedom. Indeed, Hegel would approve the principles and goals of welfare liberalism, but he would chastise us for adopting only half measures. But how many Americans would opt for the full Hegelian solution to our problems?[144] We have indeed gone half way in a Hegelian direction, but now, in panic at our failure, we are

142. See his four-count indictment of "Interest Group Liberalism" and its works in ibid., 295–98. See also Neil Gilbert, *Capitalism and the Welfare State* (New Haven: Yale Univ. Press, 1983).

143. *Philosophy of Right*, 204–07.

144. Cf. George Armstrong Kelly's essay on "Hegel's America," *Hegel's Retreat from Eleusis*, chapter 7, which presents Hegel's view of the typical American of his time—a person who "finds his being in the most primitive and individualistic rudiments of *buergerliche Gesellschaft*," and of the political-civilizational backwardness of American society (188). Kelly attempts to draw out a constructive message for our times by extrapolating from Hegel's theory of the historical development of the state to the American situation today.

ironically seeking help by reasserting the principles of classical liberalism—the principles of Locke. One might ask, however, whether it was not the failure of these principles that sparked the movement for reform in the first place. Neither direction is valid.

Force and Freedom in Marxist Russia

In Russian political culture force had always played a large role. It was therefore not surprising that the Marxist theme of revolutionary transformation would develop an exaggerated appeal there. In the Stalinist years following the trauma of the Second World War this preoccupation became a fixation of the regime. "During the postwar period," writes Soviet specialist Robert Tucker, "transformism became the reaction of the Stalin regime whenever it was confronted with a genuinely difficult domestic situation that clearly called for remedial measures of some kind. Instead of using the materials at hand and adapting its conduct to the realities present in the situation, it habitually responded with a grandiose project of transformation."[145] Stalin's own ideas "appeared to him as natural necessities governing the development of society" (97).

We come centrally to our concern for human freedom when we observe the effects of the Stalinist transformist mentality in the field of psychology. The spur to doctrinal development here came from the disheartening apathy that Stalin's government confronted when launching its projects for postwar development. The people, it appeared, could not find meaning in the renewed calls for discipline and dogged effort. And a massive propaganda effort to stimulate public spirit by enlisting all the resources of the country's artistic and literary intelligentsia met with failure. In frustration, Stalin sought a key to his dilemma in physiological and psychological science. Perhaps it could be found in the Pavlovian conditioned reflex.

It was Stalin himself who gave impetus to the Pavlovian revival. Academician K. Bykov, in a tribute to the dictator announced:

The initiator of the events that have elevated the teachings of Pavlov

---

145. This section relies heavily on Robert Tucker, *The Soviet Political Mind* (New York: Praeger, 1963), especially chapter 5. Parenthetical page references are to this work.

in our country, the initiator of the creation of the most favorable conditions for the development of Soviet physiology for the benefit of the people is the brilliant architect of the Soviet culture—Joseph Vissarionovich Stalin. We are indebted to Comrade Stalin for the victory of the Pavlovian cause in our country and for the creative upsurge we now observe in the development of this most important field of contemporary natural science. (101)

Pavlov, declared Bykov, had put an end once and for all to the concept of the soul. He had established a material basis for the higher activity of the nervous system and had thereby put an end to "idealistic fables about the supernatural character of our minds" (102). We are reminded of Skinner's attack on human dignity and freedom and of his banishment of that homunculus, "autonomous man."

In the editorial columns of *Pravda*, the work of Pavlov was associated with that of Michurin, whose doctrines of biological determinism underlay Stalin's plans for the transformation of Soviet agriculture. Both these scientists, instead of waiting for nature to bestow her favors, chose instead to wrest these favors from nature, chose "actively to intervene in nature, to remake her" (102). In a joint meeting of the Academy of Science and the Academy of Medical Sciences of the USSR in June 1950, speaker after speaker pointed to Pavlovism as the wave of the future both in physiology and in psychology. Two years later, a Moscow conference attended by four hundred Russian psychologists deplored the slow pace of change in rebuilding their discipline on a Pavlovian basis. Change was difficult because the leading psychologists of the 1920s and 1930s had stressed self-determination in an atmosphere of socialist culture as the way to the ideal of the new Soviet man. Tucker reads this as a "reflection of the quiet resistance to the majority of Russians to the sovietization of their real selves, a resistance that had proved relatively immune to the massive propaganda pressure of the postwar years" (107). The Pavlovian revival was a testimony both to the failure of the optimistic autonomist approach to creation of the new Soviet man and to Stalin's determination to mold the Russian mind thoroughly to his will.

Fortunately for freedom, the ambitious plan of the Pavlovians did not have time to mature. After Stalin's death in March 1953, new directions gradually appeared in Soviet science. A 1954 editorial statement in *Problems of Philosophy* announced that "the subjective—man's psyche—really exists." And it sharply castigated those who would "dogmatically apply to man" the methods Pavlov had created to study the behavior of animals (115–16). In 1955, in a new journal entitled *Problems of Psychology*, Russian academia officially repudiated total environmental determinism.

Despite its decline as official ideology in the exaggerated form of Stalinist transformism, behavior modification remains a preoccupation of the Soviet regime. It is well known that political dissidents are frequently dealt with by banishment to sanitariums for the mentally ill. Coercive devices of all kinds, ranging from the propaganda barrage through psychic harassment to physical torture and forced exile, are freely employed to obtain compliance with the regime's demands. The experience of Hungary in the 1950s, of Czechoslovakia in the 1960s, and of Afghanistan at the dawn of the 1980s shows that the Russians stand ready at every moment to force their neighbors as well as their own citizenry to docile obedience to their will in the name of proletarian freedom. In the Russian case, the technologies spawned by natural science, both physical and psychological, are at the disposal of a regime that learned habits of coercive manipulation from an authoritarian tradition far older than Pavlov and Marx. Marxism merely gave that regime a new purpose for the exercise of coercion—the establishment of freedom.[146]

Millian Experiments in Living

Frightened by the mediocrity and banality of mass culture as it developed around him in Victorian England, John Stuart Mill penned an impassioned plea for free and creative thought and for "experiments in living" in his essay *On Liberty*. In modern liberal culture, of all Mill's political ideas (except perhaps for his schemes for proportional representation) the doctrine of *On Liberty* has probably found the largest interest.

---

146. On the oscillation of traditional Russian political behavior between periods of anarchic freedom and periods of authoritarian repression, see ibid., chapter 4, "The Image of Dual Russia."

Especially in the period since World War II, the liberal West has experienced an incredible erosion of established ways of life and of traditional moral standards. Though how much Mill's ideas have influenced this development is hard to measure. "Freedom to do one's own thing" has become authoritative and has revolutionized old-fashioned ways. Unconventionality and individualism in dress and hairstyle is one of the most widespread and most obvious areas of change. Family relationships have altered drastically. Divorce statistics continue to move upward and in turn the number of single-parent households. Complicated visiting arrangements involving former and present spouses and their progeny have produced in some cases a new kind of extended family, whose relationships are blurred and indistinct. New practices for settling on family names for married persons, from varieties of hyphenation to maintenance of premarital family names, have emerged. The growing number of persons of the opposite or same sex establishing relatively permanent common households has led to a change in American tax law so that married couples with two incomes do not pay a larger joint income tax than unmarried couples living together. House husbands have become a common breed. And communal living by persons of both sexes who share common tastes and interests, both in urban and rural contexts, has increased apace.

In the world of economic function, women are no longer foreclosed from venturing into occupational areas formerly monopolized by men, ranging from those that require heavy manual labor and hard-hat protection to executive positions at the top of major corporations. In many other areas, equal freedom for both sexes continues to spread, and the Equal Rights Amendment is by no means a dead letter.

Unconventionality in pleasure-seeking has led large numbers of people into the world of drugs. Beginning as a New Left device for the so-called expansion of consciousness in the 1960s, drug use has now spread widely in the broad ranks of the established middle classes. A recent article in *Time* gave the number of cocaine users in the United States as between four and five million. Drug counselors say that between 5 and 20 percent of these—between 200,000 and 1,000,000 persons—are profoundly dependent on the drug.[147] The incidence of marijuana use is probably even higher.

Along with widespread and diverse experiments in living (I have named only a few) has gone a deep erosion of the traditional value systems of Western life. The one implies the other. And with this has come, for some, deep-seated anxiety and anomie. (More about anomie in the next chapter.) What the ultimate impact on the stability and direction of modern society of these large changes in life-style might be is not clear. Some may be of use in the development of "man as a progressive being." Others have the potential for badly destabilizing both the psychic structure of the individual and the structures and functions of society. And all this is happening at a time when the incredible freedom-giving powers of modern technology require an intricate division of labor and a sound and stable psychological, moral, and social underpinning.

As we have seen, Mill's belief in experiments in living and in the value of what we today call doing one's own thing had its limits. Oddly enough, as we have also noted, Mill believed that the movement of history was toward ever greater consensus on a growing number of doctrines, though *On Liberty* and our present experience seem to show the opposite. Mill also looked forward to the establishment of a moralizing clerisy—something resembling Hegel's universal class but less distinctly delineated than that idea—to preside over this consensus and to provide a moral cement for his society of the future. Mill never produced a plan for the development or installation of such a clerisy however. And in political action he and his fellow Philosophical Radicals remained a group of individuals.[148] Nor would any free person have had it otherwise. Mill simply lived with his contradictory ideals. And so do we—the ideal of experimental living and the clerical assertions of the moral majority.

All the theories discussed in this chapter have attempted to solve the problem of freedom through various schemes of moral regeneration for the creation of a "New Man." All their authors,

147. *Time*, April 11, 1983, 23–31.
148. Joseph Hamburger, *Intellectuals in Politics: John Stuart Mill and the Philosophical Radicals* (New Haven and London: Yale Univ. Press, 1965), 295.

with the possible exception of Mill, seem to have been prepared to approve the exercise of force, both physical and psychological over long historical periods, to achieve this end. In the West we have followed some of them incoherently and half way. The East has been more thoroughgoing in its discipleship. And we have all failed to achieve the freedom they promised. In our time, at least in the West, a time that has gone "beyond the end of ideology," the old man remains pretty much what he was, except that today he is more of an individualist than ever, conforming to no single type, either "regenerated" or "unregenerated."

Though none of us might wish to go to school to a Millian clerisy or to a Hegelian universal class, many have recognized with unease the problem of increasing moral dissensus in our time and the problems inherent in that fact for the health of society, as the Western world moves ambivalently toward the pole of Cartesian subjectivism. The multiplication of disciplined and irrational religious cults in recent years is a testimony that unhealthy antibodies to an unhealthy situation will appear unless reasonable persons apply their energies to the problem. After a look in the next chapter at the dark face of nihilism, the ultimate fruit of Cartesianism, and in the penultimate chapter at recent efforts to establish new holistic categories of thought, I will in chapter 7 venture my own suggestion for an approach to the problem of the crisis of freedom.

5

Reduction to Will: Nietzsche and Nihilism

In each of the theories we have examined so far, whether materialist or idealist, the world appears as ultimately rational, in a Cartesian sense. Mind and body are joined in a lawful pattern, an order that either remains a permanent possibility (Hobbes, Locke, Rousseau, Kant, Mill), or one that will necessarily result at the end of a historical process (Hegel, Marx). Whether reduced to the mechanical order of materialism or as pregnant Idea alienated into matter so that it may grow and unfold, mind as rational order, and working through necessary processes of law, furnishes the ultimate structure of the world. Will in each case is treated as a subordinate category. For Hobbes it is "the last passion in deliberating," conceivable only in a causal (rational) framework. (But if Strauss is correct, as vainglory it may frustrate the rationalization of matter.) For Rousseau, the irrationality of the particular will is removed by its subsumption under the general will, which is operative only when enlightened by the political engineer, working with materials at hand. Only in the asociality of the solitary walker does individual will have free play. For Kant, a good will cleaves to the rational dictate of the Categorical Imperative. "Wille" and reason are the same. As rational, the world defined by each theorist is also a public world, for mind is universal reason composed of necessary laws.

With Nietzsche we shall explore an entirely different Cartesian possibility—the possibility that derives from reflecting on the idea "that there is nothing that truly pertains to [one] but the free disposition of his will."[1] As we have seen, this can be understood as resignation to determination by the objective order. As such, all the theorists we have discussed conceived it. Freedom and power are achieved by self-conquest or self-mastery within the given public order. On the other hand, it is a Cartesian act of will that must finally guarantee knowledge of the whole. For with the myth of God dissolved by his subterranean argument, Descartes is left with "clear and distinct ideas" as the sole hallmarks of truth. But as Caton points out, Descartes's method adds nothing to the indubitability of mathematical and logical truths. Only an act of will can affirm the validity of the whole body of evidence.[2]

This reflection leads us to the possibility that it is by our own fiat that we create the world in which we live. In his Fourth Meditation Descartes tells us that, subjectively considered, a person's free will is as ample as that of God. "I experience it to be so ample and extended that there are no limits which restrict it."[3] In the pursuit of the objective order of truth and existence, we end up with a subjective truth about reality, a reflection of individual existence. *I* make up the world. Rousseau's *promeneur solitaire* in this fashion created his own world; but it was a purely private and solitary affair. Nietzsche both faced and embraced this way out of the puzzle of Cartesian dualism for the public political order. "Pereat mundus, fiat philosophia, fiat philosophus, fiam!" he cries in the *Genealogy of Morals*. "Though the world perish, let there be philosophy, the philosopher, *me!*"[4] The concept by which he expressed his voluntarist reduction we know as "the will to power."

Apollinian and Dionysian Dualism

In the preface to his first book, *The Birth of Tragedy* (1872) which he dedicated to Richard Wagner, Friedrich Wilhelm Nietzsche

1. Cited in Caton, *Origin of Subjectivity*, 57.

2. Ibid., 125.

3. *Meditations*, in Lafleur, ed., *Discourse and Meditations*, 112, 113.

4. In *Basic Writings of Nietzsche*, Walter Kaufmann, ed. (New York: Random House, Modern Library, 1968), 544. Quotations from this volume are with permission of the publisher, Random House, Inc., copyright© by Random House, Inc., 1968.

(1844–1900) speaks of his conviction that "art represents the highest task and the truly metaphysical activity of this life."[5] This is his way of asserting that man as artist creates the world. As the text opens, we learn that the development of art is bound up with the duality of "Apollinian" and "Dionysian" qualities— Nietzsche's formulation of the body–mind dichotomy. The book is an essay in metaphysics that takes the form of a commentary on the Apollinian and Dionysian aspects of ancient Hellenic art, especially as they are represented in the works of Attic tragedy. At the same time it constitutes a gloss on Arthur Schopenhauer's *Welt als Wille und Vorstellung* (*The World as Will and Representation*).[6]

For Nietzsche Apollinian signified matter that has been formed and shaped by patterns of reason—a world of order, proportion, of law. As I have noted, this is a conception of ultimate reality shared by all the thinkers in earlier chapters. But for Nietzsche, Apollinian meant "the beautiful illusion of the dream worlds," *"mere appearance"* (34). As the principle of individuation it represents the material world of our experience, "the reality in which we live and have our being" (34, 36). But this is nevertheless mere appearance. For Nietzsche, as for Schopenhauer whom he cites at length, "another quite different reality lies beneath it" (34, 36).

Nietzsche compares the Dionysian world to a state of intoxication—a condition exemplified by the Bacchic choruses of the Greeks and the orgiastic medieval dances of St. John and St. Vitus. In both, the individual is lost and reunited to his fellow man and to nature. In Dionysian intoxication "the slave is a free man; now all the rigid, hostile barriers that necessity, caprice, or 'impudent convention' have fixed between man and man are broken" (37). The orgies of the Greeks in particular were redemptive festivals, times of transfiguration (40). But in all other parts of the ancient world, Dionysian signified another kind of intoxication. In Rome and Babylon, for example, the Dionysian orgy unleashed savage instincts. They revealed "that horrible mixture of sensuality and cruelty which has always seemed . . . the real 'witches' brew' " (39).

5. In ibid., 32. Parenthetical page references are to this edition.
6. Leipzig: F. A. Brockhaus, 1859.

Thus considered, Apollinian and Dionysian stand for two kinds of artistic energy that "burst forth from nature herself, *without the mediation of the human artist*" (38). Their ontological interrelationship is not clear at first; but as his exposition unfolds, Nietzsche clarifies it for us. Dionysian comes to stand for active will, the will to create, and thus for life itself. "The satyr chorus," Nietzsche writes, "represents existence more truthfully, really, and completely than the man of culture does who ordinarily considers himself as the only reality" (61). A little later he tells us that "in all productive men it is instinct that is the creative-affirmative force" (88). Further on we learn of "the exuberant fertility of the universal will," and of "infinite primordial joy in existence" (104–05). Quoting Goethe, Nietzsche makes the Dionysian principle into a will "to 'live resolutely' in wholeness and fullness" (113).

The Apollinian principle, by contrast, becomes "the aesthetic, purely contemplative, and passive frame of mind" (55). And, as such, it is illusory. The Apollinian "man of culture" is a liar, a "mendacious caricature" of "the true human being . . . , the bearded satyr jubilating to his god" (61). Socrates—the archetype of Apollinian mind—Nietzsche treats, ironically, as an exception to his rule. For in Socrates "it is instinct that becomes the critic, and consciousness that becomes the creator" (88). But Nietzsche could understand Socrates only as "a monstrosity *per defectum,*" a defect that was to be revealed plainly in his successors. He found himself unable to approve of Socrates's "instinct-disintegrating influence." For in the work of Plato, "the *Apollinian* tendency has withdrawn into the cocoon of logical schematism" (88–91).

Lively reality, for Nietzsche, is thus will, understood as existential action. Mind, as the principle of individuating order contemplating itself in the creations of active will, is derivative. It is the means employed by "insatiable will" to "detain its creatures in life and compel them to live on, by means of an illusion spread over things . . . the Socratic love of knowledge and the delusion of being able thereby to heal the eternal wound of existence" (109). In the measure and constraint that it lays upon the exuberance of will, the Apollinian also appears as the death principle, the cause of decay. But this is also an illusion, for nothing can really dam up and stop the tumbling torrent of willful life.

In its raging flood, which defies all form and limit, Nietzsche's Dionysian will is a tragic reality, because its endless creativity requires endless destruction. Nietzsche speaks at one moment of the "raging desire for existence and joy in existence" of this "primordial being," and at the next of "the struggle, the pain, the destruction of phenomena" that appear to us to be necessary "in view of the excess of countless forms of existence which force and push one another into life" (104). Nietzschean wholeness has "all of nature's cruelty attaching to it" (113). Nietzsche is even ready to describe creative will as "this demon rising from unfathomable depths" (119).

The Apollinian illusionist is an optimist. He denies the tragedy that life inevitably must be. Nietzsche writes of "the cheerfulness of the *theoretical man*." This optimistic spirit

> combats Dionysian wisdom and art, it seeks to dissolve myth, it substitutes for a metaphysical comfort an earthly consonance, in fact a *deus ex machina* of its own, the god of machines and crucibles, . . . ; it believes that it can correct the world by knowledge, guide life by science, and actually confine the individual within a limited sphere of solvable problems, from which he can cheerfully say to life: "I desire you; you are worth knowing." (109)

In the long run, Apollinian optimism contributes to its own undoing and to the destruction of the peaceful and harmonious world enshrined in its vision of goodness and happiness. For such a world is a literal impossibility. It must finally be exposed as the illusion that it is.

The Fragility of the Alexandrian World

To philosophize à la Nietzsche means to prophesy and to criticize. The truth that his philosophy discloses is the torrent of ever-rushing life, an eternal outpouring of sheer power of which philosophy is the herald and spokesman. Philosophy therefore does its proper work when it expresses the lively will of the future and, in so doing, lends the future a temporary form. It must also clear the ground for the future. Hence its role as critic of the outlived forms of the present, which must be swept aside as the chaff and illusion that they are.

The Birth of Tragedy, as philosophy, is largely critical rather than prophetic. It is a critique of science as the dominant yet outworn world view of modern times. The centrality of this theme is muted, almost hidden, in the text itself. But in a new preface to the book, which he composed sixteen years after its original publication, Nietzsche gives it stark emphasis. "What is the significance of all science," he asks, "viewed as a symptom of life? For what—worse yet, *whence*—all science? How now? Is the resolve to be so scientific about everything perhaps a kind of fear of, an escape from, pessimism? A subtle but last resort against *truth*? And, morally speaking, a sort of cowardice and falseness?" (18).

Nineteenth-century scientism, as world view rather than as investigative method, was an optimistic doctrine of progress, which looked ahead to a hedonic utopia in which the technical control of nature, in a context of democratic polity, would produce the final satisfaction of all human desires. Its primary textbook was Part 6 of Descartes's *Discourse on Method*, which optimistically looks forward to the conquest of nature by a race of hedonic pragmatists. To this brief gospel, eighteenth-century rationalism and nineteenth-century utilitarianism had added an entire library of canonical books. Nietzsche's role, as the philosopher of will, was to reveal it all as a tissue of illusion. The ideology of science had to be displayed not as the key to human happiness but as a sign of cultural decline and collapse.

The Achilles' heel of scientific (or perhaps, more appropriately, technocratic) culture was the contradiction Nietzsche presumed between its egalitarian political and social aspirations and the hierarchical organization that he took to be a technical necessity of such a culture. He wrote: "The Alexandrian culture, to be able to exist permanently, requires a slave class, but with its optimistic view of life it denies the necessity of such a class, and consequently, when its beautifully seductive and tranquillizing utterances about the 'dignity of man' and the 'dignity of labor' are no longer effective, it gradually drifts toward a dreadful destruction" (111).

In the order of prophecy, Nietzsche limited himself to a Cassandra warning of doom. Dionysian will, formless but powerful, embodied in the frustrations of technocratic slaves would soon rend the delicate structures built by scientistic utilitarianism. "There is nothing more terrible," wrote Nietzsche, "than a class of barbaric slaves who have learned to regard their existence as an injustice, and now prepare to avenge, not only themselves, but all generations" (111). The elemental forces of constricted life as free will would sweep away the fantastic illusions of utilitarian freedom.

The Last Man and the Overman

Thus Spoke Zarathustra (1883–1885), Nietzsche's favorite work, is prophecy—a prophecy of the overman. In it Nietzsche speaks through the Persian seer and prophet Zoroaster (Zarathustra), for whom the worst sin was to lie. Nietzsche, as Zarathustra, becomes the great truth-teller who proclaims the death of God and the coming of the overman.

> But when Zarathustra was alone he spoke thus to his hearth: "Could it be possible? The old saint in the forest has not yet heard anything of this, that *God is dead!*" . . .
>
> "Behold, I teach you the overman. The overman is the meaning of the earth. Let your call say: the overman *shall be* the meaning of the earth! I beseech you, my brothers, *remain faithful to the earth*, and do not believe those who speak to you of otherworldly hopes."[7]

The time had come to cast off the dead weight of Christian tradition and its notions of good and evil. A dreary hypocrisy, it had stifled the healthy animal spirits of Europe and sapped its will. By focusing attention on the afterlife, it had denied life itself and made men into pygmies, devoid of strength and devoid of creativity. It had produced "the last man." "Let me speak to them of what is most contemptible," writes Nietzsche, "but that is the *last man*" (129). " 'What is love? What is creation? What is longing?

---

7. Friedrich Nietzsche, *Thus Spoke Zarathustra*, in Walter Kaufmann, trans. and ed., *The Portable Nietzsche* (New York: Viking Press, 1968), 124–25. Parenthetical page references are to this edition.

What is a star?' thus asks the last man, and he blinks" (129).

Synoptically, Nietzsche ties together the secular egalitarianism and utilitarianism of his time with the Christian culture from which they had emerged—as a sort of final form or phase of the logic of Christianity. All stand together under Nietzsche's condemnation:

> "We have invented happiness," say the last men, and they blink. They have left the regions where it was hard to live, for one needs warmth. One still loves one's neighbor and rubs against him, for one needs warmth.
>
> One still works, for work is a form of entertainment. But one is careful lest the entertainment be too harrowing. One no longer becomes poor or rich: both require too much exertion. Who still wants to rule? Who obey? Both require too much exertion.
>
> No shepherd and one herd! Everybody wants the same, everybody is the same: whoever feels different goes voluntarily into a madhouse.
>
> . . . One still quarrels, but one is soon reconciled—else it might spoil the digestion.
>
> One has one's little pleasure for the day and one's little pleasure for the night: but one has a regard for health.
>
> "We have invented happiness," say the last men, and they blink. (130)

The dead god was, of course, like all meanings, a human creation. He was the product of a "weariness that wants to reach the ultimate with one leap, . . . a poor ignorant weariness that does not want to want any more." The old god had turned out to be a poor kind of man (143). Getting rid of him would thus be a self-overcoming for man, a going beyond, a new creation.

But who is the overman, the new meaning that is to come? He is "the lightning and a heavy drop from the cloud," "the lightning out of the dark cloud of man" (128,132). He puts aside the commandments of the tradition, and for "Thou shalt" he substitutes "I will." He creates "freedom [for himself] for new creation." He assumes "the right to new values." He "wills his own will" (139). He is above praise and blame (188). And he gives himself his own evil and his own good as an act of will (175). He is one who laughs and who dances (153, 272, 406–07). He is a lover—not of neighbor (that is only for the little men) but "of the farthest and the future," of himself, and of his friend (173–74, 284, 403). He is a free man, for "willing liberates" (199). Even his knowledge is a product of his will. In knowledge he feels his "will's joy in begetting and becoming" (199). He is a superior man, who laughs at the doctrine of equality. To Zarathustra "justice speaks thus: 'Men are not equal.' Nor shall they become equal! What would [his] love of the overman be if [he] spoke otherwise?" (213). The overman is a striver and a struggler who wars "for power and more power," even in beauty (213–14). He is innocent and open in his desire—so different from the sentimental hypocrites of the old religion, those secret lechers (234–35). The overman embraces life. He affirms the earth and the body against the old dream of an afterlife. "Their body is to them their thing-in-itself," "the healthy body that is perfect and perpendicular: and it speaks of the meaning of the earth" (145).

In rejecting the vapid spirituality and somber otherworldliness of the German Lutheranism in which he was raised, Nietzsche appears to confuse the ontological categories he had so clearly defined in *The Birth of Tragedy*. Now will becomes assimilated to body and becomes body. "Body am I entirely, and nothing else," cries Nietzsche. "And soul is only a word for something about the body" (146). Body and self are also one. "Body does not say 'I', but does 'I' " (146). In one passage Nietzsche appears to separate the two by saying that sense and spirit are "instruments and toys." "Behind them still lies the self. The self also seeks with the eyes of the senses; it listens with the ears of the spirit" (146). Here a third and more fundamental reality seems to be joined to mind (or spirit) and body. But in the very next paragraph Nietzsche writes that the self not only dwells in the body, "he is your body." And on the following page we learn that "the creative body created the spirit as a hand for its will" (147).

Does this mean that Nietzsche has changed his ground from voluntarism and turned to materialism? Clearly not. He is simply emphasizing this-worldliness. His ever-moving, ever-creative will is a force within empirical nature, not a transcendent spirit. It is at one with nature—its principle of dynamic growth and self-renewal. It is the elemental power of nature from which flow the ever-changing forms and manifestations of earthly life, the phenomena of sense. It is an embodied, not a disembodied, will. But it is still will.

There is little that is specifically political in *Thus Spoke Zarathustra*, but much is implied. In one passage, Nietzsche scoffs at the "new idol," the state, which he calls "the name of the coldest of all cold monsters" (160). "It will give you everything if you will adore it." But those who give themselves to the state find that they have committed slow suicide. "A dying for many was invented there, which praises itself as life" (162). To the annihilating state Nietzsche opposes creative "peoples."

> A people . . . does not understand the state and hates it as the evil eye and the sin against customs and rights. . . . Every people speaks its tongue of good and evil, which the neighbor does not understand. It has invented its own language of customs and rights. But the state tells lies in all the tongues of good and evil; and whatever it says it lies—and whatever it has it has stolen. (163)

He urges his listener to "break the windows" of the state and to "leap to freedom." Only where the state ends, beyond the state, will we find the overman (162–63).

The idea of the state does not seem to exhaust the political for Nietzsche. Perhaps by it he intended no more than the dead hand of bureaucratic order. The creative peoples whom he praises are plainly engaged in politics. "Whatever makes them rule and triumph and shine, to the awe and envy of their neighbors," he writes, "that is to them the high, the first, the measure, the meaning of all things" (170). Although in one place he indicates that the creativity that belonged first to peoples has now passed to individuals, in another he prophesies that "it will not be overlong before *new peoples* originate and new wells roar down into new depths. . . . In earthquakes that strike ancient peoples, new wells break open" (171, 323). (But this is not a celebration of nationalism. Nietzsche saw European nationalism in particular as an impediment to the completion of nihilism and to the coming of a new age of culture.)

The coming of new peoples implies the coming of new values. And in order that new values be created, old ones must be de-

stroyed. "Change of values—that is a change of creators. Whoever must be a creator always annihilates" (171). The creator "is a
breaker, they call him lawbreaker" (324).

Nietzsche's necessary "highest evil" appears to involve the use
of force and violence. What else can be meant when he asks, "O
my brothers, are you evil enough for this truth? The audacious
daring, the long mistrust, the cruel No, the disgust, the cutting
into the living—how rarely does all this come together. But from
such seed is truth begotten" (312). The commandments against
robbery and killing must be cast down. "O my brothers, break,
break the old tablets," Nietzsche cries. "Is there not in all life itself
robbing and killing? And that such words were called holy—was
not truth itself killed thereby?" (314). Nature, life, are cruel. And
the overman embraces the way of nature, of life. "Man must
become better and more evil. . . . The greatest evil is necessary
for the overman's best" (400).

The overman will come as a new nobility, which is required "to
be the adversary of all rabble and of all that is despotic and to
write anew upon new tablets the word 'noble' " (315). The society
of the future will be strictly divided into two classes of rulers and
ruled. "He who cannot obey himself is commanded. That is the
nature of the living." "That the weaker should serve the stronger,
to that it is persuaded by its own will, which would be master over
what is weaker still." "Only where there is life is there also will:
not will to life but—thus I teach you—will to power" (226–27). It
will become very clear that "only a few are *able*!" (312). Thus only a
few will wield power.[8]

8. Some writers have interpreted Nietzsche's violent language about the nihilistic destruction of the present world and the coming of the age of the overman as
metaphorical. In this view, the language of blood and thunder is presumably there
for its shock value—to jolt each man into thinking about the emptiness of his
present life and the need for him to seek the way of the overman. On this reading,
the doctrines of nihilism and of transvaluation of values are addressed to the
individual. Walter Kaufmann, for example, tells us that the overman is "the man
who, in the face of universal disintegration . . . performs his unique deed of
self-integration, self-creation, and self-mastery." And he expressly denies a social
role for him: "For Nietzsche, the overman does not have instrumental value for
the maintenance of society: he is valuable in himself because he embodies the
state of being for which all of us long; he has the only ultimate value there is."
"Tyranny over others is not part of Nietzsche's view." The overman is an elite

Nietzsche describes all becoming as "the prankishness of gods." The world as it unfolds seems "free and frolicsome and as if fleeing back to itself—an eternal fleeing and seeking each other again of many gods." Necessity he describes as "freedom itself playing happily with the sting of freedom" (309). "This freedom and heavenly cheer I have placed over all things like an azure bell," he writes, "when I taught that over them and through them no 'eternal will' wills." In all the other theories I have examined, necessity ultimately takes the form of reason, which swallows up the spontaneous freedom of the individual in impersonal rational process. But Nietzsche declares that "In everything one thing is impossible: rationality" (278).

It is to the overman, the nobleman and ruler of the future, that the freedom of Nietzsche's world is confided, for "willing liberates: that is the true teaching of will and liberty," and it is to the overman that willing belongs, par excellence (199). By his free will the overman brings new values into being, he creates new peoples, new societies. But is anyone else free? The rest are to be

---

person, because there are few of them; but presumably he does not form an elite class. *Nietzsche: Philosopher, Psychologist, Antichrist,* 3rd ed. (New York: Vintage Books, 1968), 313, 316.

This interpretation flies in the face of too much evidence from Nietzsche's texts: "the frank call for the destruction of 'The Old Tablets,' " which forbid murder; the celebration of barbaric behavior, and behavior that we today call "evil"; the insistence that "the weaker . . . serve the stronger"; the open celebration of cruelty; the speculation that a "fundamental value for life might have to be ascribed to deception, selfishness, and lust"; the detailed prediction of "large scale politics" and wars as the age of nihilism is worked through and new creators of culture appear, ready to mold and discipline new peoples to high culture—a new "ruling caste." These and similar statements appear in citations from various of Nietzsche's major works and to some extent in the citations noted here. As David Lowenthal writes: "We cannot avoid Nietzsche's concentration on politics, on war, on conquest, on ruling men tyrannically, that is, for the sake of the rulers alone. This is plain for all to see in the last works; indeed it is a strain that was present from the very beginning." "Nietzsche's Critique of Reason and Its Political Consequences" (Paper delivered at the 1959 Annual Meeting of the American Political Science Association, Washington, D.C., September 1959). See also Tracy Strong, *Friedrich Nietzsche and the Politics of Transfiguration* (Berkeley: Univ. of California Press, 1975), especially chap. 7. For a diverse selection of interpretations of Nietzsche see David B. Allison, ed., *The New Nietzsche: Contemporary Styles of Interpretation* (New York: Dale Publishing Co., 1977).

formed, molded, shaped by the overman; and these are the large majority, for "only a few are *able!*" In speaking of the operation of will, Nietzsche uses metaphors of force and compulsion—"the hammer impelled toward the stone"; "something invulnerable and unburiable, something that explodes rock: that is *my will*" (199, 224). Once more, force is the midwife of freedom. This time the many are led not through force to freedom, but through the freedom of the overman to the yoke of limitless force.

Beyond Good and Evil: A Prophecy of Large-Scale Politics

In *Beyond Good and Evil* (1886) Nietzsche continues his prophecy of the overman. His language is now more direct, and political comments are more explicit and pointed. A lengthy critique of contemporary philosophy opens the book, in the course of which the overman is introduced as a new kind of philosopher of the future. The language of philosophy is transposed into the language of psychology, and concepts of self-conscious reflection are reduced to epiphenomena of unconscious urges. Rational thought becomes a disguise for the "will to power." Only blind instinct can give this will its authentic voice. Nietzsche does not believe that a desire for knowledge is the father of philosophy. Rather, "another drive has . . . employed understanding (and misunderstanding) as a mere instrument."[9]

But philosophy is, indeed, a genuine instrument not a mere false face. "We are fundamentally inclined to claim," writes Nietzsche,

> that the false judgments (which include the synthetic judgments *a priori*) are the most indispensable for us; that without accepting the fictions of logic, without measuring reality against the purely invented world of the unconditional and self-identical, without a constant falsification of the world by means of number, man could not live—that removing false judgments would mean removing life and a denial of life. (202)

But the world of moral concepts Nietzsche treats very differently from the epistemology underlying science. "To recognize un-

9. *Beyond Good and Evil*, in Kaufmann, ed., *Basic Writings of Nietzsche*, 203. Parenthetical page references are to this edition.

truth as a condition of life," he writes, "—that certainly means
resisting accustomed value feelings in a dangerous way; and a
philosophy that risks this would by that token alone place itself
beyond good and evil" (202). Here truth is simply the accepted
moral code, and untruth therefore merely a denial of convention—a denial required if we are to affirm nature and life.

> For all the value that the true, the truthful, the selfless may deserve,
> it would still be possible that a higher and more fundamental value
> for life might have to be ascribed to deception, selfishness, and lust.
> It might even be possible that what constitutes the value of these
> good and revered things is precisely that they are insidiously related,
> tied to, and involved with these wicked, seemingly opposite things—
> maybe even one with them in essence—Maybe! (200)

We may have to recognize that things considered false and evil
are necessary to promote life (201). Nietzsche is particularly hard
on Kant, whose moral philosophy he labels a "stiff and decorous
Tartuffery," that is, a hypocrisy and a fraud. We must beware lest
Kant lure us along dialectical bypaths to seduce us with his "categorical imperative" (203). We are also warned against the "hocus-
pocus of mathematical form" in which Spinoza dressed his philosophy. We must recognize what every great philosophy is—not
a profound and insightful statement about the truth of things,
but "the personal confession of its author and a kind of involun-
tary and unconscious memoir" (203). A writer's philosophy simply
represents *his* will to power—a great effort to enthrall and control
the world.

Nietzsche comments caustically both on the materialist and
idealist fruits of Cartesian dualism. "Materialist atomism," he tells
us, "is one of the best refuted theories there are" (209). And he
warns us that "physics . . . is only an interpretation and exegesis
of the world (to suit us, if I may say so!) and *not* a world-
explanation"; in other words, physics is *useful* in our quest for
power over nature (211). Nor, on the other hand, should we fall
into the trap of considering that the organs of sense are "phenomena in the sense of idealistic philosophy" (211–12). We must
also avoid the "immediate certainties" of idealism. In the sentence
"I think" Nietzsche finds a series of daring and unprovable
assumptions—that there is an I who thinks, or that there is a being

whose thinking activity is conceivable as a cause (213). Willing is also much more complicated than voluntarists such as Schopenhauer have described it. Nietzsche finds it "not only a complex of sensation and thinking, but . . . above all an *affect*, and specifically the affect of the command. That which is termed 'freedom of the will' is essentially the affect of superiority in relation to him who must obey" (215). The idea of a free will is simply the feeling of delight we experience in successfully controlling our environment. Willing is thus not the work of an I, who causes something to occur, but the process of overcoming and the affect experienced in that process by an organism (216).

Nietzsche's approach to philosophical questions also dissolves the problem posed for free will by determinate relationships of cause and effect. Cause and effect, Nietzsche reminds us, are properly scientifically useful concepts, not metaphysical truth. "One should not wrongly reify 'cause' and 'effect' . . . according to the prevailing mechanical doltishness." They are only "conventional fictions for the purpose of designation and communication" (219). And as such they are human constructs, symbols made by men. Hence, the " 'unfree will' is mythology; in real life it is only a matter of *strong* and *weak* wills" (219).

Nietzsche closes part 1, "On the Prejudices of Philosophers," with the thought that the psychologist is "entitled to demand . . . that psychology shall be recognized again as the queen of the sciences. . . . For psychology is now again the path to the fundamental problems" (222).

In the other eight parts of *Beyond Good and Evil* Nietzsche applies his psychology of the will to power to the domains of religion, ethics, scholarship, and national culture. In each part he announces the overman and tells us something of his nature and of his origins. One sign of his approach is the wearing thin of tradition, the decline of dominant ideas. Such is the waning of the ethic of intention—a fruitless effort at self-knowledge that had become a "calamitous superstition." We have "reached the necessity of once more resolving on a reversal and fundamental shift in values" (234). Perhaps the genuine value of an action lies in what is *not* intentional in it. Conscious intention is a superficial aspect of action, which "belongs to its surface and skin" (234). The ethics of intention is a prejudice, which must be overcome, along with the "feelings of devotion, self-sacrifice for one's neighbor, the whole morality of self-denial," which are part and parcel of it (235). "O Voltaire! O humaneness! O nonsense!" exclaims Nietzsche. The time has come for a radical transvaluation of values (237).

On the horizon Nietzsche sees "a new species of philosophers . . . coming up," philosophers who will work the needed transvaluation. The men of the future "have a right—it might also be a wrong—to be called *attempters*," a play on words that in German combines the concept of experimenter with that of tempter (*Versucher*) (242). These men will have a new truth, which will be manifestly *their* truth. They will not care whether others are ready to share it or whether it will be commonly accepted. "One must shed the bad taste of wanting to agree with many" (243). The new truth in its profundity may be shared only among the new philosophers themselves. The new philosophers will be "free, *very* free spirits,"

> curious to a vice, investigators to the point of cruelty, with uninhibited fingers for the unfathomable, with teeth and stomachs for the most indigestible, ready for every feat that requires a sense of acuteness and acute senses, ready for every venture, thanks to an excess of 'free will,' with fore- and back-souls into whose ultimate intentions nobody can look so easily, with fore- and backgrounds which no foot is likely to explore to the end; concealed under their cloaks of light, conquerors even if we look like heirs and prodigals, arrangers and collectors from morning till late, misers of our riches and crammed drawers, economical in learning and forgetting, inventive in schemas, occasionally proud of tables of categories, occasionally pedants, occasionally night owls of work even in broad daylight; yes, when it is necessary even scarecrows—and today it is necessary. (245–46)

Along with the ethics of intention the new philosophers will overthrow the religion that gave it birth, Christianity—the religion of the slave who "revenged himself in this way on Rome and its noble and frivolous tolerance" (251; cf. 298). They will also cast out the secular offshoots of this religion and terminate the "last great slave rebellion which began with the French Revolution" (251).

Religion itself, however, will not be overthrown. The new philosopher will make use of it for "his project of cultivation and education, just as he will make use of whatever political and economic states are at hand" (262). For the religious instinct remains strong and is growing (256). Nietzsche emphasizes that religion, not reason, trained the European spirit to "strength, ruthless curiosity, and subtle mobility," in the past, even though this cost much in the way of strength and spirit (290). The rationalist quest, the effort of the eighteenth and nineteenth centuries "to supply a *rational foundation* for morality" he finds laughable (287). It is religious faith that commands obedience, and this is the foundation of civilization. "You shall obey—someone and for a long time: *else* you will perish and lose the last respect for yourself." This is "the moral imperative of nature" addressed not to the individual, to nations, or classes but "to *man*" (292).

Obedience, however, may become passivity and softness. And the race of men who issue commands may disappear, as in modern Europe.

> The herd man in Europe today gives himself the appearance of being the only permissible kind of man, and glorifies his attributes, which make him tame, easy to get along with, and useful to the herd, as if they were the truly human virtues: namely, public spirit, benevolence, consideration, industriousness, moderation, modesty, indulgence, and pity. . . . Where one considers leaders and bellwethers indispensable, people today make one attempt after another to add together clever herd men by way of replacing commanders: all parliamentary constitutions, for example, have this origin. (301)

Such softness comes typically in an age of decay when races are indiscriminately mixed, a condition that gives rise to a war of values; and the herd man seeks, above all, rest from the strife. But such times also produce new strong men, new leaders, "those enigmatic men predestined for victory and seduction, whose most beautiful expression is found in Alcibiades and Caesar (to whose company I should like to add that *first* European after my taste, the Hohenstaufen Frederick II)" (302). The moral decay that today takes the form of the democratic movement, a movement that diminishes man and makes him mediocre, must come to an end. And it will if we reach out "toward *new philosophers*; there is no choice" (307). These will come to "revalue and invert 'eternal values'. " And they will teach man "the future of man as his *will*" (307).

The new philosophers will come, Nietzsche predicts, in the midst of "large-scale politics." He foresees the occasion as an increase in the menace of Russia where will is still strong and waits to be discharged. To defend itself, Europe, where sickness of will is spread unevenly, "would have to resolve to become menacing too,"

> *to acquire one will* by means of a new caste that would rule Europe, a long, terrible will of its own that would be able to cast its goals millennia hence—so the long-drawn-out comedy of its many splinter states as well as its dynastic and democratic splinter wills would come to an end. The time for petty politics is over: the very next century will bring the fight for the dominion of the earth—the *compulsion* to large-scale politics. (321)

Characteristic of the new philosophers will be a "certainty of value standards, the deliberate employment of a unity of method, a shrewd courage, the ability to stand alone and give an account of themselves." They will take pleasure in saying "No," and also "in taking things apart, and to a certain levelheaded cruelty." They will also be "*harder* . . . than humane people might wish." And they will restore severity in manners and discipline to European life. Above all they will be creators of value—"commanders and legislators: they say '*thus* it *shall* be!' " Their knowing will take the form of creating. "Their will to truth is—*will to power*" (324–26).

Nietzsche reminds us that the coming of these new philosophers will not be a unique occurrence. They will do what has been done at the foundation of every higher culture that the world has known. These have always been the work of "barbarians in every terrible sense of the word,"

> men of prey who were still in possession of unbroken strength of will and lust for power, [who] hurled themselves upon weaker, more civilized, more peaceful races, . . . or upon mellow old cultures whose last vitality was even then flaring up in splendid fireworks of spirit and corruption. In the beginning, the noble caste was always

the barbarian caste: their predominance did not lie mainly in physical strength but in strength of the soul—they were more *whole*
human beings (which also means, at every level, "more whole beasts").
(391–92)

And so it will be again in the future when the new philosophers
appear and strive to "*live beyond* the old morality." They also will
be hard. "Indeed they want hardness; every aristocratic morality
is intolerant in the education of youth, in their arrangements for
women, in their marriage customs, in the relations of old and
young, and in their penal laws . . . they consider intolerance itself
a virtue, calling it 'justice' " (400). They will be inspired by Dionysus, "that great ambiguous one and tempter god," to whom they
will also offer sacrifice. It is Dionysus who will make the man of
the future "stronger, more evil, and more profound; also more
beautiful" (423, 426).

The Transvaluation of Values

In 1887 Nietzsche published *On the Genealogy of Morals*, a sequel to
Beyond Good and Evil. In the subtitle he specified his intention "to
supplement and clarify" the earlier book. It was his last major
work. *The Genealogy of Morals* consists of three essays in which
Nietzsche conducts an exploration of the structure of moral systems and of the psychological and political processes whereby
concepts of good and evil are developed and analyzes the contemporary state of European morals. Once more the need for
renewal, for a transvaluation of values, is given voice.

Nietzsche first explains the meaning of good and evil etymologi-
cally and discovers that in all language they stood originally for
the aristocratic and common man, respectively. From words that
designated ruling and ruled classes, they developed into names
for abstract moral principles. To rule is to be good, to serve is to be
bad. Hence, what rulers approve is ipso facto good. What they
disapprove or shun is bad. "It was out of the *pathos of distance* that
they first seized the right to create values and to coin names for
values."[10]

10. *On the Genealogy of Morals*, in Kaufmann, ed., *Basic Writings of Nietzsche*, 462.
Parenthetical page references are to this edition.

In our Western experience the healthy beginning of morality, as ruler morality, was subverted by the Jews—or, more specifically, by the Christian offshoot of Judaism. Good, from a term designating the qualities of the noble, was converted to a morality of slaves—concepts such as pity, mercy, and long-suffering came to be called good. The religion of the Jews conquered the arrogance of Rome and thereby radically transvalued the aristocratic morality of the empire.

> It was the Jews who, with awe-inspiring consistency dared to invert the aristocratic value-equation (good = noble = powerful = beautiful = happy = beloved of God) and to hang on to this inversion with their teeth, the teeth of the most abysmal hatred (the hatred of impotence), saying "the wretched alone are the good; the poor, impotent, lowly alone are the good; the suffering, deprived, sick, ugly alone are pious, alone are blessed by God, blessedness is for them alone—and you, the powerful and noble, are on the contrary the evil, the cruel, the lustful, the insatiable, the godless to all eternity; and you shall be in all eternity the unblessed, accursed, and damned!" (470)

As with all rational, consciously held concepts, those of morality derive from the irrational, the unconscious, the affective levels of life. It was from their sense of power and command that the early aristocrats brought forth their ideas of value—of good and evil. And, conversely, it was from their sense of weakness, from their resentment and hatred against their overlords, that the Jews produced their slave morality of suffering and mercy. "Was it not part of the secret black art of truly *grand* politics of revenge, . . . that Israel must itself deny the real instrument of its revenge before all the world as a mortal enemy and nail it to the cross?" (471).

With the Renaissance the proud morality of the Romans made a brief comeback. But the Reformation brought a new Jewish victory. And from then to the present, the history of morals in Europe has been a working out, in a variety of secular forms, of the leveling, egalitarian implications of this slave morality. "With the French Revolution, Judea once again triumphed over the Classical ideal . . . the last political noblesse in Europe . . . collapsed beneath the popular instincts of *ressentiment*" (490). Only briefly, "like a last signpost to the *other* path," appeared Napoleon, a "synthesis of the *inhuman* and *superhuman*" (490). Nietzsche closes the first essay with an apostrophe to the future—a wish for yet a new transvaluation that will restore the harsh but splendid values of the ancient elites to moral authority. "Must the ancient fire not some day flame up much more terribly, after much longer preparation? More: must one not desire it with all one's might? even promote it?" (490).

In his second essay Nietzsche attempts to trace the psychological effects of substituting the slave morality of Christianity for the earlier morality of aristocratic arrogance. The animal in man, the brute instinct for power and for cruelty must have its way in us. Denied and inhibited by the new morality, the brute took its revenge by turning against the self in the form of self-flagellation. He "impatiently lacerated, persecuted, gnawed at, assaulted, and maltreated himself; this animal that rubbed itself raw against the bars of his cage as one tried to 'tame' it" (521). Thus originated the "bad conscience"—and with it a moral illness, a gradual eating out of strength and life which has culminated in the flat, lifeless culture of our own time. The final result has been that all our natural inclinations "have finally become inseparable from . . . 'bad conscience' " (531).

Nietzsche ends the second essay, as the first, with a hope, with a kind of taunting call for a new revolution of values. An attempt at reversal is itself possible, he declares, "but who is strong enough for it?"

> That is, to wed the bad conscience to all the *unnatural* inclinations, all those aspirations to the beyond, to that which runs counter to sense, instinct, nature, animal, in short all ideals hitherto, which are one and all hostile to life and ideals that slander the world . . .
>
> . . . It would require even a kind of sublime wickedness, an ultimate, supremely self-confident mischievousness in knowledge that goes with great health; it would require, in brief and alas, precisely this great health! (531, 532)

He closes with the prediction that "this Antichrist and antinihilist . . . *he must come one day*" (532).

The third essay is devoted to an explication of the meaning of "ascetic ideals"—to a spelling out of the meaning of Christian culture during the two millenia of its ascendancy. It is also intended as an analysis of the sickness of the European will in Nietzsche's time and as an effort to show how in such circumstances a new beginning might be made. Once more science comes in for criticism—as a final phase of the ascetic ideal, which points to and brings the nihilism of our time. With all the other authoritative ideas of contemporary culture, it points to weakness and enervation. "A predominance of mandarins always means something is wrong; so do the advent of democracy, international courts in place of war, equal rights for women, the religion of pity, and whatever other symptoms of declining life there are. (Science posed as a problem; what is the meaning of science?)" (590).

But there is hope for the future. For despite the debilitating effect of the aversion to life implicit in ascetic ideals, these ideals have not destroyed man's will. Even though they have willed nothingness, they have still willed. "Man would rather will *nothingness* than *not* will" (599).

In *On the Genealogy of Morals* Nietzsche speaks of freedom. Before being tamed by the state and religion, by bad conscience, mankind gave vent to "the old instincts of freedom," "those instincts of the wild, free, prowling man" (521). The instincts have now forcibly been made latent—"pushed back and repressed" (523). But they are still there, and Nietzsche equates them with "the will to power" (523). It is therefore freedom that he prophesies and promotes. But whose freedom? The freedom of his new philosopher, his free spirits of the future, his overman. He likens them to the Assassins encountered by the Christian Crusaders in the Middle East, whose watchword was "Nothing is true, everything is permitted." "Very well," Nietzsche remarks, "*that* was *freedom* of spirit" (586). But it is the freedom of animal spirit, the freedom of animal instinct. It is a freedom inseparable from determining power, inseparable from cruelty and coercion.

Nietzsche, who winds up our parade of Cartesian witnesses, inverted the relationship between law (or reason) and will characteristic of the other systems I have reviewed. Though the will of the overman is free, driven only by its own inner dynamic, it is interesting that Nietzschean history, for example in the *Genealogy of Morals* or in *Zarathustra*, like all the others examined here, is going somewhere—toward the age of the overman. It is not simply a string of events but a patterned story, a lawful pattern perhaps. In any case, even though the overman is free, for all of us lesser beings, his word—his imaginative view of a new society—has the character of a necessary law.

In all his major works, Nietzsche presents us with a paradox of force and freedom. His concept of freedom necessarily implies unleashing force. It passes over into force; it becomes, in substance, the exercise of force.

Nihilism

With the work of Nietzsche, freedom loses the universalist and rational characteristics of its bourgeois (liberal) and proletarian (communist) formulations. It becomes a radically private and radically irrational reality. As in the materialist reductions of Descartes's duality, the intellectual aspect of spirt becomes assimilated to body as the principle of its orderly motion. But mind and body together become radically subordinated to that other aspect of spirit that remained limited and harnessed, both in the efforts at materialist reduction and in the dialectical resolutions of the Cartesian puzzle. Freedom, as sovereign will, emerges as a voice of irrational destruction—of active nihilism, which Nietzsche thought to be the necessary prelude to the action of will in the reconstruction of culture.

Nietzsche should perhaps be regarded as a prophet rather than as an influential cause of the cataclysmic events, both political and cultural, that have characterized our time. Nevertheless, he saw himself as a contributor to that cataclysm. According to Tracy Strong, Nietzsche thinks

> that the structures holding society and life together . . . have slowly broken down over the evolution of the West to such an extent that they are now only maintained by various moral, epistemological, and political strongarm techniques. If they are to be replaced with new foundations, they will have to be shattered. This task, which Nietzsche sets for himself, can only be accomplished by breaking that which still holds culture together. Nietzsche is willing to risk all on the desperate gamble that, with proper preparation (that is why

he writes), a transvaluation may be accomplished, once the genealogical chains of the past are definitely shattered. As such, the enterprise might be thought to be political; through volition and domination it seeks to replace one form of existence by another.[11]

The age of nihilism began for Nietzsche with religion's loss of power to serve as a base and cement for the political order. Into religion's place came nationalism as a force that holds up the spread of atomizing nihilism by presenting the individual with an object of moral loyalty. At the same time democracy brings society down to a herd level and saps the will of superior men. The age of the last man sets in. But "ultimately . . . the modern state fails in that, by democratization and nationalism, it drains the potential sources from which creation of new values could come. . . . The creative 'class' of today has . . . disappeared."[12] Capitalists and socialists (the frank levelers) stand on a par in terms of their noncreativity. But socialism, like nationalism, is a reactionary force. It seeks to prevent the progress of the atomization required for the completion of nihilism—and hence holds back the birth of a new and vital culture. Socialism turns out to be "the fantastic younger brother of the decrepit despotism which it wants to bury; its efforts are thus in the deepest sense reactionary. It demands a fullness of state power, such as only despotism has had. . . . It wants the caesaristic power-state of this century, for it . . . wishes to be its successor."[13] Nietzsche seems here to prophesy the emergence of the totalitarian Communist state of our time.

Nietzsche saw a possible escape from the hindering forces of nationalism, democracy, and socialism in large-scale politics, the politics of general war, which was indeed to come only fourteen short years after his death and then again after a respite of twenty more. This would, he hoped, bring the completion of nihilism—a final leveling and atomization of society. Out of this conflict, he foresaw a new nobility of overmen that would arise to create a new civilizational matrix. Stimulated by his doctrines, individuals of potential power would subject themselves to the

11. Strong, *Friedrich Nietzsche and the Politics of Transfiguration*, 187.
12. Ibid., 205–06.
13. Ibid., 207–08, quoting from *Human, All Too Human*.

discipline that Nietzsche's writings call for and develop both their will to power and their capacity for wielding it. But on the other hand, they might not appear and might not triumph. If, instead of producing a new race of "ascetic priests," the era of "grand politics" were to produce triumph by "nationalistic and ideological tendencies" this could "possibly spell a common disaster."[14] As Tracy Strong states the dilemma: "Nietzsche wishes to launch Europe on an experiment; he finds it necessary to precipitate an inevitable, but perhaps fatal, contest for the domination of the earth which may, *just* may, have as its consequence the emergence of a new order of rank and a new culture. He holds that unless the wars that are *necessarily* going to be fought in the twentieth century are fought to bring about this new world, nothing, or anything, may happen."[15]

As indicated in the first chapter, some Nietzsche interpreters, such as Crane Brinton, have seen him as an ideological father of Nazism and Fascism. But from prominent remarks Nietzsche made about his dislike for Germans and from his condemnation of antisemitism and from the fact that the German Nazi elite displayed cruelty only (and nothing Nietzsche would have acknowledged as spiritual and cultural creativity), Nazis and Fascists could not have figured in Nietzsche's "script" for a better future. We do know, however, that these people made use of concepts that seem to be bastardized versions of Nietzschean thought. As shown in chapter 3, Hitler himself acknowledged that his sole end was personal power and that both German nationalism and the idea of the super race were but myths he thought useful to help him achieve it. Nevertheless it seems fair to say that while Nietzsche did not intentionally beget Nazism and Fascism, "he intentionally fathered some of [their] essential elements, though he would have hated those unsuspected elements which necessarily accompanied the ones he himself sought. For it was evident from the beginning that a new barbarian chief was a more likely occurrence than a Caesar with the soul of Christ."[16]

14. Ibid., 212.
15. Ibid., 214.
16. Lowenthal, "Nietzsche's Critique of Reason," 18.

In understanding another area of contemporary movement toward nihilism, Nietzsche figures quite simply as prophet, spelling out the end results of Hobbesian and Lockean Cartesianism. In speaking of liberal capitalist culture as "Alexandrian," he tells us that despite the fact that individual freedom is an ultimate value, the technological character of the system requires "a slave class" to make it function. However, "with its optimistic view of life it denies the necessity of such a class." And when the disproportion of its slogans about the "dignity of man" to the reality of industrial society is fully manifest, "it gradually drifts toward a dreadful destruction."[17]

Nietzsche wrote this in 1872. In 1964 David Apter penned a theoretical description of the present reality that Nietzsche's prophecy had heralded. He described the class structure of the modern postindustrial state as threefold: an "established" upper echelon of technocrats with specialized knowledge, a "disestablished" middle class that once had status and fights desperately to regain it, and a "functionally superfluous" layer at the bottom of the social pyramid. Power and prestige have come to be based on "functional roles germane to modern industrial society, in which science and efficiency go hand in hand."[18] But the functionally superfluous, who may be children of established technocrats as well as of the anxious and bewildered disestablished, older middle class or of the lumpen proletariat, have no skills to offer to the demanding hierarchy of industrial order. For these "truly superfluous men, there is no ideology," either Lockean, Kantian, or Marxist, "only generalized hatred. Speed, violence, a frenetic round of political activism, or perhaps more simply despair, characterizes these groups, which have been largely ignored by a prosperous society."[19] Their final recourse is nihilistic action. It is exemplified by the burning of Watts and Newark. Its voice is heard in the rifle shots that "kneecap" Italian industrialists in Milan and Turin and in the shouting of youthful rioters in

17. *Birth of Tragedy*, in Kaufmann, ed., *Basic Writings of Nietzsche*, 111.
18. David Apter, *Ideology and Discontent* (New York: Free Press of Glencoe, 1964), 33, 37.
19. Ibid., 39.

Zurich. It is heard in the pistol shots of a presidential assassin. In the burning of Liverpool, Manchester, and Birmingham, where "screaming youths fling Molotov cocktails into shops and supermarkets, turning whole city blocks into infernos," the nihilism of the superfluous man speaks to us.[20]

This is our present situation. Nihilism increases as technology improves. Our old Judeo–Christian civilization erodes, and, in irrational defense, so-called moral majorities attempt to impose their view of it on the rest of us. The ideologies of capitalism and communism still organize men to do battle, though perhaps with less conviction than earlier. Nationalism seems an exception to Nietzsche's prophecy of the ultimate wearing out of ideology and remains a powerful force, even increasing in strength in some areas. But this is not the nationalism of nineteenth-century Europe that Nietzsche knew; rather it seems to have been engendered out of the general alienation and contempt of the superfluous men our society has created in former colonial areas. In some cases an old religion, such as Islam, lends added fervor to the loyalties this new nationalism begets. What would Nietzsche make of that? Just another rearguard action? We do not seem to be able—or willing—to move to the condition of perfect nihilism that Nietzsche envisaged as the opportunity for his overman.

Is the overman secretly preparing himself for his day of glory, whenever it might come? I have spoken with some disciples of Ayn Rand who model themselves on what they think Nietzsche's ideal was. But is so marvelous and arrogant an individualism capable of organizing the world? Whatever a transvalued value system might look like, we must remember that only a few will exhibit it in the first instance. The rest of us will have to learn to obey, and accept in faith, the discipline of the self-chosen few.[21]

20. *Time*, July 20, 1981.

21. For a sensitive study of nihilism in literature see Charles I. Glicksberg, *The Literature of Nihilism* (Lewisburg: Bucknell Univ. Press, 1975). Johan Goudsblom, *Nihilism and Culture* (Totowa, N.J.: Rowman and Littlefield, 1980) contains a history of nihilism as a cultural concept and a useful section on Nietzsche's nihilism. Robert Moss in *The War for the Cities* (New York: Coward, McCann and Geohegan, 1972), 24, 26, 29, 17, explains aspects of the nihilism of superfluous man described by Nietzsche and by Apter. Urban political violence he describes as the result of (1) a sense of relative deprivation (using the categories developed by

The thoughtful reader will reflect that the vignettes of political culture that I have presented at the ends of chapters 3 through 5 are all extremes. Insofar as they refer to American politics, they certainly do not represent its best workings nor even the everyday. They are problematical extremes of behavior, which mirror extremes and contradictions in the high culture of the classic philosophers. My brief descriptions are not celebratory but hortatory—intended as warnings of crisis. They are problems that we must work on. We cannot bet the future on our national genius for

---

S. Huntington and T. Gurr), (2) the appeal of violence, and (3) the legitimacy gap. Moss writes that "it is striking that in western industrial societies, political violence has very little to do with the conventional Marxist idea of class struggle, and almost nothing to do with the class that was seen by Marx as the potential revolutionary force: the industrial working class . . . The present and potential advocates of political violence in the west come from two marginal social groups: from the body of alienated students and intellectuals . . . and from ethnic, cultural and religious minorities who do not share in the general affluence or are motivated by sectional chauvinism."

As individual pathology, James W. Clarke describes two cases of what he calls "The Nihilist Perspective" in *American Assassins: The Darker Side of Politics* (Princeton, N.J.: Princeton Univ. Press, 1982), 167. He presents Giuseppe Zangara and Arthur Bremer as people who "led the most isolated lives of all the subjects considered. They hate society; they were close to no one and were totally alienated from life. It was from this alienation that their perversity and hostility developed. So complete was their self-estrangement that their capacity for love or empathy for anyone or anything was moribund. . . . They wanted to end their own lives in the most outrageous display of nihilistic contempt possible for a society they hated."

Under "The Appeal of Violence" Robert Moss writes of an image of violence that "has something in common with the classical anarchist argument that 'to destroy is to create.' " He refers to the writings of the Martinique psychologist Frantz Fanon who sees violence as "a cleansing force. It frees the native from his inferiority complex and from his despair and inaction" (*War for the Cities*, 28, 27). Moss also refers to an essay by John Gerassi who writes that "the exhilaration that comes from street fighting is . . . achieving self-hood, independence, the feeling that one is a man, taking pride in oneself and one's comrades. It is, just as Fanon said, an act of growing up, not of adolescent nihilism" (ibid.). One wonders whether Nietzsche might have connected this sort of attitude with the psychology that destroys "slave morality" and grounds the development of an "overman," who might be called upon to establish a new and superior culture among those "new peoples" who, he thought would soon originate and in whom "new wells roar down into new depths" (*Zarathustra*, in Kaufmann, ed., *The Portable Nietzsche*, 171).

compromise unless we do something significant to enhance that genius—work out the problem of strong common values that the ability to compromise usually implies. Also, we need to recognize that not all compromise leads to prudent decisions for the common good. There are differences among compromise, rational decision, and prudent choice.

Or do we turn our back on these symptoms of illness and allow nihilism to proceed? Do we resign ourselves to the death of our culture and await in blind hope the coming of an overman? But how shall we distinguish the true from the false overman? And how would such a solution solve the problem of freedom?

6

Efforts at Finding a New Way:
Holistic Approaches—West and East

Martin Heidegger tells us that the work of Nietzsche brings philosophy to an end.[1] It may have, in fact, ended a certain kind of philosophy. With Nietzsche's death, all the possibilities implicit in the Cartesian world view had been stated. We have been living out the implications of these possibilities. When all the implications have been lived through, perhaps we shall be able at last to pass the Cartesian boundary posts. Perhaps that time is now, but the signals are not clear.

In the liberal societies of the West and behind the iron curtain, efforts are under way to find a new philosophical direction that will provide a cognitive ground for the free and responsible human personality without abandoning the gains of science. All of this effort, however, has been made within a frame of reference that remains basically Cartesian, despite self-conscious attempts by various writers to jettison Cartesian categories. As a result, in each case the kinds of tensions between force and freedom we have discovered in the classics of modern thought also mark the work of recent writers who have attempted to develop a holistic understanding of social reality. In this chapter I shall consider a number of these efforts and attempt to show that each failure stemmed from an inability to clear adequately

1. See William Barrett, *The Illusion of Technique* (Garden City, N.Y.: Anchor Press, Doubleday, 1978), 196–99.

the ontological and epistemological ground of Cartesian assumptions.

During the last sixty years a variety of schools of existentialist philosophy have affirmed the autonomy of the striving human person. In another direction, the Austrian genius Ludwig Wittgenstein, who became a Cambridge don, attempted through a common language philosophy to break down the stifling dichotomy of Cartesian mind and body. And phenomenologists, through their explorations of the prescientific life-world, have sought in yet another way to humanize and give moral value to the categories of scientific discourse. (There is also the hybrid group of existential phenomenologists.) Some members of these schools have sought to accomplish their goal within the philosophy of science by correcting or modifying the impersonalism of the logical positivist "standard position." And in Marxist circles, both West and East, humanists use the writings of the young Marx as a point of departure for criticizing the ruthless authoritarian scientism of Soviet orthodoxy.

A Note about Existentialism

Existentialism, which began as a protest against the confining abstractions of Hegelianism, seems to have run its course. Its impact has been negative—a successful critique. I mention it only briefly in passing. Affirming the reality of the existent human being and his autonomy against the deterministic flow of universals, existentialist thought was unable of itself to furnish categories of public meaning for human life. As pure existentialism it remained confined by the solipsistic freedom of Cartesian will. And in seeking to affirm a public world, existentialism has passed over into one form or another of already existing philosophical thought. In its earliest form—the anguished thought of Kierkegaard—existentialism required a leap of faith into Christianity to satisfy the need for meaning. But Protestant Christianity was not philosophy. And Kierkegaard proved not to be a missionary. Gabriel Marcel's personalism reflected the established principles of Catholicism. Karl Jaspers's need for a rational existentialism led him back to the pale categories of Kant and left him essentially inactive in the face of the powerful nihilism of Nazism. Camus's existentialist protest soon resolved into a vapid liberalism and passed quietly from the political scene. Sartre, starting with meaningless reality into which we are thrown, yielded up Promethean creativity in favor of a project, which must realize itself within the dialectical framework of a Marxist world view. In every case, the movement has been from "dreadful freedom" back to the old verities—either religious ones that lie beyond the boundaries of philosophical endeavor or rational systems grounded in Cartesian dualism, which are therefore deeply infected with the tensions of force and freedom.[2]

Wittgenstein and Ordinary Language Philosophy

The intellectual pilgrimage of Ludwig Wittgenstein is a vivid testimony to the moral constrictions of Cartesianism and also to the viselike character of its hold on the modern mind. Wittgenstein was born in 1889 to a Jewish–Catholic couple in Vienna. His father was a well-to-do industrialist, and his mother a sensitive humanist devoted to literature and to the arts. Both influences played contradictorily on Wittgenstein as he grew up, producing a man who excelled in the world of technical control but who felt morally stressed by it. To satisfy the emotional and moral side of his nature, he turned to art, literature, and religion. But religiously he found himself in a perfectly private landscape, unable to communicate with others about his deepest experiences. The categories of public discourse were for him solely those of science. William Barrett writes that he practiced a "religion of asceticism . . . a self-denial that starve[d] his own religious impulses." He was the "embodiment of the neurotic genius, and as such a thoroughgoing representative figure of our age of neurosis."[3] He was certainly the epitome of Descartes's dual model of human nature—a dispassionate, measuring mind occupied with understanding and controlling the world of body and,

2. See Marjorie Grene, *Dreadful Freedom* (Chicago: Univ. of Chicago Press, 1948).

3. *Illusion of Technique*, 4.

at the same time, an autonomous moral will and seeker after meaning. But in his early life he could find no way to join the sundered halves of his experience.[4]

Wittgenstein's first professional commitment was to engineering, but this changed suddenly to philosophy. He trained as an engineer in Vienna and in 1911 went to Manchester, England, to take a position in an aeronautics firm. But in the same year we find him at Cambridge, enrolled as a pupil of Bertrand Russell. Russell was later to say that he learned more from Wittgenstein than he taught him.[5] Wittgenstein's early philosophizing, which was to culminate in his *Tractatus Logico-philosophicus*, carries forward and embellishes Russell's historic effort to create a perfect logical language as an adequate vehicle for the burgeoning truths of Cartesian science.

When war broke out in 1914, Wittgenstein left the academy to return to Austria, where he joined the army in a spirit of religious self-sacrifice and served on the eastern and Italian fronts as an artillery officer. His constant spiritual companion during this period was Tolstoi's *New Testament*. At the same time he continued to work on his *Tractatus*, which he finished in an Italian prison camp at the time of the armistice of 1918.[6]

We learn from Bertrand Russell's correspondence that after the war Wittgenstein continued his spiritual pilgrimage through communion with the writings of Kierkegaard, Tolstoi, and Dostoevski and that he thought of entering the monastic life. Even in the severe logic of the *Tractatus* Russell detected a "flavor of mysticism."[7] But instead of becoming a monk, Wittgenstein be-

---

4. Cf. the comparable psychic pattern and personal experience of Max Weber, the father of the fact–value formula, a contemporary device for expressing the paradox of the body–mind dualism. See Arthur Mitzman, *The Iron Cage* (New York: Knopf, 1969) for a good psychological study of Weber's dual self. See also the biographical sketch of Wittgenstein by Georg H. von Wright, *Wittgenstein* (Oxford: Basil Blackwell, 1982). For useful collections of assessments of Wittgenstein's work see K. T. Fann, ed., *Ludwig Wittgenstein: The Man and His Philosophy* (Atlantic Highlands, N.J.: Humanities Press, 1967) and Irving Block, ed., *Perspectives on the Philosophy of Wittgenstein* (Cambridge, Mass.: M.I.T. Press, 1981).

5. Barrett, *Illusion of Technique*, 29.

6. Ibid., 30.

7. Ibid., 31.

came a gardener in a monastery and later a teacher in a rural school. In the quiet humility of these pursuits he escaped for a while the analytical rigors of the intellectual life to pursue the deepening of his religious life. Russell once remarked to a friend that he thought what Wittgenstein liked best in mysticism was "its power to make him stop thinking."[8] What sentiment could be more typical of the harried Cartesian mind? To think is necessarily to think the world of body and to measure its motions. Autonomous will, when it is not called upon to legislate our certainty of the world, is free only in perfect silence and absolute detachment to contemplate the holy. Here we find a dimension of the self never experienced by Descartes's pragmatist. But true to the requirements of Cartesian ontology, the God-seeker must experience the holy in perfect privacy and subjectivity, if he is to have such an experience at all. Publicly such an experience is ineffable.

In his *Tractatus* Wittgenstein attempted to represent the world for us insofar as it can be experienced in the language of mathematical logic. Since logical language can be reduced to atomic primitives, the world, which it mirrors, must also be an aggregate of disconnected particles or facts, Wittgenstein thought. "Any one fact can either be the case, or not be the case, and everything else remains the same."[9] Reality, for Wittgenstein, is made of elements that bear no necessary relationship to one another but are merely observed by the senses empirically to covary in one way or another. We are in a Humean world in which we can describe and predict what facts will be found to coexist with what other facts. But we are unable to explain why this is the case.[10] We are therefore in a meaningless world.

Wittgenstein's logic is a Cartesian logic. Its tautological statements, in the definitional necessity of their structures, serve to chart the world to which we apply them. As Barrett notes, "logic is thus a human instrument devised for certain practical human purposes."[11] By it we can predict and control the world, but we

8. Ibid., 7.
9. *Tractatus*, I, 21, cited in ibid., 33. See also 34.
10. Ibid., 36, 38.
11. Ibid., 42.

cannot say what it is or what its meaning is. So far as philosophy is concerned, we are restricted to discriminating empirical (factual) from logical (analytical) statements and to applying the analysis appropriate to each case. The most that ethical analysis can do in such a world is logically to analyze the syntax of value statements. And metaphysics gives way to the descriptions of natural science.[12]

In Wittgenstein's *Tractatus* we have the founding charter of logical positivism, a school of philosophy that was to furnish the groundwork for the philosophy of science for the next thirty years. Under its metaphysical aegis, the behavioral science of politics was born. Fathered and nurtured by Charles Merriam and Harold Lasswell of the Chicago school during the 1920s and 1930s, by 1950 it was to become the dominant persuasion of American political scientists, in the work of David Easton, Gabriel Almond, and others. And this in turn was to work its influence on the European study of politics, bringing Wittgenstein's and Russell's ideas back home. It was a science of logically ordered and predictable facts, but it knew nothing of values except as a kind of fact—the expression of emotional preferences. Easton would even caution his colleagues against instrumental recommendations. Until all the facts were in, descriptive scientists must avoid a "premature policy science." But above all, they must avoid the corruption of their factual analyses by infusing into them emotionally grounded private values. Political science was to be objective and, in order to be so, value-free.[13]

In casting out value, the new behavioral science also cast out freedom, for the metaphysics of the *Tractatus* had eliminated this from the outset. As Barrett notes, "Human freedom in a world of atomic facts, lies only in our ignorance of the future. 'The freedom of the will consists in the fact that future actions cannot be known now.'"[14] Max Weber, whose fact–value dichotomy also underlies the structure of positivist science, concludes that freedom exists but that it is necessarily capricious or arbitrary. We may will what values we choose, but they have no cognitive sta-

---

12. Ibid., 43.
13. See David Easton, *The Political System, An Inquiry into the State of Political Science* (New York: Knopf, 1953).
14. *Illusion of Technique*, 45.

tus.[15] The new behavioral science of politics, which reached its heyday in America in the 1950s like its sister science behavioral psychology, could envisage the world only in terms of its technical perfection. But the social science of liberal America, the leader of the free world as it entered its time of trial in the 1960s, could not know the category of freedom. Wittgenstein himself was to supply in his later work an antibody to the technologism of social science. Logical positivism would soon run its course both for Wittgenstein and, later, for the social scientists.

When Wittgenstein returned to Cambridge in 1929, he brought with him the everyday world of gardens and schoolhouses in which he had lived after the war. Once more he would philosophize, but no longer from the standpoint of transcendent Cartesianism—summing up the world or reducing it to primitives with the symbols of formal logic. His genius immersed itself in ordinary language. He would give an account of the every day from inside it. The philosopher had become an actor in a world that knew no distinction between mind and body, word and event, but simply flowed with life experience, in which language is itself an action, and action is language. "A split between inner and outer, private and public worlds becomes . . . unfeasible," writes Barrett. "Ordinary language moves between these opposed poles."[16] The new way of ideas would find expression in Wittgenstein's lectures and in a slender volume of *Philosophical Investigations*, which would be published only after his death in 1951.

Like life itself, the *Investigations* rambles along, without clear form though not incoherently. In it Wittgenstein explores the question: "What is it we do when we find ourselves engaged in 'thinking, cursing, praying?'"[17] He likens the language of our purposive endeavors to games and seeks to understand the structure of them. The whole he envisages as a family of overlapping "language games."[18] No longer is mind something we impose from without on the moving world of body. Mind inhabits our

15. See E. A. Shils and H. A. Finch, trans. and eds., *Max Weber on the Methodology of the Social Sciences* (Glencoe, Ill.: Free Press of Glencoe, 1949).

16. *Illusion of Technique*, 69.

17. Number 23, cited in ibid., 65.

18. Ibid.

action and our action inhabits language, as rules that grow and change with the ebb and flow of our activity. Mind becomes the ordered process of human living. And philosophy is a showing forth of the meanings hidden in this process. It does not legislate but describes. Philosophy "leaves everything as it is."[19] It reveals what *is*—an ontology of the every day. In such a view of things, value-free science becomes impossible. For all that science investigates is pregnant with value and meaning, including the categories of science itself. Every language game is fundamentally evaluative. Wittgenstein writes an end to the dichotomy of mind and body that has plagued us throughout this book—and to all its variations: fact and value, self and other, object and subject, private and public. Has he also exorcised the tensions between force and freedom?

How far we have come from the science of Descartes is manifest in an architectural metaphor that Wittgenstein employs in the *Investigations*. "Our language," he writes, "can be seen as an ancient city: a maze of little streets and squares, of old and new houses, and of houses with additions from various periods; and these surrounded by a multitude of new boroughs with straight and regular streets and uniform houses."[20] We recall the similar metaphor of Descartes's *Discourse* in which we find an impatience with the irrationality of convention. Descartes refrained from pulling down all the old buildings at once. And yet to pull them all down eventually was indeed his intention, to replace them with the abstract and regular forms of scientific engineering. Wittgenstein instead lives content in the ancient structures but also in the more modern buildings that do not replace but surround them, in a (hoped for) organic developmental unity that is our life. Just so he teaches us to be at home in the complexities of our many language games, rich in purposive meanings as they are, and not to seek to reduce them to one single form of language as he did in the *Tractatus*. Philosophy should not reduce reality to some simple

19. Ludwig Wittgenstein, *Philosophical Investigations*, G.E.M. Anscombe, trans. (New York: Macmillan, 1958), I, 124, 49e.
20. Ibid., I, 18, 8e.

uniformity but rather interpret it in all its complexity. Philosophy does not seek in its investigations the general form of language but tries to understand the relatedness of all languages.

Wittgenstein himself did not employ his new concept of language to investigate problems of ethics, either social or individual, or the world of politics.[21] But his students have displayed a special interest in these fields. In doing so they have mounted a severe critique of the impersonal and mechanistic categories of Cartesian social science. A leading work in this literature of critique is Peter Winch's *The Idea of a Social Science*, which appeared in 1958 at the apogee of the career of the natural science of politics.

Winch attacks T. D. Weldon's view of the function of philosophy for social scientific investigation. Adopting Locke's under-labourer conception of philosophy, Weldon regards philosophy as having a purely negative role in advancing the scientific understanding of social life. The philosopher is essentially a methodologist. He sorts out and corrects the eccentricities of social language and clarifies and sharpens the concepts of scientific analysis. With this work accomplished by philosophers, the scientist, using methods of empirical investigation, is enabled to go forward to find out the truth about society.

Weldon's approach, says Winch, assumes a divorce between the world, somewhere "out there," and the language through which we describe it. It assumes the possibility, by logical procedures, of improving the latter in such a way as to make the former intelligible. But following the later Wittgenstein, Winch denies the world–language dichotomy (another version of the body–mind dualism), because our only way of knowing the world is through pregiven concepts that we have of the world. He writes: "In discussing language philosophically we are in fact discussing *what counts as belonging to the world*. An idea of what belongs to the realm of reality is given for us in the language that we use. The concepts we have settle for us the form of the experience we have

---

21. Except for one brief lecture. See "Wittgenstein's Lecture on Ethics," *Philosophical Review* 74 (January 1965): 3–12.

of the world."[22] For Weldon, a priori statements are merely statements concerning linguistic usage. He does not realize that the analytical reworking of language also changes our understanding of the way the world is. It alters our frame of reference and thereby alters our conception of what is real. Linguistic analysis becomes in this way a form of metaphysics.

To display his own understanding of the relationship between language and social reality, Winch refers to Wittgenstein's explanation in the *Philosophical Investigations* of what it means to follow a rule. To explain the nexus between A and B, one should not, à la J. S. Mill, search for a psychological covering law comparable to a law of physics but rather explore the intentionality of the actors involved in the two events. Thus to connect A with B is to show what rule was employed by the actor in A to produce B. The causality of the event is mediated by the meaning of the rule and the intention of the actor. Thus the act is not conceivable as a mechanical motion of body but as an intentional action of mind. "Explanations of human behaviour must appeal not to causal generalizations about the individual's reaction to his environment but to our knowledge of the institutions and ways of life which give his acts their meaning." Understanding this latter is not simply "a matter of grasping empirical generalizations which are logically on a footing with those of natural science,"[23] for the generalizations of natural science are made according to rules laid down by the scientist himself. Those of the social scientist must be derived from the self-understandings of the society he is investigating. "It is these rules, rather than those which govern the sociologist's investigation, which specify what is to count as 'doing the same kind of thing' in relation to that kind of activity."[24] The social scientist cannot, à la Descartes, stand outside the reality he is investigating as an impartial observer. He must become a participant in that reality.

22. Peter Winch, *The Idea of a Social Science* (London: Routledge and Kegan Paul, 1958), 15. For a critique see William P. Brandon, "'Fact' and 'Value' in the Thought of Peter Winch," *Political Theory* 10 (May 1982): 215–44.

23. Winch, *Idea of a Social Science*, 83.

24. Ibid., 87.

Winch's concept of social science, unlike that of the Cartesian positivists, is not predictive but explanatory. An observer might, in seeking to predict an actor's behavior, learn the actor's frame of reference. If he also has good acquaintance with the actor's character, he might confidently predict the decision the person will make in a given instance. "But the notions which O uses to make his prediction are neverthelesss compatible with N's taking a different decision from that predicted for him." This would not mean that the observer had made a mistake in his calculations, for in a decision, "a given set of 'calculations' may lead to any one of a set of different outcomes."[25] Unlike the Cartesians, Winch has not tried to fit human behavior into determinate or necessary patterns in order to understand them. He has allowed for human freedom.

Winch recognizes that his understanding of human behavior does away with charting the course of history in the mode of the dialecticians we have studied. Historical progress to a determinate social condition becomes a will-o'-the-wisp. We will not be able, writes Winch, "to predict any determinate outcome to a historical trend because the continuation or breaking off of that trend involves human decisions which cannot be *definitely* predicted: if they could be, we should not call them decisions."[26] In this view, freedom is not the outcome of a necessary history; it triumphs over history.

Phenomenology

Phenomenology is yet another way of restoring a specifically human dimension to modern science. Born of the philosophical endeavors of Edmund Husserl (1859–1938), another Viennese genius, phenomenology aims at the unfolding of human meaning. As Paul Ricoeur puts it, phenomenology unites three general theses: "(1) meaning is the most comprehensive category of phenomenological description; (2) the subject is the bearer of mean-

25. Ibid., 91.
26. Ibid., 93.

ing; (3) reduction is the philosophical act which permits the birth of a being for meaning."[27]

The work of Husserl was a response to the challenge posed by positivistic science to the wholeness of human life. In Cartesian science, the subjective pole of reality exists merely as dispassionate scientific observer rather than as moral person. And the reality and truth available to that observer is wholly a quantitative truth about the motions of body. Hwa Yol Jung, a political philosopher and phenomenologist, has put the matter succinctly:

> Objectivism is the philosophical claim that reality is objective in the sense that it is separable or ought to be separated from the realm of subjectivity. It claims that no reality is subjective. . . . So methodologically speaking, the objectivist claims that the human or social sciences are amenable to the same treatment of [sic] the natural sciences in the name of causal explanation and prediction (i.e., scientism).[28]

The starting point of the phenomenologist in attempting to restore the wholeness of human life is the "life world" (Lebenswelt), Husserl's term. The life world is the prescientific, preconceptual world of daily action and experience in which the human actor makes no distinction between mind and body, subjective and objective, value and fact. It is an unriven unity in which one simply acts. And it is the data of this life world that the phenomenologist takes seriously in his quest for the understanding of human meaning. We are reminded of Wittgenstein's conception of forms of life, of which the common language is an integral aspect.

Philosophically approaching the life world, the phenomenologist brackets all problems of Cartesian dualism—the question of whether there is a world beyond the thinker and, if so, where the boundary between the two might be—all references to subjective and objective in a metaphysical sense. In this bracketing— or *epoché*—the life world takes on the character of an "inten-

---

27. Paul Ricoeur, *The Conflict of Interpretations* (Evanston, Ill.: Northwestern Univ. Press, 1974), 246, cited in Hwa Yol Jung, *The Crisis of Political Understanding* (Pittsburgh: Duquesne Univ. Press, 1979), 8.

28. *Crisis of Political Understanding*, 8–9.

tional" reality, something that is "real-for-me."[29] It contains both 'noematic' and 'noetic' aspects—the first referring to the object as I think it, the second to the characteristics of my thinking. Such intentional realities were for Husserl "'the things themselves,' the noematic unities originally given to a transcendentally purified consciousness."[30] The work of phenomenological analysis takes place within this setting. It is "an essentially descriptive examination of the noetic and noematic structure of intellectual acts as grounded in transcendental subjectivity, and its concern is with a total reconstruction of consciousness, in terms of which science will achieve its rationale, art and religion their validation, and philosophy its own consummation."[31] In this way phenomenology restores the "two cultures" to a unity.

The phenomenological quest for meaning is 'eidetic'; it seeks to comprehend 'essence'. We seem to have moved back beyond the beginnings of modern thought into the teleological tradition of Scholasticism. But the phenomenologist quickly puts us on notice that he is not attempting to restore Platonic forms, Thomistic essences, or Aristotelian entelechies. For the idea that he contemplates is not transcendent absolute reality but rather the meaning of an object "as it is constituted by the activities of our mind."[32] "The *eidetic reduction* is a method by means of which the phenomenologist is able to attend to the character of the given, setting aside that which is contingent and secondary and noting that which shows itself as universal."[33] It embraces "possibly imaginable things," the basic categories of meaningful intentionality.[34]

Until now, phenomenologists have confined themselves to a detailed critique of behavioral (or naturalistic) approaches to social science (Jung and Dallmayr, for example) and to a phenomenological exploration of the problem of realistic and ade-

29. Maurice Natanson, ed., *Essays in Phenomenology* (The Hague: Martinus Nijhoff, 1966), introduction, 15.

30. Ibid., 19.

31. Ibid.

32. Alfred Schutz, "Some Leading Concepts of Phenomenology," in ibid., 37.

33. Natanson, ed., in ibid., introduction, 12.

34. Schutz, in ibid., 37.

quate concept formation in the social sciences (writers such as Schutz). In both these enterprises, the intention of the scholars has been to show that human subjectivity has been lost sight of in the impersonal mathematizing methods of social scientists. Following Husserl, their objective is to perform "an archaeology of subjectivity in relation to the life world" and to show how its content and structure are relevant for the conduct of social inquiry.[35] However, no phenomenological method of social science exists that is distinguishable from established anthropological methods of "verstehen."[36] Nor is it yet clear whether there ever will be, for there is an ambiguity about the ultimate intention of the phenomenologists. This ambiguity is present, for example, in Hwa Yol Jung's discussion of the role of phenomenology vis à vis social science. In one place Jung tells us that "phenomenology is not simply a methodology; it is also a complete philosophy of man and of social reality." It is also to be understood as science, for Jung writes that phenomenology "denies neither the concept of 'objectivity' nor that of 'science.'"[37] These formulas lead one to suppose that someday there may be a developed phenomenological science of human society. Yet in another of his writings, Jung seems to indicate that phenomenology's role is solely critical—the role of a Socratic gadfly. Thus he writes that "phenomenology is not so much a particular body of knowledge as it is a vigilance or constant reminder not to forget the *human* source of political knowledge."[38] The philosopher in this role is a "perpetual beginner who takes nothing for granted and for whom everything is in principle questionable."[39]

Jung criticizes behavioralism for insulating fact from value in its quest for conceptual rigor and scientific objectivity. Standing outside the reality he observes, strictly in the role of dispassionate

35. Jung, *Crisis of Political Understanding*, 83.
36. See, however, for a possible beginning, Don Ihde, *Experimental Phenomenology* (New York: Putnam, 1977).
37. Hwa Yol Jung, "A Critique of the Behavioral Persuasion in Politics: A Phenomenological Review," in M. Natanson, ed., *Phenomenology and the Social Sciences*, vol. 2 (Evanston, Ill.: Northwestern Univ. Press, 1973): 136, 139.
38. *Crisis of Political Understanding*, 96.
39. Ibid., 97.

observer, the political scientist develops findings that contain no moral judgment on the events described or theorized. As Jung sees it, "the logical consequence of value neutrality breeds social and political irresponsibility detrimental altogether to society."[40]

Alfred Schutz has written extensively on the implications of phenomenology for conceptualization in the social sciences. He warns against adoption in the social sciences of the principles of concept and theory formation that prevail in the sciences of nature. For these exclude "persons with their personal life and all objects of culture which originate as such in practical human activity." But this is precisely the layer of the life world that the social sciences need to investigate.[41] A refined behavioral science could be constructed, but it would tell us nothing "about social reality as experienced by men in everyday life."[42] A principle of subjective investigation must be incorporated in scientific inquiry so that this everyday life is illuminated. "All scientific explanation of the social world *can*, and for certain purposes *must*, refer to the subjective meaning of the actions of human beings from which the social reality originates."[43] We are reminded of Winch's advice that social science must explain social reality in terms of the rules and self-understandings of the cultures under investigation.

The concepts that social scientists create to accomplish the illumination of social reality Schutz refers to as "constructs on the second level." They can and should be fashioned by the procedural rules employed in all empirical science. These are "objective ideal typical constructs" that are different from the first level, commonsense concepts of social reality and can be used to develop "theoretical systems embodying testable general hypotheses" in the sense of the standard position in the philosophy of social science.

Creating these concepts of the second level is a complicated and difficult affair, since they are "constructs of constructs," and yet

40. Ibid., 106.
41. Alfred Schutz, "Concept and Theory Formation in the Social Sciences," *The Journal of Philosophy* 51 (April 29, 1954), cited in Hwa Yol Jung, ed., *Existential Phenomenology and Political Theory* (Chicago: Regnery, 1972), 97.
42. Ibid., 98.
43. Ibid., 102.

we intend them to remain faithful to the reality they explain and to be intelligible to the actors they describe. Schutz distinguishes two kinds of experience in relating to others—the "we" experience and the "they" experience. In the "we" experience I am in direct contact with the other as a person whom I confront as a unique reality. The "we" experience, because it is shared with the other, is a subjective and concrete reality for me—at least in part an aspect of my intentionality. The "they" experience is an indirect one, in which I stand at a distance from the other, who is an object for me, only abstractly understood in terms of typical attributes. Since this is the case, the observer runs the danger that he "will naively substitute his own ideal type for those in the mind of his subject." The observer may reduce the other in these circumstances to an abstract "case history." And in doing so, he may not only be "using the wrong ideal type to understand his subject's behavior, but he may never discover his error because he never confronts his subject as a real person."[44] Great care must be taken in such circumstances to insure "meaning-adequacy." This requires that "given a social relationship between contemporaries, the personal ideal type of the partners and their typical conscious experience must be congruent with one another and compatible with the ideal-typical relationship itself."[45]

Phenomenology insists that valid social science must avoid conceiving the social world in an external way, as Cartesian body in motion. The observer, to understand and chart what he studies, must, in a sense, become one with his object. He must conceptually work his way into the subjectivity of the reality he is examining. It would seem that he is, in effect, enjoined to bring his subject from the objective to the subjective pole of reality—that is, from the impersonal necessity of body to the freedom of creative personal mind.

A Critique

How far have the proponents of ordinary language philosophy and of phenomenology succeeded in overcoming the wrenching

44. Alfred Schutz, *The Phenomenology of the Social World* (Evanston, Ill.: Northwestern Univ. Press, 1967), cited in Jung, ed., *Existential Phenomenology*, 266.
45. Ibid., 227.

dualism of Cartesianism and in resolving the paradox of force and freedom? It may be a sign of failure that, after years of critique, no positive restructuring of political science has been accomplished by either school. At the time it was published, Winch's book expressed quite well a philosophy that fit the participant–observer method of anthropology, a method that had long been employed in that field and one that in no sense was produced by Winch's work. Since then, two books about Wittgenstein and political science have appeared.

The first of these applications of Wittgenstein's thought to politics is a lengthy volume by Hannah Pitkin, half of which is devoted to an explication of Wittgenstein's thought and half to "possible applications" of his thought "in the work of political and social science, political and social theory."[46] In the latter part Pitkin, among other things, performs a common-language analysis of the concept *political*. She notes the prevalence in political theory discourse in America today of two divergent sets of meanings—one emphasizing popular participation in pursuit of the public good, the other turning on the ideas of interest and the exercise of coercive power. Pitkin's conclusion from this finding is that "duality is itself central to the conceptual area in which those words function, that it is built into the grammar and therefore into the essence of what is political."[47] More accurately, her common-language analysis has turned up the two central and competing strands of American political culture, which may be labeled the Jeffersonian (or populist) and Hamiltonian (or Federalist) traditions. But these, in combination, define a particular political culture—a specific ideological configuration—not the "essence of what is political." One wonders whether a philosophy that confines itself to the exploration of particular usage can do anything more than this. Furthermore, we know about the incoherent symbiotic relationship of Jeffersonian and Hamiltonian culture quite apart from Wittgensteinian common-language analysis.

47. Hannah Pitkin, *Wittgenstein and Justice* (Berkeley: Univ. of California Press, 1972), 169.
47. Ibid., 215.

Pitkin also analyzes the fact–value dichotomy asserted by positivist social science and concludes that "no word is by nature
'expressive' or 'evaluative,' or 'factual' or 'objective.'"[48] What is
important, rather, is how the word is used in a particular context,
in a particular "language game." But this doesn't help to resolve
the long-standing debate about the comparative cognitive status
of scientific descriptions and individual moral standards. It begs
the question. Pitkin also reviews John Searles's discussion of the
"is–ought" problem, which represents one variety of Wittgensteinian thought. But Searles's showing that moral obligations are
sanctioned by social practices, and therefore constitute institutional rather than scientific facts, also begs the question of the
cognitive status of concepts of right. As we all know, revolutions
periodically overturn established institutions and with them the
obligations they enshrine. Pitkin's analysis in this area shows only
that Barrett's judgment on Wittgenstein's philosophy is probably
correct. Its cultural descriptivism reduces the mystery of freedom
and right to *mere* facts—to descriptions of objective body.

In the second half of her Wittgenstein study Pitkin also evaluates the rival claims of intentionalist schools of thought and
of the exponents of objectivist causal theory to ownership of
the sole legitimate mode of explaining political behavior. She
concentrates her scrutiny on the work of Peter Winch, who she
claims is not an orthodox Wittgensteinian in the intentionalist
approach he adopts. Her own conclusion is that both modes are
legitimate and, indeed, complementary. Each proceeds within a
different "language game" and so offers us a different perspective on the same reality. She writes that "action is confined neither
to what is behaviorally observable nor to what is phenomenologically given in experience; which suggests that our need is for
forms of social and political study that can do justice to the full
complexity of action, that are not rigidly doctrinaire on such
questions, but open, inventive, observant, flexible."[49] Replying
to the rejoinder that at some point the student of politics must
explain how "objective" and "subjective" explanations are to be

48. Ibid., 223.
49. Ibid., 285.

systematically related to one another, she denies that there "must be a single, consistent reality."[50] The understanding of social reality to be rich is necessarily plural and unsystematic. She recognizes that the different perspectives "have logically incompatible implications, and reality is not supposed to be logically contradictory." Her only response to the implicit problem, however, is to say that Wittgenstein acknowledged the ambiguity of experience.[51] This is simply to walk away from the force—freedom paradox, not to grapple with it.

The second recent extension of Wittgenstein's thought to politics is a brief study by John Danford entitled *Wittgenstein and Political Philosophy*.[52] Danford shows that Hobbesian language furnishes a vehicle for the natural science of politics. After laying out the common-language theory of Wittgenstein, he compares this with the ancient common-language approaches of Plato and Aristotle. He concludes that "Aristotle's approach has a great deal in common with what we might imagine a political science based on Wittgenstein's understanding of language to look like."[53] But he does not try to show how such a political science could meaningfully be brought to bear upon contemporary politics. In the conclusion, Danford comes back to Wittgenstein to say that a political science based on his theory of language, which would relate phenomena to "one another in their concrete particularity," might be superior to one like that of Hobbes, which makes "reduction to other, simpler phenomena."[54] He also suggests it might be "wise to place less emphasis on the generality of an explanation" and to moderate "what Wittgenstein called 'our contemptuous attitude towards the particular case.'"[55] Were we to do this, we might also find it important to pay "more attention to the perspective of the members of a political community."[56] Yet in a final paragraph Danford tells us that as of now

---

50. Ibid., 286.
51. Ibid., 273.
52. Chicago: Univ. of Chicago Press, 1978.
53. Ibid., 153.
54. Ibid., 204.
55. Ibid.
56. Ibid., 205.

"we do not have sufficient grounds to reject . . . Bacon, Descartes, and Hobbes."[57]

One writer has said that neither Wittgenstein nor Husserl ever really freed himself from Cartesianism. If he is correct, this may account for the sterility of the philosophies of science that proceed from these two sources. William Barrett notes that it was Wittgenstein's intention to abolish Cartesian dualism. But to get rid of mind as a "distinct container, or closet" for mental events, he identified meaning with use. In Barrett's view this produced an emphasis which is "plainly behaviorist throughout." Wittgenstein has reduced mental life to observable bodily behavior. All of his examples show "how a statement referring to consciousness is to be replaced by one that refers to overt behavior."[58] Barrett concludes that "the streak of positivism, the simplemindedness of the engineer, runs deep in Wittgenstein, and he was never quite free from it."[59] If Barrett is correct, Wittgenstein, in exorcising the ghost of mind from the Cartesian machine, has left us with only the machine! Unintelligible freedom has been transmuted into intelligible force.

Barrett suggests the continued existence of a hidden Cartesianism also in the work of Husserl and specifically in his *epoché*, the phenomenological bracketing of the world. The *epoché* builds a wall between consciousness and the world (or what Barrett in Heideggerian language calls 'Being'). Phenomenological inquiry aims at the definition of essences, but it excludes itself from existence. It also produces a dichotomy of existence and appearances. It is only the appearances of intentionality that are open to us.[60]

There is also a kind of Cartesian paradox in Husserl's phenomenology. We begin the analysis by bracketing all reality beyond consciousness. Our explanation is of consciousness only and, indeed, of our own consciousness. We start at the subjective pole—"the pure primacy of mind." But as we develop our description, we find that mind or consciousness turns into the ob-

57. Ibid., 206.
58. *Illusion of Technique*, 70.
59. Ibid., 72–73.
60. Ibid., 126.

jects that it intends or projects. Like Kant, Husserl sought "the *a priori* constituents of knowledge in the structure of the human mind. But for Husserl consciousness has no structures in itself; it is characterized only in relation to the objects it intends."[61] Conversely, since all philosophizing takes place within consciousness, we remain, in a sense, throughout at the subjective pole.

In summarizing Husserl's thought in *Cartesian Meditations*, Fred Dallmayr gives this account of how Husserl tried to build a method for getting at intersubjective life. The method begins with the "bracketing or screening out of all *alien* features of the world, including all social or cultural meaning patterns referring to other human beings. What is left . . . is the ego's own *proper* or *primordial* sphere, containing both the ego's actual or potential intentionalities and the intended features of the world or 'nature as experienced by me.'"[62] How like this is to Descartes's reduction of consciousness to the cogito! Husserl's end point is also, as Descartes's, not a disembodied but a bodied thinker—a "unity of mind and body, . . . an integral *monad*."[63] But this primordial context remains a radically private one from which "fellow-men first appear as mere corporeal objects in the outer world."[64] Only by a complex process of analogical perception is Husserl able to obtain access to "the Other's monadic existence," and thus to a shared world.[65] "Empathy opens the door to a transcendental community of monads . . . which . . . in a strict sense is nurtured only from sources of my own intentionality."[66] Philosophy merely leads us around the solipsistic halls of our own minds and the meanings they legislate in the objects it produces. We never come in contact with a world other than that of our own minds. The world outside us remains in brackets. Even Husserl's disciple Alfred Schutz found his teacher "incapable of escaping the bonds of solipsism."[67]

61. Ibid., 124, 127.
62. Fred R. Dallmayr, *The Twilight of Subjectivity* (Amherst: Univ. of Massachusetts Press, 1981), 45.
63. Ibid.
64. Ibid.
65. Ibid., 46.
66. Ibid.
67. Ibid., 48.

And Michael Theunissen also tells us that for Husserl "intersubjectivity remains an outgrowth of the *ego cogitans*."[68]

Not all of Husserl's successors, however, criticized him for egoism. Jose Ortega y Gasset's criticism focused rather on Husserl's use of appresentative empathy as a basis for intersubjectivity; he thought it "jeopardize[d] the uniqueness of the ego"![69] For Ortega, human life is and remains "essentially *solitude*, radical solitude."[70] The outer world is simply an "immense thing."[71] And the life of another person is never more than "a presumed or assumed reality."[72] For Ortega, solitude is not something to be merely described; he celebrates it. "In solitude, man is his truth; in society, he tends to be his mere conventionality of falsification."[73] Echoes of Rousseau's "solitary walker"!

Schutz's critique of Husserl, as we have noted, was quite different. He sought a way to escape solipsism and did this by judging intersubjectivity to be "the fundamental ontological category of human existence in the world."[74] But his phenomenology remained nevertheless fundamentally Cartesian in its pure descriptivism. It is not possible to address questions of good and bad within Schutz's frame of reference. And in the end, his system remains egological. Since there is no access to public values, human experience is fundamentally subjective. The lifeworld is simply "an environmental context surrounding individual human designs."[75]

The thought of other phenomenologists remains equally focused on the individual subject. Thus the commentary on Heidegger generally finds his concept of *Dasein* (being-in-the-world) as egological.[76] Karl Loewith thought the concept "signified a deliberately cultivated solitude and non-involvement."[77]

68. Ibid., 54.
69. Ibid.
70. Quoted in ibid., 49.
71. Ibid.
72. Ibid.
73. Quoted in ibid., 51.
74. Ibid., 52.
75. Ibid., 53.
76. Ibid., 61.
77. Ibid., 62.

And in Sartre's phenomenological existentialism, life is not merely basically egoistic but basically antagonistic, "synonymous with a struggle for power."[78] Merleau-Ponty, by contrast, attempts to move outside the egoistic self with a conception of a "reciprocal being-in-the-world" and a "lateral inherence of ego and *alter* in each other," as fundamental reality.[79] But his concepts are unable finally to cope with solipsism, which in the end he simply accepts as a problem: "Consciousnesses present themselves with the absurd spectacle of a multiple solipsism: such is the situation which has to be understood."[80] Merleau-Ponty also sees this as a situation in which we live and which we need to confront in all its problematical character. The phenomenological perspective thus precipitates us either into the solipsistic freedom of the private mind or dissolves the self who is that mind into the objective, impersonal objects it intends—into "quasi-body," a field of force.

Let us dwell a bit more on the problem of subjectivity. Interpretive modes of explanation have not culminated in a new humanistic social science perhaps because they are designed to explain the private intentional meanings of unique realities, despite the Husserlian preoccupation with universal essences. "The point of hermeneutical understanding," writes J. Donald Moon, in a valiant effort at interpretive–nomological synthesis, "is to explain the meanings of particular actions, texts, practices, institutions, and other cultural objects, by setting out the internal relations which link each particular to other particulars and to the social wholes of which they are parts." The task of the investigator is thus "limited to the analysis of historically unique configurations."[81] But the idea of science implies a concern for *general* explanations based on the comparison of similar events. And even in the social world the scientist properly takes cognizance of unintended events in seeking such general explanations. "The outbreak of World War I, the scale of violence following the

78. Ibid., 80.
79. Ibid., 95.
80. Ibid., 87.
81. J. Donald Moon, "The Logic of Political Inquiry: A Synthesis of Opposed Perspectives," in F. I. Greenstein and N. W. Polsby, eds., *The Handbook of Political Science*, vol. 1 (Reading, Mass.: Addison-Wesley, 1975): 182.

partition of India, and the pattern of American involvement in Indochina are a few examples of events which were, to some degree, the unintended (and undesired) consequences of the actions of large numbers of individuals, each responding to his own particular situation and concerns," Moon tells us. And it is clear that no one of these events was unique, that each fits an endlessly repeated historical pattern. We have known this since antiquity, as Thucydides's *Peloponnesian War* testifies. Understanding the structure and causality of these recurrent patterns in order to predict and, possibly, to control them is plainly the proper province of political science, but interpretive explanations, which deal only with human intentionality, can only furnish the beginnings of such an analysis by defining the meaning of such terms as *war*. Moon points out that the structures of social and political systems, and especially changes in them over time, also are not explicable by intentional analysis. He writes:

> Rarely do the "gross" characteristics of social and political systems correspond to the intentions or conscious designs of anyone, even (or especially?) revolutionaries and "nation-builders" who try to shape them. It is a commonplace that practices change gradually as people confront new situations and adjust their behavior and expectations accordingly. Likewise, a given set of conventions can result in dramatically different effects, and its meanings can be subtly transformed, as changes in its context occur. Population movements, to take an obvious example, may have a seriously disruptive effect on patterns of representation. Similarly, an electoral system reform designed to provide for the representation of new groups, such as proportional representation, may have the effect of impeding the consolidation of older parties. And a revolution to destroy clerical power and consolidate secularism may have the effect of creating a permanent religious cleavage within a society, ultimately culminating in deep splits within the working class—a class not even in existence when the revolution occurs![82]

To explain such events as these we must go beyond the purely interpretive categories of common-language philosophy and phenomenology in the direction of causal explanation. It is nevertheless true that interpretive methods can be of great use in doing

82. Ibid., 183.

this. Moon shows that in the work of Lewis F. Richardson, Georg Von Wright, Bruce Russett, Donald S. Zagoria, Ted Gurr, Ralf Dahrendorf, and others intentional and nomic factors have been ingeniously combined in such a way as to furnish what can be called quasi-causal explanations, in which the practical inferences of individuals furnish some of the essential linkages among events.[83] To create scientific and predictive quasi-causal theory, however, requires an agreed-upon model of man, "a set of fundamental assumptions regarding human behavior, in terms of which the actions the theory requires are intelligible."[84] But it is unfortunately the case that most such theories in political science are vague and unstable. "They are shifted as one moves from one context to another."[85] If a clearly defined and agreed model could be found, Moon thinks that it might "provide the basis for the development of systematic theories similar to those of the natural sciences, while at the same time providing the interpretative explanations required by the subject matter of the social sciences."[86] But it would appear that such a model of universal man will not be produced by any of the interpretive schools because it must be stated at a very high level of abstraction. And in the view of interpretive philosophy, it is precisely such abstraction that is to be mistrusted, because it departs too far from the particularity of subjective intention, which to them is the criterion of the real.

Moon himself, however, is sanguine and ready to opt for just such a model of man—the "rational-choice" model that has recently been ably articulated by economists such as Kenneth Arrow and Anthony Downs and by political scientists such as William H. Riker and Peter Ordeshook.[87] But it can be shown that the clear and distinct ideas of this model are plainly Hobbesian in origin, a mechanical order of determinative passions (preferences) in

83. Ibid., 184–191.

84. Ibid., 192.

85. Ibid.

86. Ibid., 194.

87. See, for example, Anthony Downs, *An Economic Theory of Democracy* (New York: Harper and Row, 1957) and William H. Riker, *The Theory of Political Coalitions* (New Haven: Yale Univ. Press, 1962).

which rationality is wholly an instrumental faculty. Once more the problems of Cartesian dualism and of the force–freedom paradox assert themselves. For if we are to base our scientific analysis on the side of determinate body, which adoption of a maximizing or satisficing rational-choice model implies, how shall we combine with it the intentional categories of personal mind? Moon suggests that "rational choice theories depend on interpretative explanations to provide the context within which these theories function."[88] But what is the investigator to do if one of these contexts requires that he modify a basic principle of the rational-choice model such as instrumental rationality and the notion of logical self-consistency it involves? As Moon himself notes, the point of rational-choice theories is "to exhibit political behavior as continuous with 'economic' behavior."[89] But would the intentional aspects of every cultural situation imaginable be bound to fit with the constraints of economic rationality? On the face of it many would not, for example, the culture of Christian self-sacrifice. It does not seem to be a happenstance that nearly all the concrete examples of behavior employed by rational-choice theorists can be characterized as hedonistic and selfish. At the very end of the essay I have been citing, Moon seems to take back his hopefulness about the synthesis of interpretive and causal political science when he writes:

> The rational choice paradigm constitutes a particular interpretation of the constitutive meanings of politics and political activity—or at least radically restricts the range of possible interpretations. The conceptions of political activity espoused by a long tradition of political thinking, from Aristotle to Arendt, fall outside the pale of acceptable interpretations, given this paradigm. And by so restricting interpretations at this level, the rational choice paradigm limits the kinds of *interpretative* explanations of political actions and practices which can properly be given as well.[90]

Moon's effort to build a new political science is thus at present thwarted by the dilemma of finding a way to combine rational

88. Moon, "Logic of Political Inquiry," 205.
89. Ibid.
90. Ibid., 206.

necessity with the freedom of particular wills and intentions. Moon does not suggest that we cut the Gordian knot by reducing one pole to the other or by any kind of dialectical method, either of which would simply precipitate the force–freedom paradox. Instead we are left with a kind of Kantian standoff, an unworkable dualism of unrelatable poles.

The Wittgensteinians, phenomenologists, and existentialists, in interpreting human experience, all seek to find a way around the impersonal law concepts of Cartesian social science by emphasizing the particular local usage, the group's self-understanding. But in so doing they all sacrifice meaningful comparison across societies and cultures, and they sacrifice the values of general theory because they equate generalizing with the framing of physicalist, abstractive laws, which is a Cartesian view of law. Danford writes, "Do we really learn very much by seeing the general and abstract which ignores particular differences? We should be on our guard against explanations which do not really help us to understand but which make us *think* we have discovered the real essence of something."[91] But this begs the question as to whether there might not be some way of doing general theory that, while being general, does not become abstract in an impersonal and nonhuman way and that allows us to capture the specifically human. None of these schools of thought is ready to admit that there might be a discoverable something that could be called "human as such," which embraces all cultures and which can be discussed without employing the category of law. In the last chapter I shall explore precisely such a way beyond Cartesianism.

Marxist Reinterpretations and Cartesian Dualism

Wittgenstein and the phenomenologists have taken the world of Hobbes—the world of positivist science—as their point of departure and have attempted to humanize it in the ways reviewed here. Other thinkers have set out from the categories of Marxism–Leninism toward a more human standpoint. Jean Paul Sartre has

91. *Wittgenstein and Political Philosophy*, 205.

made one of the most original and ingenious efforts in this direction.

Sartre did not start out as a Marxist but as a liberal existentialist, as noted at the beginning of this chapter. His wartime liberalism was of a hopelessly utopian sort, one that ultimately denied the constraints of objective body in favor of the freedom of mind and will—"the most radical view of human freedom to appear since the Epicureans. . . . The individual consciousness was splendidly independent—and alone."[92] The sterility of pure existentialism led Sartre toward Marxism, a system of public meaning that he found powerfully alive in the life of the working people of Paris. It was not the reading of Marx that worked his conversion. "What did change me," he wrote in *Search for a Method*, "was the reality of Marxism, the heavy presence on my horizon of the masses of workers, an enormous, somber body which *lived* Marxism, which *practiced* it, and which at a distance exercised an irresistible attraction on *petit bourgeois* intellectuals."[93] Ironically, to make such a judgment was to take a page from Hegel rather than from Marx. For Sartre's embracing of Marxism rested on the assumption that something like an Hegelian zeitgeist exists within which a thinker must work if he is to speak meaningfully to his time. "For you would never at the same time find more than *one* living philosophy—under certain well-defined circumstances *a* philosophy is developed for the purpose of giving expression to the general movement of the society. So long as a philosophy is alive, it serves as a cultural milieu for its contemporaries."[94] Be that as it may, Sartre has felt constrained to find existential freedom within the categories of Marxist philosophy. Solipsistic freedom of itself cannot yield meaning.

In *Search for a Method*, the prefatory essay to the *Critique de la raison dialectique*, the philosopher attempts to present a method of analysis "by which the existentialist Marxist may hope to understand both individual persons and history," a method to fix the place of freedom in a dynamic but determinate world.[95] If Sartre

92. Jean Paul Sartre, *Search for a Method*, Hazel E. Barnes, trans. (New York: Vintage Books, 1963), vii.

93. Ibid., 18.

94. Ibid., 3.

95. Ibid., ix.

needed Marxism to give meaning to existential praxis, Marxism needed existentialism to rescue it from becoming an abstract Scholasticism. For in the political life of the world's major Marxist state, Marxist theory had become a lifeless system. Theory and practice had grown apart from one another, which "resulted in transforming the latter into an empiricism without principles; the former into a pure, fixed knowledge."[96] In the interest of social discipline and party control, "the Marxist intellectual believed that he served his party by violating experience, by overlooking embarrassing details, by grossly simplifying the data, and above all, by conceptualizing the event before having studied it" (27). The problem was a priorism run rampant, divorced from experiential reality. And the omnipresent party bureaucrat was the "kept" intellectual's willing ally.

In Sartre's view, Marx himself had not been guilty of this sort of distortion. Though he approached history with "universalizing and totalizing schemata," he always immersed himself in the facts of the subject of his study, always stayed with particulars, saw in the reality under investigation "a *unique* totality" (25). He allowed the shape of the universal to emerge *only* from specific events, to be formed inductively by them. The result was that his totalities "are living" (26). But his intellectual heirs had, instead, moved further and further from the facts, "denatured" them (27). "The totalizing investigation had given way to a Scholasticism of the totality" (28).

The remedy for this sad state of affairs was existentialist analysis within the bounding concepts of Marxist philosophy. For existentialism reaffirms "the reality of men." It seeks man "everywhere *where he is*, at his work, in his home, in the street" (28). Unlike Kierkegaard, Sartre does not say this man is unknowable— a mystery of freedom—"only that he is not known" (28).

In tying existentialism into Marxism, it is clear that Sartre's problem is somehow to unite Cartesian mind and free will to objective body without destroying the reality of either pole. Freedom must be worked together with necessity. Sartre attempts to do this with the following epistemological formula.

---

96. Ibid., 22. Parenthetical page references are to this edition.

The truth is that subjectivity is neither everything nor nothing; it represents a moment in the objective process (that in which externality is internalized), and this moment is perpetually eliminated only to be perpetually reborn. Now, each of these ephemeral moments—which rise up in the course of human history and which are never either the first or the last—is lived as a point of departure by the subject of history. "Class-consciousness" is not the simple lived contradiction which objectively characterizes the class considered; it is that contradiction already surpassed by *praxis* and thereby preserved and denied all at once. (32, fn. 9)

This seems to say that freedom is manifest only in its transformation of some objective reality. The free praxis comes to grips with the objective givens of historical process, internalizes them, and at the same time changes them into a new objective given. And then the process begins all over again. We are confronted with a generalized statement of Engels's affirmation that "it is men themselves who make their history, but within a given environment which conditions them and on the basis of real, prior conditions among which economic conditions . . . are . . . in the final analysis, the determining conditions" (31). In fact, Sartre quotes this passage just a few pages prior to the enunciation of his own formula. But if this idea is already incorporated in Marxist theory, why then is existentialism required?

Sartre's answer is that Engels's concept is itself not knowledge, as many Marxists today believe, but only a "regulative idea." Marxists do not seem to know how to employ it to obtain knowledge. "Everything remains to be done; we must find the method and constitute the science," writes Sartre (35). He thinks that the way to do this is by analytically developing a "hierarchy of mediations" between the historical actor and the situation he confronts. But it turns out to be the Western sciences of man, not existentialism, that he employs to construct a theory of mediations. To understand the unique person, we must understand all of the *"human relations"* by which he is conditioned—relations that are not reducible to relations of production. The experience of the unique person "is not *lived* so simply" as relations of production (66). The person lives and understands his life with reference to a number of face-to-face groups—in the factory, in the neighborhood—and it is sociology that helps us understand these things. Sartre is especially sanguine about the usefulness of Kardiner's research, for example, because it "does not contradict dialectical materialism" and because it sets forth "real relations" that are actually lived (73). Its utility is insured if we empty sociology of its general theoretical content and employ it as a "hyper-empiricism," which can readily be integrated with Marxism (82).

Beyond the sociological and psychological mediations (which are really determinations) that Sartre adds to more general economic factors so that he might grasp the special character of particular events in the causal chain, there must also be something that we can call freedom, which has causal value. Otherwise Sartre's endorsement of Engels's dictum that "Men themselves make their history" would be meaningless; he would also wholly have yielded up his claim to be an existentialist. In the last analysis man would be "a passive product, a sum of conditioned reflexes." "There would be no difference between the human agent and the machine" (85). But this Sartre vehemently denies. He insists that in a period of exploitation and alienation, man "is *at once both* the product of his own product and a historical agent who can under no circumstances be taken as a product" (87).

Sartre attempts to formulate his concept of human freedom as "The Project." This he describes as active, subjective transcendence by a person of his given situation within the field of alternative possibilities historically open to him. "It is by transcending the given toward the field of possibles and by realizing one possibility from among all the others that the individual objectifies himself and contributes to making History," he writes (93). Examples he presents include resisting the stepping up of work quotas in a popular democracy and voting a strike in a capitalist society. They also include the alternative of subjective revolt against the limitations of one's field of possibilities by oppressive social circumstances. Sartre invents the example of a black member of the ground crew at an airbase near London who, though without experience, flies a plane across the Channel. By thus refusing to accept the prohibition against blacks becoming flying personnel, this man, in his particular, unique act, also expresses "the *general* revolt on the part of colored men against colonialists," and thus moves history forward toward the day of universal emancipation (95). In this way freedom and historical necessity move together toward the future, even though this future for the time being is "shattered immediately by prison or by accidental death" (96).

Thus far we seem to have something that can be called an act of freedom—one of radical particularity whose cause is within itself. But we are puzzled by the fact that this act of freedom dovetails so neatly with necessary movement toward the future—unless that movement is not truly necessary. However, Sartre, following Marx, does in fact understand it as necessary—as an "objective process" (97). He writes:

> The project, as the subjective surpassing of objectivity toward objectivity, and stretched between the objective conditions of the environment and the objective structures of the field of possibles, represents *in itself* the moving unity of subjectivity and objectivity, those cardinal determinants of activity. The subjective appears then as a necessary moment in the objective process. If the material conditions which govern human relations are to become real conditions of *praxis*, they must be lived in the particularity of particular situations. (97)

In this formula we discover that human freedom, for Sartre, must in reality be an illusion. The human act becomes equated simply with the particular act, understood as an empirical event in a perfectly determinate causal order. Sartre has indeed saved his theory from bloodless abstraction but only at the cost of freedom. He has transmuted freedom into a richly detailed, highly articulated process of empirical necessity. For to do otherwise would have been to give up the Marxian dream of certain happiness—the certainty of a classless society free from exploitation of man by man.

Though we become absolutely sure of the necessitarian character of Sartre's thought only when we have reached his adumbration of "The Project," the earlier discussion of mediations had already pointed to this conclusion. There Sartre had said that sociological analysis employed *merely* as a hyperempiricism would "congeal in essentialism and discontinuity" (82). It could acquire meaning only when integrated into Marxism, as its overarching philosophical frame of reference. Also, there was "no question of adding a method onto Marxism" (82). Contemporary Marxism was to be reproached only for its abstractness, "for throwing over to the side of chance all the concrete determinations of human life and for not preserving anything of historical totalization except its abstract skeleton of universality" (82–83).

To exemplify his meaning, Sartre criticized the argument that "Napoleon as an individual was only an accident; what was necessary was the military dictatorship—as the liquidating regime of the Revolution." Sartre tells us he finds this formula uninteresting, "for we had always known that." But after this misleading sentence he affirms a rigid historical determinism.

> What we intend to show is that *this* Napoleon was necessary, that the development of the Revolution forged at once the necessity of the dictatorship and the entire personality of the one who was to administer it, and that the historical process provided *General Bonaparte personally* with preliminary powers and with the occasions which allowed him—and him alone—to hasten this liquidation. (83)

Engels, though known as a mechanical determinist, had at least allowed for freedom in the idea that every *particular appears* to us to be a random or chance event; only the *general* movement of history (whatever that might mean) can be conceived as necessary. We see that in the upshot, having faced the paradox of Cartesian dualism head on, Sartre's clear analytical mind was compelled to choose between the meaningless subjective freedom of his early persuasion—existentialist absurdity—and the meaningful objective rigors of Marxism. He chose the latter—force over freedom.

Kolakowski's Revision of the Marxist Canon

The pervasive coerciveness of Russian Communism has provoked a humanist response among Marxist intellectuals on the Eastern side of the iron curtain as well as in the West. A major voice among them is Leszek Kolakowski, a Polish philosopher whose penchant for freedom led to his flight to the West. He lives and writes today in Great Britain and in the United States.

While Sartre's existentialist commitment caused him to accent individuality or particularity in his reading of the Marxist gospel,

Kolakowski's humanism prompted introduction of a concept of individual moral responsibility into the doctrine. Such a concept is lacking in the theoretical message of Marx and Engels, and the practical results of the omission are manifest in the callous ruthlessness of Leninist and Stalinist political practice. Nowhere in the Soviet sphere has this been more keenly experienced than in Poland.

Kolakowski flatly rejects the idea that the problem of good and evil can be resolved simply by referring all political behavior to the outcome of historical process—the idea that all actions are good that are designed to further the realization of the classless society of free and sociable men. "There is no reason to treat morality as the tool of history," writes Kolakowski, "in the sense of being obliged to seek criteria of moral good or bad in the realization of general historical progress. Crimes which were the tools of the *Weltgeist* are nevertheless crimes."[97] He wishes to hold individuals morally responsible in the here and now for their acts and to teach the human importance of such responsibility. "Only human beings and their deeds are subject to moral judgment . . . It is impossible to evaluate morally the good or bad results of an anonymous historical process" (128).

But how is such moral responsibility possible? Marxism declares that, prior to the overthrow of capitalism, people are forced by economic circumstance into social roles that require of them a predetermined behavior. And Kolakowski has no intention of revising this determinist assumption. He accepts it explicitly: "Opinions about good and evil and about the morality of people's behavior are determined by the way an individual participates in society. Under 'participation' we include upbringing and the influence of tradition, as well as membership in all the social groups from whose influence arises that unique thing called personality" (128–29). Yet Kolakowski finds no contradiction between these two assumptions, for he holds that even though a person may view his moral values and behavior as determined, he cannot *know* that they are in fact good or bad. "That a person

97. Leszek Kolakowski, "Conscience and Social Progress," in *Toward a Marxist Humanism: Essays on the Left Today*, Jane Zielonko Peel, trans. (New York: Grove Press, 1968), 134. Parenthetical page references are to this edition.

knows he judges something to be good or bad because specific circumstances inclined him to do so does not mean that this something is good or bad" (129). We cannot, therefore, deduce moral values from purely theoretical propositions. "The question of determinism or nondeterminism of human activity has no logical connection with the confirmation or denial of man's moral responsibility, for neither the affirmation nor the denial is a theoretical proposition" (130). He calls this assumption "the humanistic interpretation of values," which requires that we accept the right of a given society to evaluate the moral behavior of its members as a natural fact. "Denying society the 'right' to approve or condemn is somewhat like decreeing that earthquakes may not occur or that rain may not fall. In this respect we follow the ideas of Spinoza" (130). By extension, granting this right to society "means that one grants it to himself as well, and to some extent he becomes the voice of society" (131).

Invoking as authority the positivist tradition "from Aenesidemus and the Sophists, through Hobbes and Spinoza, to Schlick and Carnap" is not a very convincing way for Kolakowski to ground the concept of moral responsibility—a concept that certainly implies moral freedom. It is difficult to see how any persuasive concept of freedom can be derived from positivism, which reduces all reality to a field of force. Kolakowski must have recognized this himself, for he adds to his "humanistic interpretation of values" the idea that "the deterministic theory . . . can not in any case logically support or violate [the] type of proposition [that moral responsibility entails], for one belongs to the world of knowledge and the other to the world of duty" (131). Here we seem to have been transported into a Kantian world of phenomenal determination and noumenal freedom, though Kolakowski does not mention Kant. He tells us that although the Marxist evaluates a social process within the rubrics of determination in terms of its "progressiveness," this is not to be understood as a moral judgment (132). Only "individuals are the object of moral judgment, the rest are the objects of historical judgment" (132). This reminds us, in its view of historical process, of Kant's "mechanism of nature," to which we supply the teleological concept of "destiny" in order to give it moral meaning, though we cannot *know* that divine providence is at work in the phenomenal development we observe. In the conception of morality in hand we seem to find a Kantian note as well, for Kant assigns moral duty only to individuals. But it is an attenuated and incomplete Kantianism to which Kolakowski here has recourse. For Kant, the providential "mechanism of nature" is a guarantee of moral responsibility because our phenomenal observation of progress lets us know that the norms that we experience noumenally as our duty can meaningfully be acted upon. (*"Ultra posse nemo obligatur."*)[98] Kolakowski does not attempt any such wedding of his own view of freedom with determinism. He simply leaves them as two either unrelated or opposed perspectives in which "certain concrete human behavior must be judged negatively as to its morality and positively as to its role in the historical process, and vice versa" (132). Nor does he make any adequate effort to specify and philosophically ground a fundamental norm for moral behavior, such as the Categorical Imperative, yet he writes as though some such norm or norms have been established. For how otherwise would it be meaningful to describe any action as a crime?

To the class of crimes Kolakowski assigns theft and murder. But he grounds them in nothing more explicit than our "moral sense" (132, 142). If Kolakowski is not a Kantian, he is certainly not an adherent to the natural law tradition. Yet he writes as though theft and murder are self-evidently immoral—one might say unnatural—acts. The closest he comes to a theoretical ground for his conception of moral responsibility is a brief reference to Descartes's conception of free will:

> Thus we profess the doctrine of total responsibility of the individual for his deeds and of the amorality of the historical process. In the latter we avail ourselves of Hegel; in the former of Descartes. It was he who formulated the famous principle, whose consequences are not always visible at first glance, "There is not a soul so weak that it cannot, with good guidance, gain an absolute mastery over its passions." This means that we cannot explain away any of our actions on the grounds of emotion, passion, or the moral impotence to act

98. Kant, *Perpetual Peace*, in *Kant on History*, 106–14.

differently, and that we have no right to transfer the responsibility for our conscious acts to any factor which determines our behavior; because in every instance we have the power to choose freely. (141)

Kolakowski fails to note that Descartes never worked out a complete moral theory and that all evidence points to a purely instrumental and utilitarian significance for Descartes's conception of freedom to master the passions—to a maximizing concept of free rationality like that of social choice theory, not to a moral idea. To recur to Descartes in order to ground his concept of moral responsibility, and thus to escape the force–freedom paradox, is hardly a persuasive approach for Kolakowski to adopt. It does not lead him away from the tensions of force and freedom; it simply brings the problem full circle, back to its progenitor.

Conclusion

I have traced the genesis of the force–freedom problem in the writings of authoritative philosophers of Western culture and in political practice. I have examined its culmination in both contemporary social thought and practice, west and east. The problem stands squarely at the center of the intellectual, moral, political and social dilemmas of our time. Yet contemporary philosophers seem incapable of coming to grips with its implications, unable to turn them another way. Their efforts to place force, even in idea, at the service of human freedom have failed.

We seem invited to a council of despair; let the aging world rock on to imminent catastrophe, for our intellectual and moral resources are exhausted. So bitter an end to human history rests on a large and, happily, unwarranted assumption—that the dual categories of thought inherited from Descartes, and assumed as a point of departure by all our philosophers, accurately define the boundaries and form of reality. Is it inevitable that we seek a way out of the paradox by starting with the dualistic framework employed by each of these writers?[99] Perhaps the inability of Witt-

---

99. Space does not permit the analysis of still other significant schools of recent sociopolitical thought such as that of Juergen Habermas and the Frankfurt School of Critical Philosophy. It is my view that this group in particular has not found its way beyond Cartesian categories.

genstein and the phenomenologists, for example, to find a way beyond the paradox derives from the fact that they attacked the problem on the ground that Descartes himself constructed—the dual metaphysics of body and spirit. But these are not a self-evident reality that inevitably constrain our thought. They are merely Descartes's construct, despite the pervasive influence they have exerted. In the final chapter I shall explore an alternative way of thinking about reality—not starting with or containing dichotomies such as body and mind, fact and value, subject and object, self and other, noumenal and phenomenal—or force and freedom.

7

Toward an Unparadoxical Way of Ideas:
The Dialogue of Right and Interest

The occasion for philosophizing, the moment that requires a new way of ideas, is not the discovery of a flaw in the argument of a formerly authoritative text; rather it is the discovery that the world is collapsing. We have reached what Alberto Moravia has called our "time of desecration."[1] It is existential incoherence that both prompts us to chart a new way of ideas and gives us freedom to do so. The old way has not only been thought through but lived through and found wanting.

Other political philosophers have voiced similar misgivings about the intellectual tradition within which we stand. Thus Alasdair MacIntyre, in his acclaimed *After Virtue*, tells us that the philosophies by which our world has taken its bearings must be rejected:

> Marxism's moral defects and failures arise from the extent to which it, like liberal individualism, embodies the *ethos* of the distinctively modern and modernising world. . . . Nothing less than a rejection of a large part of that *ethos* will provide us with a rationally and morally defensible standpoint from which to judge and to act—and in terms of which to evaluate various rival and heterogeneous moral schemes which compete for our allegiance.[2]

1. See Alberto Moravia, *Time of Desecration*, Angus Davidson, trans. (New York: Farrar, Strauss & Giroux, 1980).
2. Alasdair MacIntyre, *After Virtue: A Study in Moral Theory* (Notre Dame, Ind.: Univ. of Notre Dame Press, 1981), viii.

MacIntyre finds our world of values in disorder today. Several lines of moral argument exist, but we have no agreed means for comparing or testing them, he asserts. We are a prey to "arbitrariness in our moral culture."[3] And just as arbitrary as other values, he finds, is the claim to personal autonomy that each of us likes to make for oneself. We have no basis for such a claim, and we become involved in contradictions when we seek to exercise it.

> Contemporary moral experience . . . has a paradoxical character. For each of us is taught to see himself or herself as an autonomous moral agent; but each of us also becomes engaged by modes of practice, aesthetic or bureaucratic, which involve us in manipulative relationships with others. Seek to protect the autonomy that we have learned to prize, we aspire ourselves *not* to be manipulated by others; seeking to incarnate our own principles and standpoint in the world of practice, we find no way open for us to do so except by diverting towards others those very manipulative modes of relationship which each of us aspires to resist in our own case.[4]

MacIntyre has given us a good example of the paradox of force and freedom.

In earlier chapters I examined in detail eight of the most significant modern philosophies of politics and found them riven with contradictions and tensions in their treatment of the salient concepts of force and freedom and in the way they related these ideas to one another. In addition, I traced patterns of popular political culture that are symbiotically connected with these classic works—patterns that are also replete with contradiction and ambivalence. Our world of political values and our ways of conceptualizing that world, like the moral world in general of which MacIntyre writes, is disorderly and arbitrary. I attempted to trace the origins of contradiction and of arbitrariness to the ontological system of René Descartes, whose categories all modern political philosophizing takes as its point of departure.

In the previous chapter I examined a number of recent efforts to overcome the fragmenting thrust of our dualistic world view and to move toward holism, and I found them lacking. Despite

3. Ibid., 38.
4. Ibid., 66.

the fact that each is explicitly anti-Cartesian, none has been able to free itself from the basic categories and ontological assumptions of the dualistic system legislated for us so long ago by Descartes. I now address myself to that task.

A Working Hypothesis

Perhaps a useful working hypothesis is that a theory of the whole ought not assume that the world and its history can be represented in terms of necessary laws and processes. Natural science long ago abandoned necessity for probability and indeterminacy. Remember, it was the metaphysics of logical and dialectical necessity that produced the force–freedom paradox. This metaphysics was also a rationalist myth that the genius of a Nietzsche could readily lay to rest, working from the very ground on which the myth was constructed. Let us then give up necessitarian history and the Newtonian model of law and begin our inquiry.

Let us also suppose that body and mind are not useful starting points for theorizing. Ludwig von Bertalanffy writes:

> May it not be that the mind-body problem was created by *wrong categorization*? In one way or the other, and with whatever minor modification, *all* [modern] theories took for granted the Cartesian dualism of matter and mind, things and consciousness, object and subject, *res extensa* and *res cogitans*, accepting them as indubitably given and trying to bring them into some intelligible relationship.[5]

This is a perfect characterization of the endeavors of all the theorists I have scrutinized. But we are now ready for a paradigm shift, because large anomalies have developed in the old categories. The early science that helped beget them has taken on a new form and no longer fits the Cartesian framework. "By now," writes Bertalanffy, "it has become obvious that neither 'matter' nor 'mind' stood up to the test of scientific investigation. Cartesian matter has 'dematerialized' in physics—see Einstein's equations and atomic explosions. And mind, originally conceived as con-

---

5. Ludwig von Bertalanffy, *Robots, Men, and Minds: Psychology in the Modern World* (New York: G. Braziller, 1967), 94.

sciousness, has become no less problematic since the exploration of the unconscious."[6] Werner Heisenberg agrees:

> The old division of the world into objective process in space and time in which these processes [of mind] are mirrored—in other words, the Cartesian difference between *res cogitans* and *res extensa*—is no longer a suitable starting point for our understanding of modern science. Science . . . is now focussed on the network of relationships between man and nature, on the framework which makes us as living beings dependent parts of nature, and which we as human beings have simultaneously made the object of our thought and actions. Science no longer confronts nature as an objective observer, but sees itself as an actor in this interplay between man and nature. . . . The scientific world view has ceased to be a scientific view in the true sense of the word.[7]

Let us then suspend the Cartesian judgment that the world consists of sense experience that gives rise to but is also in some sense produced by private wills and minds. Let us reflect instead on the public world that Descartes attacked and see where that reflection carries us. Let us consider whether we have access to a public mind, which is also an embodied mind—embodied in a human experience of which it is both cause and effect. (I am not contemplating a mysterious *Weltgeist* à la Hegel, battling its way to self-realization, but a reality of the common sense.) If such an embodied public mind exists, can it tell us what humankind believes it should seek as its good and avoid as evil? What could be more authoritative for defining and placing the ideal of freedom in a hierarchy of human values than what the human sense of the just and the prudent has in its long experience pronounced? What we seek is an understanding of human moral principles as such, which the nihilism of our time, despite much battering, has left standing.

The Virtues, Local Community, and Universal Norms

In searching for a solution to the problem of arbitrariness in modern ethical culture, Alasdair MacIntyre rejects the concept of

6. Ibid.
7. *The Physicist's Conception of Nature* (New York: Harcourt, Brace, 1958), 29.

principle in favor of that of virtue. As a starting point for his argument he reaches back to the conception of virtue associated with life-styles of ancient heroic societies. In doing so he observes that the idea of virtue was always related to the performance of a social practice in which a society's values inhered. "A virtue," he writes, "is an acquired human quality the possession and exercise of which tends to enable us to achieve those goods which are internal to practices and the lack of which effectively prevents us from achieving any such goods."[8]

Though moral principles may not be universal, according to MacIntyre, apparently the virtues (or at least some of them) are. "From the standpoint of those relationships without which practices cannot be sustained," he tells us, "truthfulness, justice and courage . . . are genuine excellences, are virtues in the light of which we have to characterise ourselves and others, whatever our private moral standpoint or our society's particular codes may be."[9] They are imperative both for good present relationships and for learning a tradition, "the relationship to the past" that a given practice embodies.[10] Also, in his effort to develop a viable morality, MacIntyre wishes to keep his attention focused on the local and the particular. "It is always within some particular community with its own specific institutional forms that we learn or fail to learn to exercise the virtues."[11]

MacIntyre's emphasis in this passage is as much on "community" as on "particular." For he is critical of the justice claims of John Rawls and Robert Nozick—the well-known contemporary articulators of the opposing American political cultures of welfare liberalism (egalitarianism) and classical liberalism (libertarianism). What they have in common, MacIntyre claims, is a failure to refer to "desert" in their accounts of justice. Each sees only individuals with interests as the primary reality, whereas the idea of desert requires a community with a shared understanding of what is good, with reference to which individual interests are defined—a common good.[12]

8. *After Virtue*, 178.
9. Ibid., 179.
10. Ibid., 181.
11. Ibid., 181.
12. Ibid., 231–33.

MacIntyre's book is an exploration, not a complete philosophy. It appears to point toward a more thorough investigation of ancient virtue, and especially of moral reasoning, as embodied in the Aristotelian conception of the practical reason. MacIntyre believes that "the Aristotelian tradition can be reestablished in a way that restores intelligibility and rationality to our moral and social attitudes and commitments."[13] Like Aristotle, he insists to the end that we always focus on the particular. He tells us in closing that we need "constructions of local forms of community within which civility and the intellectual and moral life can be sustained through the new dark ages which are already upon us."[14]

MacIntyre's rejection of any sort of universalizing approach to morals is extreme. "The notion of escaping . . . into a realm of entirely universal maxims which belong to man as such . . . is an illusion and an illusion with painful consequence," he writes. "When men and women identify what are in fact their partial and particular causes too easily and too completely with the cause of some universal principle, they usually behave worse than they would otherwise do."[15] He is reacting here, no doubt, to the self-righteousness of opposed claims about the content of God's will or of the law of nature, which brought about the conflicts that destroyed the premodern moral tradition. He may also be reacting to the universalist character of Cartesian philosophies that, as we have seen, express moral truth in a pseudophysical manner, as "necessary law."[16]

While I find much that is valuable in MacIntyre's approach and believe with him that further scrutiny of Aristotle's practical reason has much to offer in mastering the moral dilemma of our time, I cannot accept his rejection of the idea of universal principles. It seems to me that in any complete moral philosophy, one must ultimately come to grips with the question of how to define

13. Ibid., 241.

14. Ibid., 245.

15. Ibid., 205–06.

16. Cf. MacIntyre's approach to morals with that of Stephen Toulmin, who also stresses the importance of understanding in terms of the local and who eschews universalist terms. See *Human Understanding*, vol. 1 (Princeton, N.J.: Princeton Univ. Press, 1972).

"right as such" or be left adrift in a sea of cultural relativism. And in a time of technological unity, when the world has indeed become one society of highly interdependent parts, it is more urgent than ever to find our way to first principles. In places in his book MacIntyre himself, in fact, seems to grant the point. He notes, for example, that the definition and explanation of virtues with reference to a practice "in no way entails approval of all practices in all circumstances."[17] And he follows this with the statement that "a morality of virtue requires as its counterpart a conception of moral law" and also a conception of the best life.[18] If these assertions are true, they *must* involve us ultimately in a consideration of the question of universal moral norms. I now address myself to this knotty problem, and, as MacIntyre did, I begin with an appeal to Aristotle.

A Search for Universal Norms

Some years ago, while still a graduate student, I came upon a pregnant passage in Aristotle's *Ethics* that grounded the idea of right in broad public experience. The passage occurs in book 2, chapter 6, just following the summary and review of Aristotle's doctrine of moral virtue, which he characterizes as "a state of character concerned with choice, lying in a mean, i.e., the mean relative to us, this being determined by a rational principle, and by that principle by which the man of practical wisdom would determine it."[19] At this point, Aristotle wants to make it clear that the rule of the mean is not the sole norm of moral virtue, though up to this point in the argument it appeared that this might be so. He wants to establish that there are parameters beyond which it would not be morally meaningful to act according to the mean. He writes:

> But not every action nor every passion admits of a mean; for some have names that already imply badness, e.g., spite, shamelessness,

17. *After Virtue*, 187.
18. Ibid.
19. Aristotle, *Ethics*, in R. McKeon, ed., *The Basic Works of Aristotle* (New York: Random House, 1941), 1107a 1–3, 959.

envy, and in the case of actions, adultery, theft, and murder; for all these and suchlike things imply by their names that they are themselves bad, and not the excesses or deficiencies of them. It is not possible, then, ever to be right with regard to them; one must always be wrong. Nor does goodness or badness with regard to such things depend on committing adultery with the right woman, at the right time, and in the right way, but simply to do any of them is to go wrong. It would be equally absurd, then, to expect that in unjust, cowardly, and voluptuous action there should be a mean, an excess, and a deficiency; for at that rate there would be a mean of excess and of deficiency, an excess of excess, and a deficiency of deficiency. But as there is no excess and deficiency of temperance and courage because what is intermediate is in a sense an extreme, so too of the actions we have mentioned there is no mean nor any excess and deficiency, but however they are done they are wrong.[20]

Nowhere in *Ethics* or elsewhere does Aristotle argue to this judgment. He argues only from it. And the judgment is based on the names of the things listed—that is, on social convention or tradition. Spite, shamelessness, adultery, theft, and murder were all framed for the purpose of identifying actions and passions that society had agreed to be bad or wicked.

It is significant that Aristotle does not attempt to *prove* that "these and suchlike things . . . are themselves bad." He constructs no ontology of nature or of moral law to do this. He simply asserts it, for no one would ever try to make a case for the morality of theft, murder, adultery, spite, or shamelessness. Philosophical discussion is foreclosed by the "names" of these things. One philosophizes only about what is problematical or controversial. Or as Wittgenstein said so many centuries later: "Doubt may be entirely lacking. Doubting has an end."[21]

We know, of course, and Aristotle knew that societal conventions about what is moral or acceptable behavior vary with time and place and that the meanings of words change with changed circumstance. In the generation before Aristotle's, during the moral chaos that accompanied the political disasters of the Peloponnesian War, the Greek historian Thucydides wrote that

20. Ibid., 1107a 10–25, 959.
21. *Philosophical Investigations*, II, v, 180e.

words had to change their ordinary meaning and to take that which was now given them. Reckless audacity came to be considered the courage of a loyal ally; prudent hesitation, specious cowardice; moderation was held to be a cloak for unmanliness; ability to see all sides of a question, inaptness to act on any. Frantic violence became the attribute of manliness; cautious plotting, a justifiable means of self-defence. The advocate of extreme measures was always trustworthy; his opponent a man to be suspected.[22]

To translate this statement into Aristotle's frame of reference, Thucydides seems to be saying that in times of revolutionary violence, when an entire social and political system is in flux, the name of the mean is frequently given to actions that in more settled times would be called an extreme and the name of the extreme to behavior that would otherwise be approved with the language of the mean. The norm of the mean might itself give way, and measures frankly labeled as extreme might be approved: "the advocate of extreme measures was always trustworthy." But it is interesting that the norm that gives way in such "state of nature" situations is the mean, not the conceptions of inherently wrong behavior underlined by Aristotle as permanent moral guideposts. Thucydides does not tell us that theft, murder, or "suchlike things" were approved as right, even in his description of such desolating events as the revolution in Corcyra or in the bald discourse of the Athenians and the Melians about principles of moral action. Evidently, actions that in peaceful times of social agreement and civic order are socially condemned as theft, murder, spite, and shamelessness, and punished as such, were blatantly performed during the Peloponnesian War with impunity. But it is important that Thucydides, in recounting these horrors, does not tell us that anyone tried to make a moral case for them. He writes instead that

in peace and prosperity states and individuals have better sentiments, because they do not find themselves suddenly confronted with imperious necessities; but war takes away the easy supply of daily wants, and so proves a rough master, that brings most men's

22. *The Complete Writings of Thucydides: The Peloponnesian War*, John H. Finley, Jr., trans. (New York: Modern Library, 1951), 189.

characters to a level with their fortunes. Revolution thus ran its course from city to city, and the places which it arrived at last, from having heard what had been done before carried to a still greater excess the refinement of their inventions, as manifested in the cunning of their enterprises and the atrocity of their reprisals.[23]

In a text that is usually described as a masterpiece of dispassionate and precise historical reportage—a model of value-free scientific history—Thucydides interjects a poignant judgment on the tragic behavior that he so carefully recounted in detail. It appears in his description of the revolution in Corcyra, which he ends with the following moral and political lament:

> In the confusion into which life was now thrown in the cities, human nature, always rebelling against the law and now its master, gladly showed itself un-governed in passion, above respect for justice, and the enemy of all superiority; since revenge would not have been set above religion, and gain above justice, had it not been for the fatal power of envy. Indeed men too often take upon themselves in the prosecution of their revenge to set the example of doing away with those general laws to which all alike can look for salvation in adversity, instead of allowing them to subsist against the day of danger when their aid may be required.[24]

Since Thucydides wrote his history "not as an essay which is to win the applause of the moment, but as a possession for all time," he must have supposed that his brief moral comment as well as his scientific description of recurrent political processes would be meaningful to later generations raised in cultures different from his own. For he believed that the future "in the course of human things must resemble [the past] if it does not reflect it."[25] Like Aristotle, in speaking of fundamental moral questions, the Sophist Thucydides evidently believed that there are persistent transcultural norms. In time of conflict, some of these will indeed be more honored in the breach than in the observance. Nevertheless, there are things we all know to be simply wrong, by the names that human society throughout history has given to them. We do not need to justify them. Like the earth, the air, and society itself,

23. Ibid.
24. Ibid., 191.
25. Ibid., 14.

they are simply givens. They are irrefutable and undeniable existential realities.

If we reflect on the norms of Aristotle's list, we discover that they are by no means principles peculiar to Greek culture of the fourth century B.C. The prohibition against envy, adultery, theft, and murder corresponds to four of the Judeo–Christian Decalogue, whose origins are deep in Semitic history. The prohibition of spite—a warning against ill will—can be construed as a negative formulation of the Judeo–Christian injunction to have good will, that one love one's neighbor as oneself. Shamelessness, or insensibility to disgrace, is displayed in any behavior that callously flouts moral principle in general. One might render it as a lack of any sense of justice or righteousness or lack of a moral sense. And, plainly, moral sense is a prerequisite to moral behavior according to any code of morality.

Anthropological research has shown that the moral agreement I have noted between Athens and Jerusalem is even more widely shared. John M. Cooper has written that "the peoples of the world, however much they differ as to details of morality, hold universally, or with practical universality," principles that are virtually identical with those of the Ten Commandments.

> Respect the Supreme Being or the benevolent being or beings who take his place. Malicious murder or maiming, stealing, deliberate slander or "black" lying, when committed against friend or unoffending fellow clansman or tribesman, are reprehensible. Adultery proper is wrong, even though there be exceptional circumstances that permit or enjoin it and even though sexual relations among the unmarried may be viewed leniently. Incest is a heinous offense.[26]

26. John M. Cooper, "The Relations between Religion and Morality in Primitive Culture," *Primitive Man* 4 (1931): 36. On the existence of universal moral principles see also Walter T. Stace, *The Concept of Morals* (New York: Macmillan, 1937), chaps. 2–5. Stace introduces his discourse by writing that he will try to show that morality is "relative in the sense that it is relative to the universal needs of human nature. But it is not relative to the particular needs of particular nations, ages, or social groups. Consequently it does not vary from place to place or from time to time. Morality is universal, but it is not absolute," (67). He then attempts to answer three questions in detail:

What is the universal moral law? What is its actual content? What, in short, are its commands?

Thus we see that the social "names" of good and evil are very broadly shared among the cultures of the world.

It would seem that one could well begin to formulate a philosophy of freedom around such broadly shared positive and negative norms as these—the historical values of public man rather than the fantasies of Descartes's man of private will. Freedoms congenial to them would be considered rightful; freedoms inimical to their maintenance or realization would be deemed harmful and subject to limitation. The universal agreement would have the status of a set of directive or regulative principles. Not conceived as a "law," as a statement of necessary relationships in a logical, scientific, or legal sense, nothing by way of specific regulations, in the form of coercive legislation, would follow from them. They could not eventuate in a law code or in a totalitarian five-year plan aimed at moral regeneration or at forcing men to be free. The work of politics in such a view would consist of prudent experimentation of a pragmatic sort, directed by universal agreement as an expression of the moral sense of mankind. It would involve the application of Aristotelian practical reason, or one

---

In what *sense* is this law universal, and how can its universality be shown to be consistent with the actual plurality of moral codes in the world?

What is the *basis and foundation* of this morality, and of the *obligation* which it imposes? and how can it be shown that the universal "ought" which it implies is empirically meaningful? (68)

For a comparison, see A. Macbeath, *Experiments in Living* (London: Macmillan, 1952), especially 358–76, and Melvin Rader, *Ethics and the Human Community* (New York: Holt, Rinehart, and Winston, 1964), 241–45. The work of humanist psychologists such as A. H. Maslow, directed to the definition of a universal hierarchy of human needs, points toward the possibility of a universal morality but as a reality to be created rather than as one already in existence. Also compare the different approach of Arnold Brecht, *Political Theory* (Princeton: Princeton Univ. Press, 1959), 387–403. Brecht defines five "universal postulates of justice" of a very abstract and largely procedural sort that he believes are scientifically verifiable and that also seem to derive from the idea of what it is to do science. He claims that by "summing up these postulates we would obtain a minimum definition of justice. . . . It would attempt to be the exact description of a human phenomenon, of a universal, invariant, inescapable form of human thinking and feeling based on universal characteristics of human existence" (397).

might conceive such politics as a Deweyite search for or effort to construct a "great community" out of the burgeoning dissonance of our "great society." The self-definition of such a community's interests and all efforts to serve them would be framed, like Aristotle's politics of the mean, within the large parameters of the universal moral sense.[27]

No one could object that the norms described here are too abstract, because of their universal scope, to be guideposts for social policy and legislation. Murder and theft are surely "clear and distinct ideas." (We would not want to dismiss this Cartesian criterion of judgment along with the body–mind dualism.) Indeed, what constitutes murder or theft in a particular situation may be debatable. And what might be called for in the way of specific social policies to prevent them may well be fundamentally variable and radically dependent on time and circumstance and on the prudent sense of statesmen. The clarity of the norms, while directive, would thus not be unduly confining to policymakers.

But are norms of the sort described here adequate to an entire social policy of freedom? Perhaps not—we certainly cannot be sure, prior to research, what needs to be done to discover just how broad and detailed a general agreement on fundamental norms (or "names") exists. In any case, would not an understanding of universal norms be sophisticated by an understanding of the view or model of human nature that underlies them, the ideal of humanity, and the value system from which they are derived? Norms never hang in the air; they are always designed to realize some end or purpose. Those of the sort I am discussing are derived from a conception of human needs, goals, and purposes. Is there a discoverable, existentially shared ideal of humanity that might take the place of the problematical ontologies of human nature I have scrutinized in this book?

On the face of it we should have to answer "no." A brief review of the history of political thought would show us that there is no

27. John Dewey, *The Public and Its Problems* (New York: Holt, Rinehart, and Winston, 1927) and critique of this work in William T. Bluhm, *Theories of the Political System*, 3rd. ed. (Englewood Cliffs, N.J.: Prentice-Hall, 1978).

such shared ideal but a great plurality of ideals. Nevertheless, it may well be meaningful to ask whether there are common themes that link these ideals together, shared or cross-cutting concepts that evidence a certain continuity through the ages. Are there not important aspects of human being that are the same today as they were in ancient Athens, Jerusalem, or Peking—aspects from which one might derive the general norms of human comity just described?

Coming at the question in this way, one prominent commonality comes immediately to view—a historical dialogue between hedonistic self-interest and inherent or absolute right as fundamental human motives. In every time and clime these two great human ideas have had to come to terms with each other. Each has given rise to images of the just and the unjust man, images which display, if not perfect continuity, at least a constant reappearance, a continual reformulation in similar terms from age to age. Nietzsche's concept of the "eternal return" is certainly valid here. This is *not* an invocation of premodern ideas of natural law but a suggestion that we might find useful a reflection on the commonalities that exist between universal ideas of right and universal conceptions of "enlightened interest."[28]

The Dialogue of Right and Interest in the West

In the Western tradition, one of the earliest formulations of the dialogue of right and interest is found in the Genesis story of Cain and Abel. Sensing Cain's selfishness in his reluctant offering of produce, Yahweh warns him that his ill disposition invites temptation and evil acts. "If you are ill disposed, is not sin at the door like a crouching beast hungering for you, which you must master?"[29] But when the man of self-will has lived out his selfishness, which culminates in the murder of his brother, the author of Genesis makes Cain cry out his sense of guilt and injustice at his act, albeit in terms of self-concern. Reflecting Yahweh's judgment

28. For a critique of the natural law approach see Kenneth W. Thompson, *Morality and Foreign Policy* (Baton Rouge: Louisiana State Univ. Press, 1980), 133–35.

29. Genesis 4:7–8.

that he must be a "fugitive and wanderer over the earth," Cain adds: "Why, whoever comes across me will kill me!" Recognizing the enormity of his act, Cain thought that other men would recognize it too and that along with divine punishment would come human sanctions as well. In Cain's cry we have a statement by the man of self-interest of the need for sanctions against murder. For if anyone at all can exercise a license to murder, no one is safe. Out of pure self-interest the members of the community will act against the murderer, whose existence is a threat to all.[30] On the other hand, the punishment of murder in the same story is assigned to the order of absolute justice by God's reservation to himself of the right to punish infringements of his holy law. " 'Very well, then,' Yahweh replied, 'if anyone kills Cain, sevenfold vengeance shall be taken for him.' So Yahweh put a mark on Cain, to prevent whoever might come across him from striking him down." It is clear from this story that the commandment "Thou shalt not kill!" is as much a matter of social utility and enlightened interest as it is a matter of inherent justice. The norm is expressed on both sides of the dialogue.

The New Testament is replete with juxtapositions of the life of enlightened interest and the life of true righteousness. As in the Old, they frequently issue in similar behavioral norms. Thus we learn in Matthew 6:1−4 that almsgiving, helping the poor, will be practiced by men of both motivations. One can distinguish the righteous from the self-interested man not by his charity but by the manner in which he does it.

> Be careful not to parade your good deeds before men to attract their notice; by doing this you will lose all reward from your Father in heaven. So when you give alms, do not have it trumpeted before you; this is what the hypocrites do in the synagogues and in the streets to win men's admiration. I tell you solemnly, they have had their reward. But when you give alms, your left hand must not know what your right is doing; your alms-giving must be secret, and your Father who sees all that is done in secret will reward you.

30. If Richard Cox is correct, John Locke read the passage this way and employed it with this meaning at the subterranean level of his argument in the *Second Treatise*. See *Locke on War and Peace*, 55−56.

In addition, Jesus' formulation of the Golden Rule obviously speaks meaningfully to the man of self-interest as well as to the man of good will, though that may not have been his intention. "So always treat others as you would like them to treat you; that is the meaning of the Law and the Prophets."[31]

If we investigate these matters in the culture of classical Greece, we find a similar dialogue of interest and justice. In the pre-Socratic culture, self-interest and inherent right are in fact actually interwoven with each other. The outlines of the traditional Greek moral code are graphically sketched for us by Thucydides in the pages of the *Peloponnesian War,* to which I have already referred for another purpose.

Traditional Greek morality was based on relationships of power. The stronger person—or city—because of his power, has a right to rule. But with that right goes a moral obligation to protect the weak, who have an obligation to submit. Responsible rule is morally obligatory; magnanimity and moderation are the virtues of the powerful. To them are due honor and acceptance when they display these virtues. Contempt of a benevolent ruler by the weaker is injustice and punishable by stern action. On the other hand, oppression—the display of arrogance or cruelty by the stronger—is also injustice and warrants rebellion. Criminal marauding is a shameful outrage.[32]

When power relationships are equal, justice requires equal treatment and fair play. It is unjust for equals to seek to oppress or subjugate equals, and such behavior warrants resistance and contempt. Freedom, defined as independence, is deserved by cities that are equal in power. And among such free states, good will and mutual assistance are called for in the face of threats by common enemies. Gratitude is owed by those who receive help.

The morality of magnanimity and moderation are based on a hedonistic psychology in which security, material well-being, and prestige ("fear, honour, and interest") are the three strongest human motives. Considerations of right and justice are inter-

31. Matthew 7:12.
32. See Thucydides, Finley, ed., *Peloponnesian War,* 17, 21, 22, 24, 25, 44, 48, 104–06, 112, 165.

mixed, at every point, with considerations of expediency. It is also supposed that truly expedient behavior always conforms to principles of right. Right builds power.[33]

By the Periclean period, the Sophists had sharply separated interest from inherent right. But as in Judeo–Christian culture, enlightened interest and inherent justice pointed in the same direction. Thus we find Protagoras teaching the social utility of political codes of right that protect life, limb, and property, even though he can find no warrant for them in nature. It is also important, he taught, that the traditional moral virtues of justice, wisdom, courage, and temperance be instilled in a population as moral habit, if the polity is to thrive. Their inculcation, however, in Protagoras's schema had the character of what we would today call political socialization rather than the education of a natural capacity for being virtuous. The radical Sophists, indeed, taught a doctrine of radical individualism, in which it was quite acceptable—it was "by nature"—to use any means at all suitable to one's end. But in the *Peloponnesian War*, Thucydides, himself a writer in the Sophist tradition, showed that such behavior, when widespread, destroyed the unity and power of Athens and contributed significantly to her defeat.

In the pages of the *Republic*, Plato sets before us a social contract theory in the words of Glaucon that the origin of conventional justice is in its social utility.

> What people say is that to do wrong is, in itself, a desirable thing; on the other hand, it is not at all desirable to suffer wrong, and the harm to the sufferer outweighs the advantage to the doer. Consequently, when men have had a taste of both, those who have not the power to seize the advantage and escape the harm decide that they would be better off if they made a compact neither to do wrong nor to suffer it. Hence they began to make laws and covenants with one another; and whatever the law prescribed they called lawful and right . . . So justice is accepted as a compromise.[34]

33. Ibid., 20–23, 27, 44.

34. Plato, *Republic*, R. M. Cornford, trans. (New York: Oxford Univ. Press, 1945), bk. 2, 358e–359a, 43–44.

As is well known, Plato follows this with his own doctrine of justice, which he grounds on a conception of personal righteousness. He also makes it clear that judging purely by observable external behavior one will not be able to discern the truly just and good man from the clever sophist. Indeed, Plato believed that the unjust man would often manage to break the law with impunity. But this would have to be done sub rosa, not in the clear light of day. "The unjust man, if he is to reach perfection, must be equally discreet in his criminal attempts, and he must not be found out, or we shall think him a bungler; for the highest pitch of injustice is to seem just when you are not."[35] The man of self-interest must at least give the color of justice and right to his behavior if he is to succeed. In public his actions must seem to be guided by norms similar to those of the just.

Both Machiavelli and Hobbes reformulate for their times the doctrine of enlightened interest that so much earlier had been voiced by the Sophists including Thucydides. At least in the republican system of Discourses, a morality similar to that of the religious code is enforced against both rulers and ruled. Temptation to tyranny and wickedness of all kinds is prevented by stern punishment, vigorous enforcement of the law, and by a system of checked and balanced power. In Hobbes's system of leges naturales (natural laws) are also found principles of comity like the universal code I have been discussing.[36]

At the same time, in the theologies of the Reformation and of the Counter-Reformation, similar norms were grounded in conceptions of inherent right. John Calvin, in writing of Christian liberty, tells his readers that this conception will not "authorize any one to conclude that the law is of no use to believers, whom it still continues to instruct and exhort and stimulate to duty, although it has no place in their consciences before the tribunal of God." Elsewhere he writes that "it is certain that the law of God, which we call the moral law, is no other than a declaration of natural law, and of that conscience which has been engraven by God on the minds of men, the whole rule of this equity, of which

35. Ibid., 46.
36. Thomas Hobbes, Leviathan, 190, 201, 209.

we now speak, is prescribed in it. This equity, therefore, must alone be the scope and rule and end of all laws. . . . The law of God forbids theft, . . . false witness . . . murder."[37] In the writings of such late Scholastics of the Catholic Reformation as Francisco Suarez and John Cardinal Bellarmine, Thomistic concepts of natural law receive restatement as expressions in human conscience of the will of God and as principles of reason and inherent right. Heinrich Rommen tells us that

> the late Scholastics, like St. Thomas, included the Decalogue, regarded as belonging in its entirety to the *lex naturalis,* in the contents of the natural moral law. They distinguished in this connection the supreme principle, "Good is to be done, evil avoided," and equally evident though already less universal principles, which therefore embrace specific kinds of goodness. Such are the following: Give to everyone his due; Worship must be paid to God; Justice must be observed; Agreements must be kept. From these follow by way of deduction additional precepts, which concern individual goods and the institutions that protect them. Thus theft, lying, adultery, and perjury are always forbidden because they are intrinsically evil.[38]

The Dialogue of Right and Interest in Oriental Thought

If we turn to Oriental culture, we find repeated the ideas of universal right and the dialogue of justice and interest that I have been sketching in Western thought. Mencius, a Confucian sage of the fourth century B.C., went so far as to assert that not all cultures but all men have implanted in them the same sense of right and wrong. "All men have the feelings of sympathy, shame and dislike, reverence and respect, and recognition of right and wrong. These feelings give rise to the virtues of benevolence, righteousness, propriety, and wisdom. These virtues are not infused into me from without, they are part of the essential *me.*"[39]

37. John Calvin, John T. McNeill, eds., *John Calvin on God and Political Duty* (New York: Liberal Arts Press, 1950), 25, 62, 63.

38. Heinrich Rommen, *The Natural Law* (St. Louis: B. Herder Book Co., 1946), 65.

39. Quoted in H. G. Creel, *Chinese Thought from Confucius to Mao Tse-Tung* (Chicago: Univ. of Chicago Press, 1953), 88.

As in the thought of the pre-Socratic Greeks, inherent right was fused with utility. The book of *Mencius* opens with the report of an interview with the king of one of the Chinese states of his time. In response to the king's query as to what counsels he brought that might profit the kingdom, Mencius replies that to think only in terms of utility and profit brings conflict and social disintegration. "Superior and inferior will contend with one another for profit, and the state will be endangered." In the long run, the king's position will be coveted by a self-interested subordinate. The king would be wiser, Mencius tells him, to cultivate the spirit of righteousness; for putting an emphasis on right will surely turn out to be profitable to all. "There has never been a benevolent man who neglected his parents, nor a righteous man who regarded his ruler lightly. Let your majesty then speak only of benevolence and righteousness. Why must you speak of profit?"[40] H. G. Creel points out that while this appears to be a contrast to utilitarian ethics, it is itself a kind of utilitarianism. "He does not say that one must be benevolent and righteous because that is a categorical imperative. . . . Instead, he points out that action which has as its sole aim material profit will in the long run not even achieve that, for it will result in anarchy and civil war."[41] Thus, in the thought of Mencius, right and utility are intimately joined in a kind of symbiotic relationship, the first as the cause of the second.

Mo Tzŭ, a philosopher of the generation that followed the death of Confucius (fifth to fourth centuries B.C.), came close to the enlightened interest or utilitarian doctrines of the moderate Sophists. An advocate of universal love ("Suppose that everyone in the world . . . loved every other person as much as he loves himself") Mo Tzŭ emphasized the great utility of such a benevolent attitude. "Could there be any thieves and robbers? If everyone looked upon other men's houses as if they were his own, who would steal? . . . Would states attack each other? . . . If everyone in the world would practice universal love, . . . then the whole

40. In ibid., 86.
41. Ibid., 87.

world would enjoy peace and good order."[42] When one asked what good his doctrine of universal love was, Mo Tzŭ replied: "If it were not useful I myself would disapprove of it. But how can there be anything that is good and yet not useful?"[43] Five things in particular Mo Tzŭ deemed to be desirable goals: "enriching the country, increasing the population, bringing about good order, preventing aggressive war, and obtaining blessings from the spirits."[44] Here we are not far from Protagoras's program for social integration. (Mo Tzŭ's cosmopolitan world view also reminds us of the Stoics.) As in the case of Sophistic Greece, an extreme version of utilitarianism, which takes the form of radical individualism, is also found in China at this time in the work of Yang Chu. Mencius writes of him: "If Yang Chu could have benefited the whole world by merely plucking out one of his hairs, he would not have done it."[45]

To find a school of Chinese thought parallel to that of Plato, in which goodness and right are celebrated for their own sake, we must go back a generation from these writers to the work of Confucius. In Confucius's conception of the *tao* (the Way) we have "the ethical code of the individual and . . . the pattern of government that should bring about the fullest possible measure of well-being and self-realization for every human being."[46] This was not a religious but a humanist concept for Confucius, as for Plato. One of his disciples tells us that he did not discuss "the way of Heaven."[47] Nor was the *tao* for him a mystical principle of cosmic unity as it was for later Taoists. "The Way" for Confucius signified always a principle of human action.[48] Yet it was not simply a program of utilitarian reform. It stood for a way of life that was right in itself, and consequently obligatory for all men. As Creel puts it, "the idea of Heaven gave him the feeling that

42. Quoted in ibid., 56.
43. In ibid., 57.
44. In ibid.
45. In ibid., 70.
46. Ibid., 33.
47. Ibid., 35.
48. Ibid., 34.

somehow, somewhere, there was a power that stood on the side of the lonely man who struggles for the right."[49]

In the concept of *shu* , reciprocity, the "one unifying principle" of Confucius's ethical system, we have a clear parallel to the Christian Golden Rule. Reciprocity was understood to mean "what you would not have others do unto you, do not unto them."[50] For Confucius, reciprocity, so understood, was an expression of *Jen,* the cornerstone of Confucian doctrine, which can be translated as "magnanimity," "benevolence," "perfect virtue," "moral life," "moral character," and "true manhood."[51] When asked by a disciple about the meaning of *Jen,* Confucius said that it was an imperative: "Love men." A Confucian of the third century B.C. elaborated this, saying, *"Jen* is to love men joyously and from the inmost of one's heart."[52] We are close to Jesus' teaching that the one great commandment is to love God with one's whole heart and one's neighbor as oneself.

Right and Interest in the Traditional Culture of India

In Indian culture, as in China and in the West, this-worldly, hedonistic traditions are juxtaposed to otherworldly, ascetic traditions, and in some ways more sharply so. Yet at an abstract level, they are also holistically united under the principle of *dharma,* which means duty, morality, law, or natural harmony. The hedonic or utilitarian tradition is represented by Arjuna, a great Kshatrya warrior, in the *Mahābhārata* and by Kautilya's *Arthashastra*. Both claim that wealth, in the broad sense of all means of physical subsistence, is the basis of all other values. Arjuna proclaims that "performance of duty *(dharma),* enjoyment of pleasure *(kāma),* and even the attainment of heaven depends on wealth, on which life itself depends." Kautilya calls wealth the chief end of life. We are reminded of the emphasis in the pre-

---

49. Ibid., 36. See also Y. P. Mei, "The Basis of Social, Ethical, and Spiritual Values in Chinese Philosophy," in C. A. Moore, ed., *The Chinese Mind* (Honolulu: University Press of Hawaii, 1967), 153.

50. Mei, "Spiritual Values in Chinese Philosophy," 152.

51. Ibid.

52. Ibid.

Socratic Greek tradition and by the Sophists on the hedonic drives for security, wealth, and prestige, and of Hobbes's insistence on physical security as the foundation of other values. On the opposite side, we have the doctrine of the *Yoga-bhāsya* and of Bhiṣma in the *Mahābhārata*, which expresses disgust with temporal goods and sees them as the source of suffering. Here an analogue is the asceticism of Plato's guardians or of Jewish prophets and Christian monks. In the work of Manu there is an effort at synthesis, or a golden-mean position, in the view that *dharma*, wealth, and enjoyment are all of equal importance and are mutually sustaining. Perhaps the work of Aristotle is here a Western analogue.[53]

Three basic universal principles that summarize an entire ethical philosophy are presented in the *Brhadāranyaka-Upaniṣad*: "Cultivate self-control; be generous; and have compassion."[54] And in the *Taittirīya-Upaniṣad* the teacher gives the following general advice to his pupil: "Should there be any doubt regarding conduct, you should conduct yourself after the manner of those wise men who may be living in your vicinity—those who are competent to judge, dedicated to good deeds, not led by others, not cruel, and lovers of virtue."[55] In the *Mahābhārata* we find an Indian version of Jesus' Golden Rule: "What is harmful to oneself, one should not do to others. This is the quintessence of *dharma*. Behavior which is contrary to this is based on selfish desire."[56] And even in the worldly and amoral *Arthashastra*, we are told that "harmlessness, truthfulness, purity, freedom from spite, abstinence from cruelty, and forgiveness are duties common to all."[57] The aim of Indian philosophy is not, however, to

53. Dhirenda Mohan Datta, "Some Philosophical Aspects of Indian Political, Legal, and Economic Thought," in Charles A. Moore, ed., *The Indian Mind* (Honolulu: East-West Center Press, 1967), 277; S. Radha-Krishnan and C. E. Moore, eds., *A Source Book in Indian Philosophy* (Princeton: Princeton Univ. Press, 1957), headnote, 193.
54. T. M. Mahadevan, "Social, Ethical, and Spiritual Values in Indian Philosophy," in Moore, ed., *The Indian Mind*, 157.
55. Ibid., 156.
56. Ibid.
57. Radha-Krishnan and Moore, eds., *Source Book*, 198.

produce the moral life but rather to train the soul for an experience that transcends both the moral world of daily life and the mental world as well. There is a certain pessimism in Indian thought about the degree of perfection that is possible in the moral life, a factor which, along with the weight of a hedonic tradition, profoundly affects the form taken by the dialogue of right and interest in Indian culture.

The basis of the political and social order in Indian thought is *dharma*. The king and his officials are expected to develop moral discipline and to display it in their lives. "Along with intellectual education," writes one scholar, "great stress is laid on enthusiasm, moral discipline, control of the senses, speech, thought, and action. Control of passions—such as anger, jealousy, greed, egoism—is also thought necessary. Addiction to vicious habits is condemned."[58] The fullest realization of such moral virtues both in domestic and in international politics is found in the reign of the Emperor Asoka (third century B.C.) who established a welfare state at home and both concluded and lived by treaties of mutual nonaggression with neighboring states, states which were less powerful than his own. Asoka also sent out "ethical emissaries . . . to distant lands . . . to preach the universal human virtues and toleration of the faith of others as the best service to one's own."[59]

But there is also a tragic and amoral side to Indian political culture, which roots in the unhappy jungle realities of a complex state system and in moral pessimism and the hedonistic tradition just mentioned. In times of political distress and disorganization, it did not seem possible to apply the norms of *dharma*, harmonious order. When politics is fundamentally disharmonious, the conditions of harmony must first be established by the assertion of power. Thus the relationship of right to might posited by the Chinese philosopher is inverted. In the *Mahābhārata* we find it written that "might is above right; right proceeds from might; right has its support in might, as living beings in the soil. As smoke

58. Datta, "Indian Political, Legal, and Economic Thought," 280.
59. Ibid., 285.

the wind, so right must follow might. Right in itself is devoid of
command; it leans on might as the creeper on the tree."[60]

In times of disaster, then, politics achieves in Indian culture an
autonomy like that we find embraced only by the most pessimistic
and cynical political philosophers of the West, such as Machiavelli
and Hobbes, especially when one is considering the question of
admissible behavior in a state of nature. When the circumstances
of politics become equivalent to those of the jungle, no restrictions
are laid on acceptable behavior. Thus in the *Mahābhārata* we find
the following maxims:

> When thou findest thyself in a low state, try to lift thyself up,
> resorting to pious as well as to cruel actions. Before practicing
> morality, wait until thou art strong. If thou are not prepared to be
> cruel and to kill men as the fisher kills fish, abandon every hope of
> great success. If men think thee soft, they will despise thee. When it
> is, therefore, time to be cruel, be cruel; and when it is time to be soft,
> be soft.[61]

Even the very good and moral Emperor Asoka found it necessary
in the first instance to build his empire on force and violence,
though on this foundation of pure power politics he built an
ethical state and transmuted a policy of territorial conquest into
one of peaceful moral conquest.[62]

Obviously Indians did not think morality a meaningless category, nor, as in the case of Machiavelli and Hobbes, a mere name for
rules established by the stronger. Nor did they subscribe to something like Cartesian subjectivism, in which right becomes whatever an individual wishes or wills it to be. Their amorality signifies
rather that war furnished the basic model of politics—a model in
which the principles of *dharma,* understood as moral harmony,
could not apply. But in ordered times, when power relationships
are settled, moral behavior was to be expected. D. Mackenzie
Brown sums up the matter well when he writes:

60. Quoted in Heinrich Zimmer, *Philosophies of India*, Bollingen series, vol. 26
(New York: Pantheon Books, 1951), 124.
61. Quoted in ibid., 124, 125.
62. Datta, "Indian Political, Legal, and Economic Thought," 285.

The section [of the *Shāntiparva*] dealing with periods of disaster contains some of the most cold-blooded realism in the history of political theory. Unless the modern reader fully appreciates the tenacity and restraining power of Dharma in traditional Indian government, he may easily conclude that cynicism is the guiding tenet of the author. . . . But behind all the brutal expediencies there remains an ultimate accountability to the rule of Dharma.[63]

The major moral tradition in India, then, unlike that of China or the West, makes exceptions in the application of universal principles of right, though it subscribes to them as fully as does the major tradition in the other cultures. In associated traditions it gives correspondingly smaller place to doctrines of enlightened self-interest as a ground alternative to morality for norms of fair and equal behavior. We do find something similar to a code of enlightened interest, however, in some of the Hindu beast fables that figure in the *Mahābhārata*. One tells of a wildcat and a mouse, natural enemies, who had built homes in the same tree in the jungle. One day a trapper entangled the cat in the meshes of a net, and shortly afterward the mouse found itself threatened by an owl and a mongoose. The mouse sought refuge in the cat's furry bosom from these other two enemies, promising that it would gnaw through the meshes that imprisoned his friend-for-the-nonce. The mouse waited, however, until the moment that the trapper appeared, knowing that the cat would not then be able to use its freedom to devour him. Each partner to the limited bargain profited from the behavior of mutual help forced upon him by the situation.

In another fable told in the *Hitopadésa* a lion befriends a starving tomcat and shares its meals with the cat because it is being annoyed during its sleep by a mouse that lives in a hole near the lion's cave. "Mighty lions are unable to catch mice; nimble cats however can; here therefore was the basis for a sound and possibly agreeable friendship." The arrangement of mutual help goes well and profits both partners. The presence of the cat in the cave

---

63. Quoted in Richard Lannoy, *The Speaking Tree: A Study of Indian Culture and Society* (London: Oxford Univ. Press, 1971), 325.

is enough to keep the mouse from tweaking the lion's tail. But the enlightened bargain ends one day when the cat is foolish enough to catch and eat the mouse. The lion quickly turns his erstwhile helpmate out of the cave to starve. But at least for a term, we find principles of behavior resembling those called for by *dharma*, the principle of right, being performed from motives of pure self-interest.[64]

Norms of Right and Interest in Islam

The moral principles of Islam are based on revelation. They are understood as commands of God, which have been mediated to humankind from the beginning of the world by a series of virtuous prophets—Abraham, Moses, Jesus, Mohammed, and many others. Each time a messenger is sent, acceptance by mankind proves to be incomplete and imperfect. Hence another prophet must be dispatched. As one scholar puts it, "no one knows how many times throughout history persons are chosen to remind mankind of the heavenly norm, and to warn us of the terrors of failing to accept it. This much is known, that they were many, of diverse lands and people. Yet in essentials, despite the wide variety of messengers, the message is always the same."[65] In this way Islam subscribes to the idea of a universal moral law. The Koran is seen as the fullest and most perfect statement that has been made of God's word and law. And Mohammed is the prophet par excellence. *Muslim* means in Arabic "acceptor" or "submitter," a man who has accepted and submitted to God's law.

The moral code of Islam is embodied in the *Shari'ah*, which means "way" or "path." This establishes first and foremost the rights of God, and the human obligation to acknowledge and worship him. Next come the rights of the individual and his duties to himself. The latter forbid "the use of all those things which are injurious to man's physical, mental, or moral exis-

---

64. Zimmer, *Philosophies of India*, 88–89, 109.

65. Wilfred Cantwell Smith, *Islam in Modern History* (Princeton: Princeton Univ. Press, 1957), 12.

tence."[66] Third are announced the rights of others, conceived so as to "strike a balance in the rights of man and the rights of society."[67] General principles of right in this category, which correspond to norms of the other traditions examined here, include prohibitions against lying, theft, cheating, slander, murder, and adultery. Also included are positive injunctions to social responsibility and social justice—care for the poor, the sick, the orphan.[68] Specific duties for the various members of the household—husband, wife, and children—are also laid down. Indeed, the *Shari'ah* includes rules that cover every situation that might arise in one's life.

Unlike the moral doctrines of Hindu India, those of Islam do not ambivalently juxtapose worldly pleasures to transcendental asceticism. Instead, they incorporate hedonic values in the religious life. The good life is not something to be achieved by transcendence of the temporal and empirical, or only in the hereafter, but rather in the flow of empirical events. The mission of Islam is understood as the creation of a temporal world community in which all men will be brought to the enjoyment of that good life. As a consequence of this total incorporation of the holy in the secular, the dialogue of interest and right in Islam takes a form different from that in the other cultures I have examined.

A modern exponent of Islamic ethics expresses the attitude of Islam toward hedonic values in these terms:

> The *Shari'ah* stipulates the law of God and provides guidance for the regulation of life in the best interests of a man. Its objective is to show the *best way* to man and provide him with the ways and means to fulfill his needs in the most successful and most beneficial way. The law of God is out and out for your benefit. There is nothing in it which tends to waste your powers, or to suppress your natural needs and desires, or to kill your normal urges and emotions. . . . It is [God's] explicit Will that the Universe . . . should go on functioning

66. S. A. A' la Maududi, *Towards Understanding Islam*, 14th ed., K. Ahmad, trans. (Lahore: Idara Tarjuman-ul Quran, 1974), 160.

67. Ibid., 162.

68. Ibid., 153; Ilse Lichtenstadter, *Islam and the Modern Age* (New York: Bookman Associates, 1958), 85.

smoothly and graciously so that man . . . should make the best and most productive use of all his powers and resources, of everything that has been harnessed for him in the earth and in the high heavens. He should use them in such a way that he and his fellow human beings may reap handsome prizes from them and should never, intentionally or unintentionally, be of any harm to God's creation.[69]

It is obvious from this formula that the category of interest is entirely accommodated to the category of the holy and the just. The following passage explicitly indicates that this is so.

The fundamental principle of the Law is that man has the right and in some cases it is his bounden duty, to fulfill all his genuine needs and desires and make every conceivable effort to promote his interests and achieve success and happiness—but . . . he should do all this in such a way that not only the interests of other people are not jeopardised and no harm is caused to their strivings towards the fulfillment of their rights and duties, but that there should be all possible social cohesion, mutual assistance, and co-operation among human beings in the achievement of their objectives. In respect of those things in which good and evil, gain and loss are inextricably mixed up, the tenet of this law is to choose little harm for the sake of greater benefit and sacrifice a little benefit for avoiding a greater harm. This is the basic approach of the *Shari'ah*.[70]

In the doctrine of Islam, inherent right and enlightened interest not only converge, they are absolutely identical.

Conclusion

John Stuart Mill once wrote of the readiness with which the narrow utilitarian mind of Jeremy Bentham had dismissed all past philosophy as so many "vague generalities," not recognizing that "these generalities contained the whole unanalyzed experience of the human race."[71] So too, René Descartes chose to ignore the unexamined moral experience of mankind in confin-

---

69. Maududi, *Towards Understanding Islam*, 150–51.

70. Ibid., 151–52.

71. John Stuart Mill, *Essay on Bentham*, in *Utilitarianism, On Liberty*, Mary Warnock, ed. (New York: Meridian Books, 1962), 97.

ing the concept of knowledge to the clear, distinct, but entirely abstract ideas of the morally detached individual mind. In this chapter I have taken that moral experience seriously, as tested moral knowledge. But the examination has been cursory. The subject demands a full and careful exploration, for in the universal moral experience of the human race—an experience of right and interest—we can find embodied a public personality, the public reason of mankind. In that personality, which is not a mystical Hegelian *Geist* or a detached thinker of categorical imperatives but an existential, committed, historical reality, despite the progress of nihilism, we all live and breathe and have our moral being. It is in that shared personality that private will—the final recourse of Cartesian certainty—and the public motions of body are brought together as a human whole.

The knowledge we have acquired is not of a universal moral code that can readily be translated into a specific hierarchy of values, but rather of a complex dialogue between a universal code of moral right and a universal teaching of self-interest. But despite their contrapuntal character, these two codes overlap. The overlap is extensive, and we take it to be the chief source from which we may legitimately draw a hierarchy of publicly (in the broadest sense) accepted values.

The universal historical dialogue of interest with justice reviewed here gives us a time-tested conception of human nature that grows immediately out of human moral and political experience. Everywhere in the world, whether it be Peking, Delhi, London, or Baghdad, and throughout time, the human being is a creature of hedonic self-interest who longs to know and do what is right. From a person's selfishness derives the need both for strong coercive government and for constitutional limitations on the exercise of coercive authority. From that person's love of right derives a need for moral and intellectual development—and for educational institutions in which one is free to clarify and refine a conception of the just person and the just society and to be trained in the way of right. The hedonic person and the lover of righteousness require the use of power both to protect their interests and to construct the just political and social order. Since these are one and the same person, though variously proportioned, the interweaving of interest and right in political life will forever be a subtle and complicated affair. And since the circumstances of geography, climate, the distribution of resources, and technological skills vary greatly with time and place, political systems and public policies that adequately address themselves to the problems of interest and right will no doubt vary markedly.

Although the variety of human life requires a plurality of political orders, the approach to fundamental values that I propose can provide a unitary base of shared principles from which to construct a philosophy of freedom. That such a base is urgently needed is revealed by the volume of recent literature on human rights. That the base remains wanting is displayed in the discordance and incoherence of that literature.

Among philosophers the problem of an agreed view of the character of human community is revealed in the disagreements and puzzlements of the contributors to a recent volume of *Nomos* devoted to the subject of human rights.[72] Jan Narveson presents at the outset of his contribution the questions that need to be answered:

> What are these things called "rights," whose possession is in question here? Just what are to be accounted "humans" for this purpose? and anyway, most important of all, why should we suppose that humans have them? Where, so to speak, do these rights come from? And what do we say to any who might deny our claims about human rights? If we lack reasonably solid answers to these questions, we cannot plausibly claim to know which rights humans have, or even whether they have any.[73]

Narveson follows this list of questions with a critique of "the most powerful of the current theories on the subject," but his critique ends inconclusively. The inconclusion is stated frankly in the opening paragraph of the essay, in which the author hopes his exploration may lead "to an understanding of which rights we could have by virtue of being human—if any. The qualification,"

72. J. Roland Pennock and John W. Chapman, *Human Rights, Nomos*, vol. 23 (New York: New York Univ. Press, 1981). See my review of this volume in *Social Science Quarterly* 63 (December 1982):806–07. For a discussion of human rights in non-Western cultures, see Jack Donnelly, "Human Rights and Human Dignity: an Analytical Critique of Non-Western Conceptions of Human Rights," *American Political Science Review* 76, no. 2 (1982): 303–16.

73. *Human Rights*, 175.

he tells us, "unfortunately, expresses a real uncertainty, not a Cartesian doubt."[74]

The philosophical positions of most of the fourteen scholars who contributed to the *Nomos* volume appear to fall into a diverse category described by John Charvet as one that focuses on "the claim the individual has against others . . . in respect of his particular life." Charvet accords moral worth to this view because "the individual may be said to form or determine himself." The view does not necessitate egoism because the right of self-determination "is necessarily an equal right of all such individuals." But the individualistic character of the concept sets up a conflict between the particular and the moral will. And Charvet believes that it eventuates in extreme interpretations—elitist libertarianism and illiberal egalitarianism—along with compromises, like that of Rawls.[75] All the views of individual right described by Charvet fit into one or another of the Cartesian positions delineated here. That they should entail tensions between force and freedom, as Charvet's analysis indicates they do, is therefore not surprising. Charvet would substitute for each of these individualist approaches an integral model grounded on a Hegelian theory of social selves who are ends for each other and who mutually create one another.[76] But the assumptions underlying this approach fit into yet another Cartesian category—one that we have seen also produces tensions between force and freedom.

Alan Gewirth's chapter (which capsulizes the argument of his *Reason and Morality*, 1979) avoids commitment to a controversial substantive moral assumption through a "dialectically necessary approach," which grounds human rights in concepts of purposive action and rationality.[77] But critics of his thesis show that it displays all the problems found by Charvet in the individualistic model. Richard Friedman argues that Gewirth's theory is logically incomplete without the "egalitarian moral outlook" of Rawls's theory, which Gewirth had rejected. Susan Okin claims that such

74. Ibid.
75. Ibid., 31–45.
76. Ibid., 45–50.
77. Ibid., 119–46.

an outlook is present in Gewirth's philosophy as a "camouflaged premise." And Arval Morris, by contrast, thinks that Gewirth's is an "elitist theory of human rights" that would leave inactive, comatose persons like Karen Ann Quinlan without human rights. Martin Golding finds Gewirth's approach that of a "prudent amoralist."[78] That the problem of force and freedom is written in large letters in Gewirth's chapter, along with several other difficulties, is clear from these criticisms.

Louis Henkin notes in his analysis of the international law of human rights that it builds on "faith in the validity and desirability of human rights" and avoids the "philosophical uncertainties that trouble human rights discourse." But while this body of law mentions human dignity as a ground of rights, there is no agreed theory that justifies human dignity as a source of rights, Henkin remarks.[79] In yet another chapter, Golding expresses the need for "something like a common or unqualified good" in which to ground the idea of human rights, but he does not present an argument as to how it might be established.[80]

In my view, metaphysical and epistemological speculation of the sort represented in *Nomos* will never yield answers to the hard questions the volume propounds. But the moral experience of mankind, sketched here, is rich with answers if we are prepared to consult that experience. The development of a political science within an ontology of human nature such as this, to be true to the canons of its origin, will require the broadest possible comparative empirical endeavor of the most careful scientific kind. I have sketched only its barest outline. It will be an endeavor that makes use of the techniques of anthropology, sociology, psychology, and economics together with the cultural insights of humanistic disciplines such as philosophy, religion, literature, and the fine arts. It will be a discipline free of the fact–value dichotomy—the moral blindspot of the positivist behavioral sciences that have been authoritative until now. It will also be free of the pitfalls of cultural relativism into which humanistic critics, like those dis-

78. Ibid., 148–74, 230–56.
79. Ibid., 257–80.
80. Ibid., 165–74.

cussed in chapter 6, seeking to rescue the human person from the universal necessitarian laws of positivism, so ironically tumbled. To escape technological universalism, many of these writers stressed the particularity of human intentionality and the uniqueness of particular cultures and ended up in a parochial and relativistic quandary about values. I have attempted to show how the human being can be restored to social scientific inquiry as a universal moral being.

And so let us close the gap between mind and body by recognizing that we live and act within a world impregnated with values that are not identifiable with (though not exclusive of) hedonic drives and that surround and educate us and control and shape our drives. Our basic human reality is a symbolic universe that, though created by human beings, "gain[s] autonomy, or, as it were, a life of [its] own." We are cultural animals, and "symbolic entities . . . may govern man and human behavior more strongly than biological reality or organismic drive."[81] Yet it is *we* who create these symbols, and they remain open realities. "The human condition . . . is in *free decision* . . . This is the Dignity of Man."[82] It was precisely these symbols of culture that Descartes sought to discard as he attempted to plumb down to some constant entity in his discovery of *res extensa* and *res cogitans*. Reflection on the normative practice of humankind has brought us back to these discarded cultural symbols as the primary human reality.

The dichotomies of subject and object and of value and fact fall away. Our symbolic world of human value is the source of that public philosophy for which Walter Lipmann so long searched. Its re-cognition will allow the fantasies of Nietzschean ideology to fade like the will-o'-the-wisps they are. And with them also we are rid of the force–freedom paradox.

The norms I have reviewed set parameters to the freedom of individuals largely in a negative way without filling in the positive content of moral action, leaving great leeway for variety in lifestyle and in the structures of political order. The principles of human comity announce for the most part what must not be done

---

81. Bertalanffy, *Robots, Men, and Minds*, 30–31.
82. Ibid., 48.

but leave it to the creativity of free men to decide what ought to be done. With the shibboleths of necessary progress abandoned, the way is open for the pragmatic exploration of those creative possibilities. Let us embrace the living moral experience of mankind as the ground and limit of freedom.

Appendix A

A Note on Exegetical Method in the Interpretation of Descartes

An interpretation of a text that attempts to lay bare an author's hidden meaning is obviously not one whose validity can be demonstrated in a way comparable to mathematical demonstration or which can definitively be established in any other way. But for that matter, neither can *any* interpretation. An interpretation is simply that—one writer's view of what another intended to say. Its *plausibility* (not its validity) rests on the degree to which the author of the interpretation can show: (1) that his reading reveals a *pattern* of thought that bears the marks of careful construction and (2) that the pattern of meanings he unfolds embraces statements from several of the works of the writer being interpreted. If such a pattern can be expounded and documented from several sources, both internal and external to the texts examined, it seems to me that the plausibility of such an interpretation is greater than one that asserts that a brilliant thinker's work is simply confused and that explicit contradictions in such a writer's work are signs of that confusion. It should be remarked, however, that a hidden pattern does not exclude ontological ambiguity. In Descartes's dualism in particular, no matter how interpreted, residual ambiguity is a characteristic feature.

Caton argues that Descartes's theology was insincere and that its purpose was to evade official censorship and punishment, like that Galileo met. He traces the beginning of this interpretation back to Descartes's own time; Henry More, for example, said that Descartes insinuated that mind as an incorporeal substance was a "useless figment and chimera." La Mettrie agreed, and Fathers Gassendi and Daniel found Descartes's picture of the soul's spirituality "so exaggerated as to be a fitting subject for satire." "Leibniz, Locke, and d'Holbach doubted the sincerity of the proofs of the existence of God." D'Holbach declared that "one is right to accuse Descartes of atheism, seeing that he very energetically destroyed the weak proofs of the existence of God that he gave" (*Origin of Subjectivity*, 11).

Some modern writers agree with the judgment of Descartes's contemporaries. Charles Adam thinks that Descartes's metaphysics was simply a "flag to cover the goods, the physics." Gilson and Maritain thought the same and Laberthommière, Krueger, Jaspers and Heidegger "all suspect his piety." (Ibid.) Caton writes also that Descartes's ethic is nonreligious and that it might be actually hostile to religion. In addition, he finds that Descartes reduced the virtues to passions, "which are generated by entirely mechanical causes" (12). He also finds it significant that Descartes himself told Burman: "The author does not gladly write of ethics, but because of pedagogues and the like he has prescribed them, for they would otherwise say that he is without religion and faith and that by his method he seeks to overthrow them" (18).

Caton describes Descartes's strategy in dissembling his meaning: "He feigns submission to the Church and pretends to possess a metaphysics which upholds the existence of God and the immortality of the soul. This picture is made necessary by his understandable desire to avoid persecution for heterodox opinions. But it is also dictated by a long-range strategy to replace Aristotle, and the ways of thought of antiquity generally with his own teaching in the philosophical culture of Europe" (12). Caton also explains that "since all interpretations must begin with simple trust, a hermeneutics of dissimulation can legitimately be based on the author's own words when they intimate or say explicitly that he does not always mean what he says, or that he does not say all that he believes" (14). Furthermore, if he deals with the uses of disguise so as to make it clear that he is talking about his own method, "then the words provide the habeas corpus of a hermeneutics of dissimulation." (Ibid.)

Walter Soffer, another writer who holds with this school of interpreting Descartes, documents his view by pointing out that Descartes himself had explained part of his strategy to another scholar of his time, who had been too forthright in rejecting Scholastic ideas and had as a consequence stirred up a storm of opposition. In a letter to Regius, Descartes writes:

> I should like it best if you never put forward any new opinions but retained all the old ones in name, and merely brought forward new arguments. This is a course of action to which nobody could take

exception, and yet those who understand your arguments would spontaneously draw from them the conclusions you had in mind. For instance, why did you openly reject substantial forms and real qualities? Do you not remember that on p. 164 of the French edition of my *Meteors*, I expressly said that I did not at all reject or deny them, but simply found them unnecessary in setting out my explanations. If you had taken this course, everybody in your audience would have rejected them as soon as they saw they were useless, but you would not have become so unpopular with your colleagues. (Letter of January 1642, in A. Kenny, *Descartes: Philosophical Letters* [London, 1970], quoted in Walter Soffer, "Descartes, Rationality, and God," *The Thomist* 42 [October 1978]: 681.)

Soffer argues in detail against the generally accepted interpretation that Descartes's theology is the core of his metaphysics and that his rationalism is subordinate to it. In a cogent essay this writer attempts to demonstrate that the opposite is the truth of the matter; "the issue indeed comes down to rationalism vs. theology, and . . . in such a context revelation gives way to reason" (667). Taking an argument of Harry Frankfurt as his target, Soffer shows that a careful reading of the *Meditations* reveals "that reason renders faith superfluous because divine inscrutability fails to vindicate God from possible malevolence rather than being the capstone of His omnipotence" (673). Thus one purpose of the *Meditations* is to show that a benevolent God validates human reason, which enshrines the law of noncontradiction. That is, he guarantees "that what human reason cannot help but regard as true is in fact true." (Ibid.) "The limitation of God's power by His goodness cannot be demonstrated, the corollary of which is the self-grounded autonomy of human reason in the absence of a transrational guide" (690).

If Soffer's argument is correct, Descartes's theology thus serves a double purpose: at one level it establishes the preeminence of reason over faith, and at another it disguises a naturalistic interactionist version of mind–body dualism. Well suited to his enterprise was the personal motto Descartes had adopted: *"Bene Vixit, bene qui latuit"*—"He lives well who is well hidden."

Appendix B

Freedom and Necessity in Hegel's Politics

George Kelly writes that in Hegel's philosophy "a correspondence is asserted between the method and the world's actuality. The result is the necessary result of reason, a reason which cannot go beyond what is already revealed in the world, for it would find nothing there." Hegel's *Retreat from Eleusis,* 9. Patrick Riley cites a passage from Oakeshott's *On Human Conduct* that, in its reading of Hegel's view of the rational state, moderates somewhat the necessitarian character of Hegel's thought that I have emphasized:

> The "authenticity" of conduct cannot be a sufficient identification of the conditions which constitute *das Recht,* but it stands for a principle of the highest importance; namely, that the only conditions of conduct which do not compromise the inherent integrity of a subject are those which reach him in his understanding of them, which he is free to subscribe to or not, and which can be subscribed to only in an intelligent act of will. The necessary character of *das Recht* is not that the subject must himself have chosen or approved what it requires him to subscribe to, but that it comes to him as a product of reflective intelligence and exhibiting its title to recognition. (Cited in *Will and Political Legitimacy,* 193.)

I question, however, whether the expression "free to subscribe to or not" has substantial meaning, for in Hegel's thought the individual's will is formed to objective rationality by the absolute spirit working through social process. A *purely subjective* will, not so formed, is irrational in choosing not to subscribe to the commands of *das Recht,* and hence not truly free in Hegel's theory. Riley notes that none of the "traditional manifestations of will in politics—contract, consent, agreement, election, opinion, conscience— . . . have any considerable weight in [Hegel's] state." *Will and Political Legitimacy,* 193.

Index